Pedagogical Evolution: From Hard-Ass to Hippie

By Sybil Priebe

ISBN: 9798466521955
Imprint: Independently published

DEDICATION

To the teachers who have allowed an evolution inside themselves. To the teachers who have epiphanies and have followed through on them. To the teachers who reinvent themselves and who choose kindness.

To Amy, who has come to me in my acupuncture sessions to tell me it's all going to be okay.

To Marcia, who told me to keep writing.

NOTICE

Most of the parts of this book are nonfiction, but to "protect" some people and situations, some names have been changed... and details slightly fictionalized.

CONTENTS

{This page intentionally left blank.}

{This page intentionally left blank.}

Prologue, 1

This book was born of partial curiosity and the need for some partial productivity during a global pandemic. Yes, while at a cabin with my family in July of 2020, I started reading *Untamed* by Glennon Doyle. I liked the layout of her book and wondered if I could link various teaching stories I had – emails, old journal entries, recent journal entries, private and public blog posts and tweets, and current thoughts – into a quilt of something halfway interesting.

Before the pandemic smacked all of us upside the head in March, I had wondered if I should begin to edit more of my recent journal entries into more books (editions 2-6), but I always found myself "stuck" on how to fictionalize the pieces (as I had in my first book of journal entries about teaching, *Teaching: With a Side of Chicken Wings and a Shot of Vodka*) in ways that would have impact on the reader BUT prevent me from getting fired.

It's a fine line, let me tell you.

So, this book is a way for me to share ALL THE THINGS.

And all the things includes an epiphany that began right around the summer of 2019 about my approach to teaching and learning – about my approach to my students. All the things might overlap with my personal life a wee bit, too. All the things might have been edited – as evident by the use of: [...] – for the important parts only.

This is an evolution of pedagogy.
An evolution of the teacher.
An evolution of attitude.

+

A Tiny Intro to Me.

My name is Sybil. I grew up in North Dakota, and pretty much never left.

Currently, I'm starting my seventeenth year of teaching college composition & creative writing at a small, rural community college.

I live with my boyfriend and bitchy cat in a house we bought in the summer of 2011. He & I have been together for almost twenty years at this point, and the fact that we have remodeled almost every room in our house without killing each other means something.

I'm of above average weight and height for an American woman, I have awesome freckles, a bad right knee, random ice pick headaches and fatigue, and I'm constantly "fighting" the mish-mash of hair colors on my head. I think the only intimidating thing about me is my rest bitch face; it probably doesn't help that my eyes always seem kind of "sad" – a strange pale color that sometimes resemble a worn grey sweater and sometimes resemble the color of an unkempt backyard pool.

Younger Me.

I was kind of a good kid, got good grades, played in many sports, and my claim to fame my senior year of high school was that I was nominated for Miss Tennis of North Dakota... high school was chaotic for me at times with depression sinking in once in a while; I didn't party. I floated, I had a scattering of weird friends, and I really found peace in my bedroom reading "smut literature" or whatever the kids call it these days.

And that is the end of my high school summary.

It's no shock that I stated at the age of 18 that I wanted to get the hell out of our hometown. I'm sure I even said, "I'll never live in my hometown." Well, joke was on me. Never say never.

Like every other teen in 1995, I wanted to move to Seattle, be artistic (and get paid lots of money for it), become best friends with grunge bands, and continue shopping for large men's jeans at thrift stores. I was *SO original.*

Education.

After high school, I bolted but not very far away for college. My major? Architecture. I wanted to build buildings, or so I thought; I didn't realize I was destined to build lesson plans and curriculum and textbooks instead. That came after my freshman year when my math grades stunk up the place. Okay, the grades weren't that horrible, but I didn't make it into the architecture program, and I was okay with that. I didn't want to do math for the rest of my life; I wanted to write, talk to people about blasphemous ideas, and, as the Hemingway lifestyle had taught me, I wanted to have liquor-induced conversations with other smarties and write genius plans of world domination on napkins.

Prologue, 1.5

What you really need to know is this: I realize that I am no one special, and yet I am someone special: all at once. Yes, I did cringe at many of these entries while sorting and finding and editing; some of them are a glimpse into some angry teacher who wanted to be at odds with her students. But why? Why was this how I started? Is this a part of our own "teacherly indoctrination"? I don't mean to excuse my actions at all; I take full responsibility. Yet I do ponder where my attitude came from.

What I've learned is that we should always question why we're doing what we're doing, in and out of the classroom. Why are the things we think are important, important?

{This page intentionally left blank.}

Evolution (noun)[1]

- a process of change in a certain direction: unfolding
- a process of continuous change from a lower, simpler, or worse to a higher, more complex, or better state: growth
- a process of gradual and relatively peaceful social, political, and economic advance
- the process of working out or developing

[1] "Evolution." Definition. *Merriam Webster*. https://www.merriam-webster.com/dictionary/evolution

{This page intentionally left blank.}

Dear Students.

August 25, 2004.

To my dear students,

I assigned this letter not only so that all of us in class can get to know everyone else better, but also because it gives you an opportunity to talk about yourself a little more. And I think everyone has something to talk about.

These are the things that I like to talk about:
I love the sports of tennis and volleyball, and I wish that I played more of them both. One of my most favorite memories from high school was when our girl's tennis team made it to State for the first time in our school's history. Besides those two favorites, I also ran cross-country in high school. That sport taught me a lot about discipline. I never thought I would be able to run two and half miles the way I did.

Most recently, another "sport" I adore is shopping. I think this is the "gatherer" part of me from caveman days coming through. I love to spend a day shopping, even if I don't buy anything. My boyfriend says that when he's fishing, he just thinks about fishing, and that's how my hobby of shopping works. I like to go alone, and I like the time to just walk around and look at fashion.

When it comes to the second part of this assignment, the first thing that pops into my head is Mr. Wall. He was one of the best English teachers at Wahpeton Senior High. He retired this summer, and somehow, I feel like so many more students could have benefited from him. I want my students to feel the same way about me that I do about Mr. Wall.

The teachers who I have loved, in general, have always made class fun. They made us laugh and think that we weren't really learning when underneath it all, we were. In fact, I had a class at 8am when I was an undergraduate like yourselves, and the teacher was so fabulous that I actually went to that class more than my 12:30 classes.

In this class, I hope to simply be somewhat of an expert in helping you improve your writing skills. If I only teach you better ways to brainstorm or an easier way to research or how to cite what someone said in your paper, then I will have at least helped you or taught you something that will aid you in the future. Whatever you have difficulty within this class, I want to help you with. If you are an excellent writer, then I hope that my assignments make you think more about yourself and your future.

I hope you learn more about English, yourselves, and have fun in the process.

Sincerely,
Sybil

Be a Bitch.

One of the programs through the North Dakota State University allowed future teachers to student-teach at certain schools for an extended period of time (say 16 weeks instead of 12, or something to that effect), and I participated. It required me as a student-teacher to have a home base to be attached to – West Fargo Middle School was mine – and part of the pre-planning was to observe in that school before completing my student-teaching.

Mrs. Webber was a 7th or 8th grade teacher at the time I dove into the observation stage. I was too focused on her attire – very flashy and "put together" and aloof – to notice what the hell the students were being taught. Grammar? Sentence-diagramming? Who knows? Perhaps the scent of her perfume and all the memories of my teachers from k-12 had begun to mold me into some stereotype of a teacher even at that stage.

Look "good."

Implement resting bitch face.

Wear heels.

Did she like her job?

Did she like these students?

It was during this observational experience where I put in time in the special ed classrooms. My eyes were opened wide when I saw that the students were given the same textbooks as the other students, only these textbooks had the answers highlighted. How was this supposed to help these students? I realized that many of them needed attention, among other tools, and I recall just listening to many of them (instead of "helping them" with their homework, as I was required to do). It wasn't until I landed my first job that I saw the power of special education at work; the Battle Lake teachers were better equipped with compassion and literal tools.

The next semester, Spring of 1999, was when I would not get paid to try out this teaching gig. I asked for a leave of absence from Target for a few months and crossed my fingers that living off of my financial aid would suffice. I was living with my sister across from Sunmart[2], and she bought me dinners and basics from time to time. Our rent was cheap, and I had a used Pontiac Parisienne (courtesy of our mom's parents).

Mrs. Frandson was the teacher I was paired up with for student-teaching. She was close to retirement (in fact, she retired after having me as her last student-teacher; I'm unsure if that's a good or bad sign) but still the spitfire of a petite grey-haired lady. She had a flirtative quality to her, especially with the history teacher in our cohort. He was petite, too, and I towered over them[3] both whenever we met.

Speaking of cohorts, this would be the only time I experienced educational pods, which seemed to definitely have some advantages. Students were "looked over" by all their teachers, and it gave me a sense of relief that students were checked on by more than one teacher; if Isabella or Marcus were not doing well in English, it could be helpful for their other teachers to know and help out accordingly. Maybe Isabella is doing okay in Physical Education class and has a rapport with that teacher, so that teacher could reach out to the teachers in classes she wasn't doing well in. Ditto for Marcus, if he's failing English but awesome at math. And if other schools were doing this, then it was beneficial for me to learn about how they worked. There was a lot of cross-disciplinary action going on, too, due to the pods, which I assumed encouraged students to transfer knowledge from one subject to another.

I took over 8th Grade English lessons here and there and was asked to create my own module of sorts as a cumulation of all I had learned about lesson planning. I believe my module was on Creative Writing – a topic I have zoned in on since I

---

[2] We had an apartment together my senior year of college, and her freshman year; she worked at that Sunmart for many years.

[3] And I am 5'7".

started writing around the age of 9 or 10. The professor overseeing my development typically had good things to say every time he popped by to observe me. Mrs. Frandson was critical of my disciplinary strategies, but overall, fairly helpful in much of what I was doing, learning, and observing.

It was generally assumed by me and my overseeing professor that Mrs. Frandson was doing everything "right," and I just needed to copy her style. When I think back on all of this, I realize that many people saw one path for teaching, and that was the path we were all supposed to learn. To shy away from that path, to put a twist on it, was not ideal. Stay in your lane, take the $400 test, get certified and licensed, earn tenure, and THEN maybe you can create the "classroom culture of your dreams."

Maybe.

I could see it then – that some students who had a "red mark" placed upon them, just needed attention. I'm unsure why that idea faded away at times in my teaching history. So many of the "troubled students" just needed a listener, and sometimes I was that for them (Casey in Battle Lake), and sometimes I failed them. Actually, more often than not, I failed them. The girl who was labeled a "slut" from a broken home in Mrs. Frandson's class? I doubt I reached out to her in a way that mattered.

And at the end of that story, the story of me teaching 8th grade, all I can say is that I received advice I appreciated for a long time. I took it to heart. I gave that same advice to others. But now have wondered if it was really all that great... At some point, the teeny tiny history teacher said, "Sybil, if you are going to teach high school, you are going to have to be a bitch for the first month. After that, you can become more lenient. But if you aren't a bitch for the first month, the kids will not respect you."

Battle Lake Journals #1.

01.11.2000

Apparently, badgering teachers is okay to do. Rachel H. today – as well as Jessica N. – really need to learn manners! Fighting with me over answers on a test, as if that is going to make me want to give them the points back?

Changes – time has sure changed things.

Yes, teachers should respect the students, but how can I when they don't respect me? If I think back and even when Mr. Pfliger got mad, I could see that he just needed to let off some steam. Then again, my class then wasn't as obnoxious as these guys.

A picture I took of Casey, Richie, and Cody (for the yearbook) at basketball the other day – Casey was flipping me off! That little shit! I need to relax. Maybe I'll come up with some plan of attack for those freshmen? A new seating chart? Overwhelming niceness? Hm...

01.14.2000

Well, the freshmen "attacked" again. I wrote out 28 different story types and had them pick a number and put them (the title or storyline) on the top of the sheet. They had to write three lines and then give the sheet to another person, and I was hoping to get these sheets all the way around the room. Well, Richie's was "A Teacher's Life", and he wrote how I was the only able to afford my "ugly" bug by stripping at a local bar. The girls who I love so dearly wrote that I was gross and made the men puke (this was all started by the infamous Jessica, of course).

I was a bit pissed about this.

AND on another story – "An Argument Between a Teacher and a Student," they wrote about how Jessica stabbed me with a toothpick and walked away laughing. Also, it was the "funnest" day of English because Jessica kicked the shit out of me.

What to make of this for Sybil?

I could do many things about it all.

I showed Carr – the principal – and he is going to talk to them and put them on detention. So, that should be a fun week. I no longer even care to please that class with fun projects or anything. I am thinking of just giving them some good hardcore Sybil ass-whooping.

[...]

It is super hard for me not to take these childish shits personally. Why? I don't know. Maybe I haven't matured enough. Maybe I am too close in age?

[...]

The dynamics of being a teacher are drawn so thinly. Look at the age difference between me and my seniors – four years – with some of my juniors (like John) – five years. Normally, I could easily be friends with them, and if I wait a few years and go back to teach college; I'll be 25ish and my students 18-22. Crazy!

Quotes.

Battle Lake, 1999-2001.

When Casey wasn't allowed to go onto the internet: "Miss Priebe, that's like putting a piece of chocolate cake in front of me and saying, 'Casey, don't eat the cake.' Well, you know what? I'm going to eat the cake."

Brady: "If there was no suffering in the world, there would be no English classes."

Don't Be A Dick.

Tuesday October 1, 2002

[...]

Ok, after today's 9:30 class, I was a bit peeved. I assumed everyone had gotten my e-mail last week regarding the readings for today, but alas, when you assume, well you know how the riddle goes. Some of you tried to give me a line that your e-mail accounts were full, but then why didn't the messages come back to me? Good question, eh? Then there were some of you that were honest, but that's no excuse.

So, I have to refrain from getting too upset and just readjust some things. From now on, check this bad boy (aka- my teacher47 blog) many times a week. Especially on Mondays and Fridays since that seems to be when I get my ideas for what to do in the coming days. I WON'T assign something on a Monday, however, that's due Tuesday. That's too mean.

I have always had a problem being mean.. or not so much mean, but disciplinary with students. I take it internally and wonder what I DID wrong, when it wasn't my responsiblity in the first place. Gotta lower that level of taking things personally even further I suppose.

Thank you to those that DID do the homework for today.
Posted[4] 10/1/2002 at 1:48 PM

Monday October 7, 2002

---

[4] Posts with a timestamp like this are blog entries; some blog entries were private and some were public.

[...]

I checked up on your blogging thus far. Some are blogging even if I don't say they have to, and some haven't blogged in a while. I don't wish to "assign" you to write, BUT this is a COMPOSITION class..[5] so I will just "warn" you that I will be checking everyone's again next week. Try to write in there every 3 days or so... I think that is a decent goal. And remember, blogging is part of the final points too. You are graded on effort in that area.

SOME of you don't even have blogs yet. YOU are BEHIND. I suggest you get one and get going. Failing that part of the final grade won't help you. E-mail me your blog address so I can add it to my list.

On Thursday, we'll be in the lab again. You'll start your projects, hand in your summary of what your project will be, blog about Rheingold's weird chapter, and find out what to do for Tuesday.

P.S. Papers will be done when I get them done[6].
Posted 10/7/2002 at 8:17 PM

Monday November 22, 2004

Dear students,
Do not freak out on me when you procrastinate on a paper. Do not put pressure on me to give you ideas when you have had umteen times in class to ask a question when I have said: "Does anyone have any questions on the paper topic?" And do not expect me to feel bad for you when you have had a month to write a paper but failed to get it in on

---

[5] I guess I didn't know how to use ellipses back then? Sheesh.
[6] Good lord. This is cringey.

time or with any good content. Thanks much.
Sincerely,
Me
[...]
Posted 11/22/2004 at 11:20 PM

Friday November 4, 2005

Errrrrrg. Student papers without Works Cited pages? Without parenthetical citations? Those are usually the first signs of plagiarism. Very frustrating. And how come a few (so far - there may be more) couldn't get 3 complete pages of information on some of these huge topics? Should I take this personally?
Posted 11/4/2005 at 3:33 PM

Monday September 12, 2005

Why is it always hard for students to understand that late work is LATE and therefore a ZERO. Like, did their teachers in high school allow them to hand in shit after the deadline or what? I don't think I did. Well, I think I gave partial credit, but that's about all. This morning, I had some moaning over that... oh please, get your fucking assignment in on time for Christ's sake. And on Friday, when we did the email assignment, many had my email spelled incorrectly - double check your shit kids. And why are they asking me for my email - it's in the SYLLABUS. Fuck. On Wed, I need to give a quiz right at 8am. Yup. And today, I need to give a "wake-up" announcement to my 105 classes as well regarding attendance and attitude and late work.. you know, THINGS IN THE SYLLABUS.
Posted 9/12/2005 at 10:49 AM

Wednesday September 14, 2005

Note to self when creating syllabi in the future: Remember to mention the importance of deadlines. People have them in "real life" with bills and such... so that's why late work doesn't fly in my class. Also, I think I will have them sign a sheet that states something to the effect of: I am responsible for all material covered in this syllabus, all material covered in this class during class time, and all material covered on the instructor's teaching blog and web site. Technically, when they take/register for classes they are signing up for that responsibility, but it may be a good idea to remind them of that. I'd rather concentrate the class on English projects instead of reminding them of policies and procedures, however.
Posted 9/14/2005 at 10:29 AM

Tuesday January 17, 2006

Had a student today who tried to weasel his way out of putting together a resume for the job packet. It was a wonderful try and I got a good laugh, but it ended with: "Look Wayne, you may only have one job for the rest of your life and you may never move or have a wife who wants to move thus making you have to have a resume for a new job, but let's put one together JUST IN CASE that doesn't happen, shall we?" I don't think I put it that eloquently, but it was close. He's one of those students who could be good at things, possibly great, but it's like he doesn't want to set himself up for any major failure so he's just average in his assignments. Did that make sense? Note to all of my students: Make sure you are backing up your documents by saving them to your EMAIL as well as a disk or USB. Remember remember remember that I will not take: "I lost it" or "The disk doesn't work" as excuses!!
Posted 1/17/2006 at 1:47 PM

Friday January 27, 2006

My *Favorite** Students: a) those who don't listen to directions and expect me to repeat everything, b) those who don't use Work Days to work and then will moan and groan later that I didn't give them enough time in class, c) those who have really elaborate excuses that aren't considered "excused" in my book (or syllabus), d) those who don't have imaginations or don't allow themselves to imagine , and e) those who don't think you should have to have "homework" in college....
*sarcasm.
Okay. Now to be more positive! It is a BEAUTIFUL day, and it's a FRIDAY... And I have a leftover sub & Diet Dr. Pepper waiting for me in my fridge! Excellent lunch if you ask me.
Posted 1/27/2006 at 12:50 PM

Tuesday January 31, 2006

New rule starting tomorrow: ALL ASSIGNMENTS in either class I teach (105 or 110) WILL BE DUE AT THE BEGINNING OF CLASS TIME (or, for instance, if I state that the assignment is due at the end of class time on a certain date, like I sometimes do with English 105, it is due then... at 11:50am, not noon). It is just too much of a hassle for me to get things later on in the day AND it is unfair to those who come prepared for class. Essentially, this is not necessarily punishment for students, it's positive reinforcement for those who actually do their stuff when they are SUPPOSED TO. And, for those students who say that they don't have internet at home or a printer - Guess What? Our lovely campus has COMPUTER LABS. Use them; that's what they are there for. It's amazing - free access to internet & free printing!
Shockingly enough, later on in life people (bosses, supervisors, friends, family) will like the fact that you are

prepared when you say you will be or when they need you to be. Lessons learned in college actually work in the "Real World"? Yes, they do. I was/am just as shocked as my students will be someday. {There are a few who already "get it." I appreciate them.}
Posted 1/31/2006 at 1:18 PM

Friday February 3, 2006

[...]

>> When it comes to teaching at the college level, how many times should you have to tell a group of students to be quiet? I think once is enough (discipline shouldn't really have to be laid out in college, should it?) - they should be mature enough at this stage in their lives to listen for 50 minutes. And, really, they are paying for the class - if you don't want to listen and you want to talk with your friends instead, don't show up!

>> Another thought: I have heard in the past that the school I teach at is "easy" or "like 13th & 14th grades," yet the minute I am a "tough college instructor" or require as much from them as I would at, say, NDSU, then they complain. They mock it when it's easy, and they complain when it's tough.

I want to say: "THIS IS C O L L E G E." And do you think you'll get away with the same crap after you graduate?

Okay... enough with the negativity. It's FRIDAY, and I just had a fabulously massive cup of coffee.

Posted 2/3/2006 at 10:39 AM

Sunday February 26, 2006

It's two-sided: I am disappointed when students don't even try to complete an assignment when the assignment is relatively simple (or even fun!), yet because I have students who don't care to do well or don't care enough to hand in things on time, my grading process is a tad bit easier. I get to concentrate on papers and assignment that have been done somewhat well and handed in on time, and those receive my constructive criticism. Assignments that are late or not done "up to par" don't receive my full attention, and maybe that's simply karma at work - Students who care enough will get help and do better; students who don't care enough to try will not do well.

I could and sometimes do try to motivate those who don't care to do well, but shouldn't I focus in the most on those students who really want the feedback? Who are willing to try? Who want to be in class and do well? Who should get my attention?

Lastly, what frustrates me the most about this English 110 Punk class is that I tried to design it so that students would hopefully see it as somewhat fun and not "another boring English class that they HAVE to take." But it's still going to be just another required class for some.

I think when I teach this course again in the fall, I will rearrange some things. For instance, giving them their choice of deadlines has broken up my amounts of grading which is nice, but I think I will lower the choices of types of papers they can create. For example, their first deadline will be a paper that is either Narration (memoir) or Description (profile). Their second deadline will be a [multi-genre[7]?] PowerPoint Essay with the "Who am I?" theme... and the third - I was thinking of having the third be a proposal and paper. They'll propose to me what they want to do for that third individual paper. It'll be

[7] Multiple genres organized in a project that usually answer a question or revolve around one specific topic.

interesting to see what boundaries they set for themselves (page lengths, etc). I may try out that idea with the fourth paper in this semester's class. Instead of the group paper, I'll have 'em write a proposal w/paper... maybe. If I did do that this semester, I think I would have them write the proposal by sometime around Easter, and do the paper by May 3... hmmm something to think about.
Posted 2/26/2006 at 5:37 PM

Sunday August 20, 2006

Top Ten Things Not to Say to an English Teacher (or any Teacher):
10. "Do you take off points for spelling mistakes?"
9. "I don't know how to find a library book/source/web site/article."
8. "I have never liked English class." (or "I don't like this class.")
7. "How long does it have to be?"
6. "I didn't know we had to document sources."
5. "Will this hurt my grade?"
4. "I didn't know we were going to peer edit drafts in class today."
3. "Will I be missing anything important?"
2. "I don't know what to write."
1. "Why do I have to take this class?"
Posted 8/20/2006 at 2:15 PM

Wednesday August 30, 2006

Yup, this one student is going to annoy me. Arrogant! Sheesh... I talked in class about the group activity (competition), and stated that there will be options for those who don't want to participate. He comes up afterward to declare that he didn't want to be in a group because "he's only responsible for himself." Yea, didn't I just say there'd be options Mr. Know-It-All. Eeek!! And

someday you may have to worry about others keeping up with their responsibilities... that's what a WORKPLACE is all about. You can't do everything on your own all of the time... errrg. Whatever.
What's more annoying - a student who shows up and is arrogant, or one who doesn't show up at all? Hmmm...
Posted 8/30/2006 at 11:59 AM

Tuesday November 7, 2006

Interesting how students who don't show up for writing conferences sometimes have immaculate papers when they do show up to hand them in. Mm hm. To go from a so-so paper to one that barely has any punctuation problems... hmm or to write about a subject like guns to then writing about a Mexican gang when the student seems like they may be a little prejudice.
Yea, that's right. I don't think he wrote it. Imagine that.
Posted 11/7/2006 at 1:43 PM

Wednesday October 24, 2007[8]

Fonts, fonts, fonts. UGH.
So, I thought that having papers submitted electronically was a GREAT idea. A green idea, even. But now I am running into font problems. No, they aren't trying to submit papers with WingDings, but rather, they are using a bigger-than-average font like Trebuchet... and when their paper still isn't 3+ pages, then they tell me to switch it to an even larger font, like Tahoma. How about you make sure it's 3+ with ANY FONT!
The purpose of writing the memoir/profile is getting lost... they just want it to be the right length, no matter what stupid font. They don't aim for quality. And when I say

---

[8] This post is ridiculously picky about very insignificant things. Sheesh.

"they," I don't mean all my students, just some of them. I detest Times New Roman, I'll be honest. But if I require Georgia or Arial, someone is going to forget and then their paper will be longer or shorter and life won't be FAIR. Ugh. I wish I could just say that I'll grade on quality... but then the A students will still write 3+ pages, and the rest will write the BARE minimum and argue with me about the quality. That's why I stick to my 3+. Yes, kids, there's a reason for the BIG THREE. For one, it's not THAT long of a paper. Secondly, within three pages, they cover the basics and give details. Two pages is a little short for a narrative (especially when it's double-spaced) and, yea, 4 or 5 may be pushing it for many. Thirdly (hee hee), I love the number 3.

See... the font I blog in, Verdana, is nice. Maybe that'll be my required font?

p.s. Some still aren't getting the MLA required 1" programmed into their brains either. Why doesn't Microsoft Word just default to that? Another = UGH.

Posted 10/24/2007 at 10:44 AM

Monday April 28, 2008

[...]

Also, I realized this morning that the reason I may have gotten the "she doesn't answer my emails" comments in my online student evals was because I don't respond to emails filled with errors. I thought I placed that in ALL of my syllabi, but maybe not? Seriously, not only do I have no idea who some students are (based solely on their goofy email addresses) but I also get uncapitalized, misspelled emails. Since I teach them English, shouldn't that be of concern when they email me? They should remember who their audience is; this is also the reason I have no problem with crazy IM/text abbreviations because I am not their audience for that sort of communication.

I suppose I have started off today on the bad side of ... my email inbox.
Posted 4/28/2008 at 10:11 AM

Tuesday October 14, 2008

To put it bluntly, when a student claims that he/she was gone for an excused absence but then can not show documentation of the absence, I automatically assume the worst. I frown in suspicion. The student perhaps is lying or hoping I forget that I haven't seen the documentation, etc. Apparently, my syllabus' rules hold no value.
In reflecting further, I've noticed that students really haven't come up with any new argumentative strategies when it comes to arguing their excuses since I started teaching. It's the same arguments over and over. And my go-to point everytime? It's in the syllabus; I need proof. No proof, no assessment.
[...]
Posted 10/14/2008 at 10:18 AM

Wednesday September 7, 2011

Once again, I have to remind myself of the students who get their butts to class. Just the other day, I was assessing things and for every 7 students who had "figured it out and done well," there was one who didn't. And I focused on that ONE. Why? Because I like to torture myself? Maybe. But I think I have this optimism that creeps up at the start of every semester; I want them to just freaking do well. My class isn't tough, my assignments aren't hard or dull, and yet, it happens. They don't show their potential. Some just won't. I can give them knowledge, but I can't make them think. I stole that quote from someone, by the way.

And I wonder what percentage of time I spend in the classroom on assignments from the PAST. I think I may have solved that today by creating a small handout called, "So, You Want To Hand In Something Late, Eh?" I'll just give them that instead of fighting over whether their excuse is valid, etc. They have to read it, which most won't, so that'll save me some time. I'm not going to chase them or argue over excuses. I'll give them the small handout and the work they missed; they can figure out the rest.
Yeppers.
Posted 9/7/2011 at 1:9 PM

Tuesday October 18, 2011

Why don't my student know where the *&^%$#@ Dropbox is? Seriously. I wish we all could just put our assignments wherever we wanted. Maybe I'll start doing that with instructional guides. I'll just put some on Scribd.com, some on here, and some in my sock drawer. They'd be so upset. Ugh. It's like a freakin' scavenger hunt trying to find ANYTHING they handed in last week. For real. If ANY of them ask me when their papers will be graded, I'm not going to answer for fear of flippin' holy hell on them.
And this pertains to my on-campus students; my onliners typically don't shove stuff wherever they want.
Can you imagine if I sent my bills wherever I wanted? It's such a simple thing, people. Get your heads out of your phones for 5 seconds. Sheesh almighty.
Posted 10/18/2011 at 11:6 AM

Monday September 17, 2012

This is meant to be geared at my students... Who don't come to class.
I basically should tell them on the first day that I'm not going to chase them.
This is not high school.

I don't care, or believe, that you were sick on a Friday afternoon.
Posted 9/17/2012 at 1:53 PM

Sunday February 3, 2013

I don't know if "students these days," in general, don't "get" that late means late OR
if I've had one too many rare cases of confusion on this issue JUST this semester (and it'll go away in the coming semesters)...
But it's showing up more. Somewhat.

I know that this issue seems silly to some, but I detest lateness. I'm rarely - RARELY - late myself (with assignments or dates or bills, etc.), so I can't wrap my brain around this "easy to understand" rule. Isn't it disrespect at a low level? Like the same level where students/faculty send error-filled emails. It says to me, and maybe JUST me (I'm well-aware of this), "I don't care to write nicely; I don't care to get this to you on time." Maybe that's extreme, but it's my feeling.

Ugh. I've become more lenient on some things, but not this lateness stuff.
And then some will do the whole: "Just this one time, can you overlook your rule?" Sheesh. I don't want the bitch switch to go off, people. Isn't there a saying like: An emergency on your part does not constitute an urgency on my part. Would a boss give them another chance & another chance &... because I doubt they are missing deadlines JUST in my class.

Anyhow. Let's end that rant!
[...]

Posted 2/3/2013 at 8:55 PM

October 13, 2015.

In other news, some of my students are annoying and lazy. Shocking, right? I introduce the project yesterday where they get to CHOOSE between two options in either Writing Spaces book... either essay is over 10 pages.

A student (or two) groan at this.

Me: "Oh My God, I'm Making You READ!"

Student: "Is there an audio version?"

Me, squinting and tilting my head: "What did you just say?"

Student: "Is there..."

Me, agitated: "Nope, nope, nope. Zip it."

Ugh.

March 22, 2016.

The older-than-average student in my 1pm class wrote in a project's response that he felt the articles he was asked to read were not worthwhile. Oh, gosh, let me please create the class around your interests and your interests alone! I'm so sorry. First of all, why even write that in one's response? To piss off the instructor, right? And I immediately go to the if-I-had-a-penis scenario because a lot of students – whether they would acknowledge this or not – are sexist. Secondly, if you are older-than-average, are you not older and wiser and can see that I am gearing this class at the average college student who needs to fucking learn how to write better. I'm not teaching an upper-level English class here, bub. I know I'm not teaching your precious diesel classes, but wait – in another response for another project, you said the degree you were achieving was worthless. That you've learned more in the real world. Well, no shit! I had NO IDEA there was a REAL WORLD! Listen to the words of my former thesis advisor: Life is long, college is short. Why can't he enjoy himself? Why do I have to end up with Eeyores all the damn time? Like, oh my god, you have a good job when you leave this campus, and it's going to make you lots of money... I'm SO SAD FOR YOU. Give me a break.

And I so want to respond and say something snarky, but I'm going to let him think I didn't read it. I'm just going to keep it in my hat, so to say.

May 4, 2016.

[...]

So, I wrap up "teaching" today. Not the "grading" part of my job, but the face-to-fact stuff will be "over" as of about 4pm today. That's kind of a relief. I'm exhausted.

It doesn't help that I've had two conversations with nimrods who need extra credit. It doesn't help that I've had a few conversations over email and in person with 1pm students who wanted my schedule to be the rule ("It says the Tiger[9] Project is due over the weekend.") and not my actual words in class ("The Tiger is due Saturday" x 3). Huh. So, I'm supposed to reward you for not listening to me in class? The schedule even says it's subject to changes. Hell, you didn't even technically upload it "on the weekend" anyhow! I mean, I know the real request. The real request is for me to do more work (accept their late projects and assess them) and for them to do less (if their Tigers are accepted, a few don't have to complete the Wildcat). That's a lot of selfishness, isn't it? All because they can't hear me in class (then tell your buddies to shut up or ask me when it's due or whatever).

July 31, 2016.

My official "summer off" starts now: at almost 9am (the early bird assesses crap early). And I have a good sixteen days to stare at a wall or not think about school shit or binge-watch

---

[9] Many of my projects, for a time, were named after animals. I can't recall why I did this, but I think it was to spice up the typical titles of "Project #1," etc.?

chitty TV or paddleboard into oblivion or bicycle to China or drink vodka until I'm super stupid or nap until August 16.

Those final grades weren't too tough to wrap up. I had a good bunch of students in all my sections this summer; I don't think I've always been able to say that. The only oddballs have been this female student in Eng120 who has plagiarized her classmate's responses here and there; I caught her rephrasing them much too closely about four times. I doubt she read my comments as to why she wasn't earning anything on them, either. Perhaps, she thought it was normal to copy and paste others' thoughts, but I've been ON HER since day one when I was reading their comments and another student responded to her stating, "Um, that's exactly what I just said." I requested that she revise her entry, and she did, but then continued to plagiarize. I'm sure she thinks I don't read their entries [...]. Whatever the reason, I'm over it. She failed herself. If you want to plagiarize, do it smartly. And I have a zillion ways that can be done in an online class; I'll write a book about that someday.

Not.

Anyhow, beyond her, the other oddball I've had is a very recent one. An email came in yesterday from another female student about how she started off this class flustered over a car accident in late May. Now, I don't know why she waited until THE LAST DAY to tell me this, but it doesn't sound like she was hospitalized – just shook up, which I understand can be a wee bit traumatizing for a while – and she actually DID do some work within those first weeks of class in June. In fact, those assignments she sent me that she wanted credit for? Yeah, um, she did them on time in June, but did them incorrectly. Yeah. And she sent me the same exact mini-arguments (they were incorrect because it's a pass/fail assignment and she was missing a piece). I rolled my eyes intensely, gave her credit for two of them since they fell into that "first two weeks of class" area, and she still ended up with the exact letter grade as before she emailed me.

So, whatever. I guess if nothing else, I'll look like I cared enough to give her credit? For an assignment that was already completed and incorrect? Eh. I could point out all that, and that it didn't change her grade, but it's probably not worth the stress and time.

August 31, 2016.

[...]

In 8am class, more students have no idea how to log into the computers (after I asked them to hit up IT last week to find out their login shit) or how to connect to the printer in the room (um, again, use the IT center for that; I'm a teacher and my rooms change, so why should I know all that, AND didn't I put in the syllabus that you should bring a USB or email your papers to yourself or maybe use fucking Dropbox.com?), so I have to be calm and not freak out about that. Seriously, people. YOU all should figure out how to hand in your shit. Let me repeat: YOU should be figuring this out. Not me. Like jeezus. And to the girl who just wanted to email me her Google Docs for the rest of the semester? Um, what? Yes, I want everyone to choose whatever way they want to hand in their stuff, so that I have 66 students handing in things in 66 different ways. No. I want you to type your project on paper. End of story. Get it to me in that way. Your future bosses aren't going to want an email and then a Google Doc and then a URL and then a Dropbox invite. Good lord.

THEN another student has to complain – ever so slightly – about having to come ALL THE WAY TO CLASS at 8am on Monday to find out I wasn't there. I was burn victim #1, and I'll get to that later.

p.s. My officemate right now has a student talking to her that is using "like" way too fucking much. And he sounds high. And it's obvious he doesn't want to write; he wants her to do the work for him: "Should I say like three things in the intro and then like..." OMG, shoot me. Or shoot him. Whatever. "I could like basically like compare... could I like basically like, you said, like in the intro..." Holy fucking shitballs.

September 19, 2016.

[...]

I just checked my email... SO many sick students. Or should I write "sick" students. Luckily, it's built into the contract[10] that they can miss 5 small/medium projects, so I don't have to worry about late work coming in. I don't even think I put what was excused vs. what wasn't excused in the syllabus; this allows me to not have to worry about judging their absences. I think I may have mentioned that school-sponsored things were okay, but that was about it. I didn't talk about getting nurse's notes or funeral booklets. I'm just going to use those 5 small/mediums as potential "skip days" for them. Oddly enough, if they followed the schedule relatively closely – and had a buddy in class who told them what we were doing for those Medium Projects (as far as what page in the Booklet, etc.) – they'd be able to "skip" more than 5 class days. But they aren't the sharpest tools in the shed when it comes to that stuff, are they?

September 26, 2016.

The Breeder's song "Cannonball" just came on Pandora. Fuck yeah. I need to throw a cannonball at a few people. Some colleagues, maybe ten students, and Drumpf. Ugh. What a fucking Monday it's been. How can a college student email me how he "didn't have time" to upload his Alligator[11] project this weekend? I'm fairly certain a lot of them were DONE with that project last Wednesday. Yes, last Wednesday. So, he just didn't have time between Wednesday and Saturday night to press ATTACH and SUBMIT? Fuck that noise. You don't belong at college. If you can't write up three letters to some cool people

---

[10] For a few semesters, I tried out contract grading.

[11] Yep, more animal names for projects.

in 3-5 WEEKS and upload the goddamn documents on time, you DO NOT BELONG HERE. Go work at Subway with that lunatic former advisee of mine. Good lord.

MY CLASS ISN'T THAT HARD? My schedule is like organized TO THE MAX. More than it EVER HAS, and yet, they don't have a clue what they are doing. I don't know how ANYONE can not being doing WELL in my class, EVEN IF they have skipped class a few times. My schedule is amazeballs. Like, no shit. Not kidding. It's got everything fucking listed. It feels like the more organized I've become over time, the less likely they depend on that organization they have at their fingertips. They'd rather just ask me to hold their hands.

Shit. How did I get through college without knowing any one professor's detailed schedule? I must've been a genius. I must've read minds because we didn't email our professors back then. Or maybe I just asked my classmates what was going on or something. Jeezus Pete.

[...]

I'm mentally fried today. I assessed like a banshee, and then I had to prevent myself from freaking out on students who didn't listen. This wasn't the worse Monday I've had, but it hasn't been pretty. If someone had taped me in class today, they would've seen a tired woman holding back a lot of frowning... the people watching would've heard my students' questions and thought, "She just covered that," or "Why would they think she takes late work?" or "Why aren't they paying attention? Do they think she'll repeat this stuff later?" And I probably will. Now that I think about it, there were two girls in the corner of that 1pm class chatting it up while I was covering the Camel. So, note to self... I'll use Josie[12]'s questions as my response later.

"What did we talk about Monday?"

"Did you look at the schedule? Did you look online?"

---

[12] Friend turned colleague and officemate.

Put it all back in their fucking court. They are smart; they can figure shit out without me.

True fucking story.

I need to stop hand-holding in the ways I do… by answering questions they can find themselves. And when it comes to the contract:

"Am I missing anything from the contract yet?"

"Have you been keeping track? Are you using the Contract Checklist? Have you been using Gradebook as a guide for what you've handed in?"

November 2, 2016.

[…]

After my 8am class, I felt a little like I had just witnessed an impromptu shitshow. Students coming unprepared to show their presentations, students not showing up at all, and students showing up late – who always do – and then showing off a half-done presentation all before asking me what's due Friday because… yeah, they haven't been to a full class time slot in weeks, and suddenly, I'm supposed to reiterate to them what they've been missing by coming to my class late. Not.

It was a shitshow, and I'm sure the 1pm class will be a shitshow and then ditto for the 3pm. And then I'll go home and try to compose myself with a cocktail before attending the PD Day Friday where I hope I can figure out how to lower the shitshowness of my damn classes.

What can a teacher respond with – in these circumstances – that is professional and will change the action/attitude of these students? If I were to mention, nicely, that they should show up for class on time, I just get excuses that aren't related to me or the class. They fully know – yet maybe don't embrace – that coming to class late is not cool, but they continue to allow that of themselves. Zeb said in class that his phone keeps falling in between his bed and something else, and that's why he can't hear his alarm. Huh. How about you put the phone somewhere else? This literally hasn't occurred to him? And why does that excuse him? His lack of planning requires me to be flexible; perhaps students should be learning the opposite because that's the real world... working with inflexibility, yet they'd just write that kind of lesson off. THEY aren't supposed to deal with inflexibility; we are. This is shit. Hand-holding is allowing them to remain in their comfort zones when, um, college ain't a space for comfort. It's a space for learning, and learning is uncomfortable – hell, just look at me trying to learn that TYCA-MW website crap or why Outlook won't download images from other people!

Zen.

I had some zen when I got done with my 8am class because Josie had her sister Ann – one of my best friends from long, long ago – on her "dumb" phone. It was lovely to hear her voice, and I needed that little dose of Ann Happiness.

As expected, the 1pm class was a shitshow, but it wasn't 100% shit. I can't imagine how these students would do IF I were to NOT give them a sample of the project. I mean, they aren't really USING the sample as a guideline and they aren't looking at the infographic with the checklist either, so I don't know what the fuck they are thinking or doing or reading... oh wait, they aren't – some to most of them, that is – thinking or doing or reading anything.

I ignore a lot of these issues. I don't freak out in class too much when they pull out these questions of where something is or when something is due or what some assignment is... I've started to smile sarcastically and repeat myself again and again and again. Funny thing is that they don't have to ask me shit; everything – EVERYTHING – is in my schedule or online somewhere. I'm not even kidding. I'm THAT organized. So, let's say they skip class? Okay, if they take 5 minutes to READ the goddamn schedule, they'll probably figure out what is due or what is going on. I mean, jeezus. I didn't have even a 1/3 of a clue what some of my instructors wanted when it came to papers and projects; I remember Dr. Krishnan not giving out a rubric or sample or remote guide to what he wanted from us in that Literary Analysis class, or whatever it was called. I wrote four different papers before I finally achieved a B on one that I barely tossed together over beers. And, ding ding ding, I didn't go up and complain to him about the four Cs once. Firstly, he intimidated me, but secondly, I figured there was something wrong with my writing. My students – some to most of them – figure that a low grade is my burden; I have caused them grief for no real reason. They know it can't be their fault that they didn't hit the contract level; somehow, I didn't say something or hold their hand enough. They don't turn it back to themselves and ask, "Did I read her instructions thoroughly? Did I listen critically in class when she introduced this assignment?"

November 16, 2016.

So, what used to be the student plan of just throwing their assignments on the desk in the random classroom on campus – assuming that that was my actual office or something – has turned into the student plan of uploading their assignments to random Dropbox baskets in our online platform that are not designated for that assignment, or maybe they save it to the actual Dropbox.com and send a link to my email that I can't open due to privacy settings, or they'll email it after class claiming their computer blew up or something, or they'll pretend to have emailed me and spelled my name incorrectly.

All these plans they have for handing in my assignments typically fail, and then, as predicted, it's my fault.

It's always my fault.

And when you try to convince them it was THEIR fault, they get mad... and I always de-escalate my anger for their benefit. For the retention. For their egos. For my own sanity.

November 18, 2016.

We got our first "snowstorm" of the season last night. [...] Students typically use this first snow day to pretend they have no clue how to walk in snow or whatever. The lamest excuse thus far in my career has been the student who didn't want to walk back to his dorm to retrieve his book because it was too windy.

Yes, that happened.

November 21, 2016.

[...]

Two students didn't bother to come to class this morning to show off their Panthers and one – Martin[13], who comes in weekly to check his contract grade; it's always a D – came into my office before class to tell me his flash drive was missing. Oh, of course. What perfect timing for Mr. Slacker. I would bet big money he just doesn't have it done, and I didn't have to argue with him much beyond my knee jerk response of a boisterous laugh telling him that it WAS a problem. I threw his name down for Wednesday, and then he asked me if he could just show me. Um, no, this isn't how this fucking works. I think my instructions even state that the creator has to present it to the class! Sheesh.

Anyhow, Tony[14] made his using Windows MovieMaker, and that program isn't on the teacher station computer. So, after the students who signed up presented, I jumped up and downloaded it while I handed back their Medium Project #9s, but then his song and photos didn't show up anyhow. Annoying. Next time, I will tell students to use PowerPoint or iMovie. Anything but fucking MovieMaker. I also should have talked more about citing anything that wasn't your own, as well as required their poems to be uploaded somewhere, so I could double-check word count.

---

[13] Many student names have been changed.

[14] Many student names have been changed.

"I love when students come to my class 40 minutes late to show their presentation." - said no teacher ever

Big ass lessons learned from doing this visual essay project differently this semester. I already got an idea from Josie about having their presentation and poem uploaded to a spot online the Sunday before the two days of presentations. That will "cure" them of doing it during class or coming to class 40 minutes late because I'm sure they were finishing it up after I gave them over a week to do it. The truth is that I don't need to give them weeks to complete something, I suppose; the "good" students aren't going to procrastinate, and the ones who are going to wait until the last minute no matter how long I give them. So, I need intermittent deadlines. And then those deadlines count towards fulfillment of the contract.

And then Mr. Slow waits until there are five minutes left... I don't know if he was thinking I would just move him to Wednesday for presenting and give him a pass on lateness? I had seen him working on it all hour, so I ask him if he's going to present. He says he doesn't have a song in it, and I state that he could "get creative" and play a YouTube clip in the background. I follow that up with: "Why do I have to be more creative than you all?" He sheepishly walks up to present.

I've always felt a little bad when I hear that my students find me intimidating, but perhaps that's a good thing, and I should use it to my advantage. They walk all over me, and I'm sick of it. If I'm this amazingly organized teacher, and they don't appreciate it, why am I the one who feels badly about intimidating them into getting their goddamn fucking work done?

It's bullshit. I want to get away with being angry with them, and in that instance, not being called a fucking bitch. I know the first part is doable; the latter is impossible due to sexism. Ugh.

The truth is that I tippy-toe around them because I don't want to be "the bitch," but what good is it doing me? None. I should just let them have it. If they are being rude, I should point it out. I did with the quarterback – stating: "Oh, how nice of you to grace us with your presence." He smiled a smile that was as cocky as hell. I detest athletes like him; he gives them a bad name, for sure. As it turns out, his project was riddled with errors, so it's the first Redo of the day, and I'm going to require a letter of apology for him being late to class. I'll just pile up the assignments on him since his ego is large enough to carry it all.

[...]

April 10, 2017.

I get it. Students want it on paper – or email – that I said it was okay for them to skip class. They want it on paper – or email – that I declared, "Yes, that is the only assignment due," but it's not going to happen. Follow the schedule. That's my repetitive mantra to them when they message me about "having to be gone" because they don't have any classes in their discipline. So, today will be a quiet one, I guess. Some students are probably going to skip class, and I don't really care either way. What I do care about are the email messages asking what we're doing when my FUCKING SCHEDULE has been followed to a T this 8-weeks. Use the schedule, stop using me. I don't care, and it's not my job to interpret the schedule, is it? It says what is says. I could understand if I've moved deadlines on them, but the only time I've done that is when I've extended the damn deadline (not shortened it).

Anyhow, enough about them.

[...]

May 2, 2017.

[...]

In this morning's episode of "Another Email I Should Have Just Deleted," an online student wanted to know how to complete the bonus discussion for this week. It appeared that he might not have read the instructions, so I asked him to do so. Yes, I should've deleted the email as this discussion is worth extra credit, so hey students, do the extra work, but no, I asked him to READ and then I got one rude email after another about how I make him feel dumb and that he's been wanting to respond – REACT: that was the word he used – to me in this manner, in this tone, because apparently I deserve it. I make him feel dumb. Huh. Well, maybe you aren't being smart about reading the fucking instructions. Maybe you ARE being dumb about this? Maybe you shouldn't tell your instructors to search for the definition of the word reaction? Maybe you shouldn't tell them you are allowed to express your feelings as a student or react as a human because, yes, you can, but wow is that going to bite you in the butt as a coworker and employee, MAN.

All this bummed me out. Josie told me not to give it juice – this is Zooey's[15] advice always. [...]

August 28, 2017.

My first two classes have gone well today; the only hiccup was when I read one of the journal entries from a female student who dropped the "n-word" in the middle of her story about what happened this weekend. Yes, she commented mid-entry that she should not add any "n-words" to her Snapchat anymore. Oh, holy shit woman... I might have to tattoo the non-discrimination statement straight on her forehead.

And then there was the comment about how "I'm an electrician, not an English teacher" in the other class which I just smiled at; students don't know how to whisper. All I thought, in the middle of my sigh was, oh dude you are neither right now. Calm down.

Well, time to throw some controversy about gender at my English 120 students. I'm hoping for a good discussion – with ground rules established first – and then time for them to

---

[15] A wonderful friend and beloved colleague.

compose their first MAD[16] assignments: the skeleton of an argument.

So, the discussion about gender went SUPER well; I might've brought up things about my personal life that I should not have, but oh well. How much of it will they remember? Bits and pieces, if any at all. I'll focus, instead, on how they created a hashtag (#NipplesFor200), and how they all seemed to really engage in critically thinking about how girls' attire is policed, how men treat women as objects, how it's on both men and women to treat each other well and call out crummy behavior, and how the "boys will be boys" thing is over. We got lucky and had about 10-15 minutes left to chat about the MAD activity; I showed them the format, and we did a sample together. I hope they understood it, and if not, we'll figure it all out on Wednesday. One student wanted me to claim they were my favorite class... I said they were my loudest. I have a good crew in there; that's for sure.

It's a wee bit odd to observe myself not getting royally pissed – or even mildly pissed – at things that have torked me off in the past. Almost every student in every class last week nodded along when I asked them if they could all log into the classroom computers and get onto our online LMS. Today, I discovered that quite a few of them "lied." Instead of huffing and puffing at them, I've found myself simply informing them that they need to go to IT as soon as possible to figure it all out because I don't have access to their passwords, but they DO need access to these computers. A few students asked to submit things online, but that causes me to frown and tilt my head like a dog: They aren't taking an online class... but you want that little bit of convenience? Huh. It sounds lazy and a

[16] MAD was an acronym for Mini-Argument Dissection, meaning the students would dissect an argument down to its bare bones: thesis, evidence, conclusion, etc.

little bit like: "Please let me hand this in however I want to." Um, no. This is an on-campus course, so much of the stuff is done IN class.

I wondered, on my trip home to let Sadie out, if this isn't the zen in me floating to the top, but also Mark Manson's[17] book. I mean, I literally have been giving zero fucks about students' crummy attitudes thus far. I practically ignore them; I'm almost immune.

August 30, 2017.

Ah, my first "I didn't understand Blackboard and I didn't know we had something due" message this morning. From whom I assume is a fairly bright student, too – the one who started the hashtag #NipplesFor200 on Monday. Ugh. I replied back that I would help him with Bb yet wondered why he didn't ask how to complete the assignments last week when I mentioned TWICE that they were assigned and due. Huh. It's a convenient excuse, and one I will hear until the end of time.

As assignment deadlines pop up in the coming weeks, I have a feeling my zen and #ZFG[18] vibes will be challenged; I will just have to remind myself that they need to acquire autonomy. They need to fail at these small things, learn to revise their actions, and then do better. I can't allow late work "just because." I'm unsure why they think that works in the classroom or real world. Maybe it's just their "Hail Mary," hoping I'll allow them to complete an assignment that is worth 1/100 of the semester?

September 1, 2017.

As predicted by an imaginary force, I had a few email messages this morning from students who had "family emergencies" and had to miss class. I'm pretty sure the family emergency is that they want to go home early for the long

---

[17] Title: *The Subtle Art of Not Giving a Fuck.*

[18] This is the acronym for: Zero Fucks Given.

weekend; I'm no dummy. So, to those who asked, "what we were doing," I responded: "We're completing a journal entry and small project #1[19]." Then, to fend off any questions about making up the work, I added: "The contract allows you to miss a certain number of projects." I'm sure that won't deter them from asking to make up things. I'm sure the student who gave me her late MP#1 today is thinking that it counts because... she thinks it's okay to hand in late work? I don't know.

I predict a few more of those email messages for my 11am class.

Anyhow, the upside of right now contains many things. First off, I graded a lot of assignments yesterday – prompts and MP#1 for English 110 – and created my first VoiceThread. I canceled class today with the English 120 class in order to give them time to read the 14 pages I wanted them to; I uploaded that 14-page article to VoiceThread, it made the PDF into slides, and then I read certain passages aloud to get the students going. I then shared it with the face-to-face class and copied it over to the online class, too. This way, the online students can hear me, and I'm hoping it encourages all of the students to read the whole damn thing.

I'm going to zip over to that online shell and shoot out reminder about the first deadline being this Saturday.

September 20, 2017.

Oh, students students students.

First, an email comes in last night from a student who was sick the first week or two.... I clicked "exempt" for those assignments for her, and her email asks about the video online for the Week 5 MAD. Um, in class on Monday, we talked about what the MAD would be about this week – Chuck's[20] essays #16

---

[19] The contract grading I used contained X amount of small, medium, and large projects. There is a picture of one of the contracts I used in the chapter called I'll Call This Chapter: Pedagogy.

[20] Chuck Klosterman's *Sex, Drugs, and Cocoa Puffs.*

or #8. Was she in attendance (I asked that)? She responded at 11pm last night that she didn't think we had Monday classes? AND that, um, I should get back to her as soon as possible. At 11pm. Like WHAT THE FUCK? I'm 85% sure I gave her the Syllabus when she finally came to class... did she LOOK at it and READ it? I'm betting on no.

Then I've had students – constantly and consistently for years – who email me and then DON'T go back and read my response. It's like texting a person and then throwing away their phone. Why do they do that? Maybe I should stop responding to on-campus student email if they are just going to ask me in class for the very response I took the time to type the fuck out? Maybe I should ask in the email if they truly want a response or if they are just going to ask me the same damn question in class anyhow?

[...]

You know, it really doesn't matter if I start off with Resting Bitch Face in the classroom on day one or take the more zen approach because in both cases, the students slowly show their true colors. Not all of them, but many around this time embrace the laziness within them that they perhaps see in their classmates. For example, a student in my 8am this morning asks what the Medium Project #3 topic was. I mentioned in class at least twice, and I'm pretty sure he was there, but he didn't listen, and he stated that his friends in the class didn't hear what it was either. Huh. I guess I'm just fucking talking to myself.

Has no one heard about taking notes in class? Or using those damn phones as a note-taking device?

Annnnd as I start to grade [...] I am realizing that many of them aren't completing the online assignments at all, and a few are completing it half-assed. So, before I even start on the 11am class, I think I might make an executive decision to use Friday's class for them to complete the entire Small Project #4. They might say they want it due over the weekend, so they can leave early, but that's not a great plan for them when I consider their grades right now. Then again, it's their choice to not do homework that's been assigned. It's their responsibility.

October 2, 2017.

I really love when male students adjust themselves in front of me when it's just us. In the hallway. Yeah.

I also love when students procrastinate and then Blackboard goes to shit and suddenly, they're getting rewarded for procrastination.

I love it, too, when students miss deadlines by seconds or minutes and think it's no big deal when really, Blackboard wanted your fucking submission at 11:10am NOT 11:11am. Deadlines matter. Duh.

I love when they email me saying they've been trying to email me.

I love when they email me, I respond, and then they see me in class and ask me if I saw the email they sent. Yes, and I responded: did YOU see my fucking RESPONSE? Like, do you send text messages and then not look later to see if anyone responded? Why is email that different when you can set up notifications just as easily for your eMAIL as your TEXTs. Jeezus Christ.

I love when I have to be responsible for me AND them, somehow.

I love being responsible for the teaching and the learning and the writing and the deadlines and the repeating and I love how it's my fault and my problem when they can't remember my two or three or five reminders.

I should ask them, "Am I responsible for YOUR deadlines?" I have the feeling I could remind them by text message, email, voice, and Schedule... on an hourly basis, and they would STILL miss deadlines.

Wow.

Ugh.

Do I need a TYCA-MW[21] break or WHAT? Shit, man.

December 1, 2017.

[...]

To backtrack into things I haven't written about because I was happily overwhelmed with NaNoWriMo[22]:

- Did I already write about the student who came in all concerned about her grade? And stated that she'd always gotten As in English (so, like I should just GIVE her one in mine, I guess?)? Well, that day she sat on her phone in class. Yep. Moments after being all concerned, she didn't care to pay attention. And that must be her M.O. because I got an email from her this morning about something I covered in class. DELETE.
- Another email I deleted this morning: A student wondering about our Final Exam during Finals Week. I don't know HOW OFTEN I have repeated myself about that one, but SHIT. I know no one listens to me, but she didn't hear me say that ONCE in the 3+ times (in 3+ days) that I did? And even if you're not going to listen to me, LOOK AT THE FUCKING SCHEDULE.
- I have written about the student who made some "Mexican joke" (they dig ditches?) at the end of his group's Fake Company presentation? Yeah, that was super awesome. I made the comment in class that his comment was highly unnecessary, and then I reported it to a few people in his major.

[...]

- I've had one student figure out that she didn't need to come for this last week because she's due to earn an A

[21] TYCAMW stands for Two-Year College English Association for the Midwest region. These regional conferences bring together two-year college English teachers for professional development, learning, and networking... and the occasional cocktail or karaoke or disco night.

[22] National Novel Writing Month, which is typically every November.

with the contract grading system. Yeah, and then she went and turned in a plagiarized medium project. Good lord.

- A few emails have contained students begging for me to pass them at a 60%... when we're using a contract grading system. Hmmm... I guess they haven't been in class long enough to hear it repeated 14 times that we're using the points system online as a back-up? Their contract grade MIGHT be better than the points grade.

Ugh.

I have many reasons to be pissy, but it's the same shit every semester. [...]

December 8, 2017.

If one more student asks me if we have a final exam...

Ode to the last Friday of regular classes:
To the students who ask me about Finals Week, we're meeting in a remote part of Alaska at 3:33pm Wednesday.
To the students who ask me how long the last small project has to be, I'm requiring a million words.
To the students who haven't bothered me about anything and who have listened and read instructions, Godspeed to you and may I have more of you in the future.

August 22, 2018.

[...]

One student thought I looked much older than a picture in my syllabus, another student in English 120 wanted to know if Chuck Klosterman's book was a movie, and another student asked where he was supposed to type/print up his homework. Ah, yes. These Mondays and Wednesdays will be fun and chaotic. I shall look at the positive and wonder how much stretching of my own patience will occur... I'm sure it'll all be fine; I have sarcasm on my side, and if all else fails, I have the power to ignore or calmly state that they need to listen better. They need to trouble-shoot. Yeah. [...]

August 29, 2018.

[...]

Speaking of good ideas, I've been transferring major points of knowledge in my good old melon lately... taking Josie's[23] schpeel[24] about boundaries and mixing it with other kinds of teaching strategies... and wondering where I've come from in that realm ("guide on the side," "sage on the stage," etc.). I've been strict about spelling and grammar and then I moved to caring more about organization and structure. I once cared a lot about late work and was a stickler for it, but now I've thrown in late passes to make myself be and appear "less bitchy." I've had students feel intimidated by me, and I've had students adore my class and it's push to make them more creative. What I'm saying is that we evolve as people and teachers. What I'm saying is that it's possible to mesh boundaries with silliness and that a person doesn't have to put the smack down to get her point across all the time. What I'm saying is that I think it's totally possible for Josie's style and strategy to work just as much as mine can for me. And the same can be said for even those teachers who we don't find to be very effective.

Maybe I'm turning into a softie, but hell, in the "real world" those who aren't productive or effective aren't always fired... higher ed works the same way; there will always be those who I might not think are doing something the best way, or those who are just bumps on logs waiting for a paycheck. This is the norm, unfortunately, everywhere in every place, so why complain? Why not just push ourselves to be amazing and then maybe the "bumps on the logs" get inspired?

---

[23] Friend turned department member and cherished colleague at NDSCS.

[24] Definition: A funky way to say summary or monologue?

Long story short, the way one person teaches is not wrong or right: it's just different. My way isn't more right or wrong than hers; we're just fucking different. End of story. [...]

October 1, 2018.

"I'm sorry I'm taking so long to grade your papers." Maybe I should just say it instead of getting snarky; it can be a little white lie. But then again, it adds to how apologetic women are supposed to be, instead of assertive. No, I didn't assess your papers over the weekend; I don't grade shit on my weekends!

Sean knocks and asks if I'm free before my 11am class; I say yes. Then he asks how to find our textbook online. Ugh. So, one step ahead and one step back. I should give a quiz at the end of the semester JUST on simple shit like that: Where is my office? Where is our textbook online? What time is your class? It's not like I expect them to memorize items, no, I'm constantly pushing them to BE RESOURCEFUL. BE FUCKING AUTONOMOUS.

Then in 1pm class, Mr. Simonson – the other student athlete I "told on" last week – asks me about the quiz that was on the schedule and due for 2pm today. I say, calmly, "Didn't I say that I would mention what was due in class? We'll be doing that quiz this week, yes, but it's not due today." So, then he wants me to reset the grade because he did it so quickly – thinking it was due today. He had earned 6/10 points. Yeah, we're talking 10 points. But it doesn't matter. Sometimes all that matters is that I just didn't follow some rule in their head; it could be a 5-point category on a rubric (like that one student who came in to complain years ago when Troy was my officemate for a year) or a 50-point assignment. If they sniff out some apparent, imaginary wrongdoing on my part, there is hell to pay suddenly on my end. It's weird.

I will always have those students who give a shit – who write out complete sentences and come to class with a smile on their faces. I will always have those students, too, who put in the bare minimum and rarely learn even how to spell my name on their somewhat MLA[25]-formatted papers, much less in an email message. There are people in my life who will always invite me to their parties, and there are some who don't want me around them when they celebrate. This is life. There are all types. They are in my life and in my classrooms.

Oh, the 3pm class. So, Ryan spent the whole hour retyping his proposal because the computer in the classroom didn't save it; um, hi, those computers reset themselves every night – you need to put your stuff on a flash drive (as stated in the syllabus). Luckily, I can just make a note that he completed it and he won't have to retroactively produce that with the Camel Redo that's possibly in his future.

Then Jimmy comes up with puppy dog eyes wondering why he got a zero on the Panther. I ask if I had left comments in the Gradebook. Um, yep, it was late. He uploaded it on September 19, but it was due September 16. I tell him, then, that he can use the last day of class to argue to his classmates that he should get those points; he wonders why he should have to do that. I say, "Because it's late." What the fuck? He should feel lucky I've added that little piece[26] to the semester; since argument isn't a large part of my English 110, I've added that to the last day: Argue to your classmates that you should get points – or get to revise/resubmit – a large project. But, no, I don't receive any gratitude. I've added so much cushion to that class with the late passes and redos. It might be worth looking at all of it to see if I'm putting too much into making everything less harsh on them.

October 8, 2018.

[...]

---

[25] Modern Language Association. It's a citation style.

[26] I can't remember what I called these activities, but they sometimes helped students who completed work very late. Their classmates always extended them grace.

"You don't have to answer so sarcastically."

"Um, yes, yes I do." One of the students I "told on" a few weeks back says this to me in class. He had asked me if the screen I was showing him in class was from Blackboard, when it was pretty fucking obvious that it was. I mean, what else would I be showing the class? Then, at the end of class, after I put it on the board and said it aloud at least once to the whole class, he asks if the MAD is online. Yes, it's a quiz, as I HAVE ALREADY STATED. Ugh. And he wonders why he's on my shit list? Firstly, nowhere in the book of the life does it state that we have to be friendly to other humans just because. Nowhere does it say that professors have to be nice to students to begin with, nor does it say we have to AFTER a student has been disrespectful. I mean, the common courtesy – like moving over for a vehicle coming in from the ramp lane – is to be nice just to be nice, but I literally don't have to be nice to you, dude. I'm not sure why you think that's a thing, ESPECIALLY after you've been a dick. I mean, I had to ask if class was ready today because you were blabbing. That seems to be the case a lot; people working AROUND your attitude. Yeah, not fun. Not cool. I'm not civil enough to bend to that idea anymore.

So... yeah... about that clusterfuck of a 3pm class. I walk in there, and it's just the 9-10 students talking over each other. I would try to listen for any questions, but it's impossible. They're confused about what was due over the weekend, etc. etc. I hand back Medium Project 4s, I ask for Medium Project 5s, but no one listens so I walk around and pick them up... I bring up the next item on my list: Assigning Medium Project 6. No one is listening from what I can see, and so I just stop and go to the teacher station to grade/assess what they handed in. Suddenly, they want answers. It's almost ten minutes into class, and it's like I'm suddenly the person who they seek out for help. As if I magically appeared. As if they were just going to use class as their own therapy session until they found me useful. So, I lose my cool. I flipped out but did not once use profanity.

Three of them walked out. I had considered walking out myself, but I just let them go. The minute they did, Raven asked a question, and I went to sit with the ones who stayed. We had a nice chat. Sean read his intro aloud, and it was good. I think I helped Raven figure out her introduction, and I gave Casey tips on what he might ask (if he's around cars all day, and it's a technical perspective, why not ask people about the fun stuff of cars – why they drive what they drive, etc.). The others chimed in with their topics, and we found out that the planet is at 7.6 billion people. I have a feeling I saw one of the boys who walked out – Ryan– in Walter's[27] office when I went to see what was in my eyeball. They may or may not complain about me. Whatever. I should probably write to their advisor(s). [...]

April 24, 2019.

[...]

Oddly, I had a student from a class come by yesterday and ask if he could just "take someone else's story and put his own words in." Um, no. And he had no clue what I was talking about when it came to using creative commons images; I simply said that I had talked about that in class, and that he should read up on it. He smiled and walked out, but I thought, Where did he get the idea that he could steal images? Some are well-aware that that's uncool (Amanda) and some are not (Trey).

Anyhow, beyond him, there's been one student online who is convinced that I have two errors in my Chuck Test. And there was a 3am email from a female student who has an 89.5, and she wanted a few points back on some random assignments.

No. Just no to all of it, people. Go away.

May 8, 2019.

[...]

Oh, dear people of Twitter who ask me to embrace my students in constant compassion... Do you want to know why I

---

[27] One of my many bosses.

default to not trusting students some of the time? Because I've been lied to, threatened, and insulted more times than I care to count. And after all that, I still love my job; I still enter the classroom with learning and fun on my sleeve, and... I even still try to be empathetic. Please don't push the lovey dovey stuff on someone who deals with the occasional bullying email from a student who demands "I WILL pass this class," etc.

Don't Poke the Bear.

Once upon a time, I taught in a very large computer lab. It was towards the end of the class period, and the shortest technical student I've ever taught came up to me to complain about his grade in front of a few leftover classmates. I could tell he was almost on his tippy-toes as I stood and listened to his complaint, when he ended his vent with, "Do we have a problem here?"

I LEANED into him and extended my height more, and said, "DO WE?" A buddy of his giggled, and they left.

At the time, I was filled with rage; so many of my "problem students" year after year are students who identify as males. And I recall wanting him to hit me. That sounds horrible, doesn't it? I wanted him to assault me and get kicked out of school. Luckily, the little bugger walked away.

The students who "poke the bear" rarely fare well. There's been the one who didn't want to read *Rule of the Bone*[28], a few who didn't want to read *Brain Droppings* by Carlin[29] or Chuck Klosterman's book[30] (due to the swearing/content), the student who looked like a serial killer (he didn't blink!) and stared at me in class as if trying to penetrate my skull with his glaze, the student who wanted to rumble over his own pal letter and then ended up on the campus web site, the student who thought he could use his religion to get around doing assignments, and a whole host of other fun stories...

+

---

[28] By Russell Banks.

[29] Yes, THEE George Carlin.

[30] *Sex, Drugs, and Cocoa Puffs.*

Tuesday June 7, 2005

"I've written a report before. They aren't that long." I wanted to say: Look buddy, in this class, for this assignment, it has to be a page to get a decent grade... Are they getting lazy 'cuz the quarter ends soon?
Posted 6/7/2005 at 8:53 PM

Tuesday September 13, 2005

"So, if it's going to be a zero, why even hand it in?"
"Because if you hand it in ON TIME, you WILL get credit."
Imagine that. They're called deadlines, ya'll.
Posted 9/13/2005 at 2:46 PM

Wednesday September 14, 2005

"Can I hand in the obituary on Friday?" "Well, you can, but you won't receive any points because it'll be late." "It'll be a zero?" "Yes, late work gets a zero. I talked about it on the first day of classes, and it's in the syllabus." His face suddenly looked like I just shot his mother.
Posted 9/14/2005 at 10:23 AM

Monday November 7, 2005

I hand back assignments in a class.
A student, passing by near my desk, says outloud:
"You must not like me," after looking at his grade.
He kept walking back to his spot.
I continued looking through my materials not quite sure if he wanted a response.

I thought: "You [students] earn grades; I don't give out 'good' grades just to the 'nice' students." It's tough to understand where some of these students are coming from. Many don't read the material and then they expect me to run through what the document is supposed to

contain. "How about you read the booklet I just created?" I sometimes feel like I am repeating myself as much as I did when I taught high school. Whew... And another thing, why is it that A-work is looking more and more like B-work. Only if a student goes beyond the expectations of the assignment should he or she earn an A. A = excellent. To some students, if they just complete the work they want an A. Not so much...
Posted 11/7/2005 at 2:29 PM

Friday September 1, 2006

"If it ain't on there, then I ain't doing it again." Wonderful. Way to stay positive Mr. Clark. Errrg. I wish he would stop talking to me. Like I am supposed to personalize my shit for him. Camilla had some student who wanted her to meet with him on a different day than class in order to get the information from class. Um. Yea. If you aren't in class, get the info you missed on your own time. This isn't flextime dude.
I am SO ready for the WEEKEND. A 3-day-er too!
Posted 9/1/2006 at 3:56 PM

Saturday March 3, 2007

I don't think students have any clue that their emails can have a certain tone to them... a tone that isn't appreciated. This one girl who also wrote a somewhat "mean" note which was attached to her Scavenger Hunt indicating that I hadn't counted her items correctly. Now she wants the fact that she left Thurs night to head of the storm to be an excused absence. I don't think so. And she accused me in the email of not being able to control the weather - um, duh. I think whoever is doing research (someone presented on it at the RRGSC[31]) on students' emails was onto something. They are more harsh via email.

I should almost do my own research. Save emails... or even tell students that I am conducting research so they "watch" their tones or language? I wonder if that would even deter them.
Posted 3/3/2007 at 9:52 AM

Wednesday March 7, 2007

Wow. Students can be really disrespectful. I have a certain someone who won't be coming back into my classroom until I get an apology. When did students start thinking that swearing at teachers was an okay thing to do?
Posted 3/7/2007 at 2:54 PM

Tuesday April 3, 2007

For some reason, even when students in the online classroom say, "This article was a complete waste of time," I take it personally. Like, why? I didn't write the article. And, hey, it made it into *everything's an argument*, so it must have something in it that is worthwhile. Sheesh.
And this Leigh girl. Ugh. The second "Like" girl. Check my grades check my grades they are wrong online.
LIKE I CARE.
Posted 4/3/2007 at 3:20 PM

Tuesday February 5, 2008

Listening skills. Vent #409.
So, I introduce the Proposal for the Stretch Project today

---

[31] Red River Graduate Student Conference (hosted by NDSU graduate students in the English department); this might've been a conference created by me and some others when I was up there 2001-05?

in my English 110 class (the 12-week one). A few ask me how long the paper has to be. I frown.
"Were you in class on Friday when I introduced the Stretch Project?"
"Yes."
"Interesting. Um, you have to teach us the topic you choose. There isn't a paper involved."
"Really?"
"Were you listening?"
"Um, no."
"Huh."

And this is how/why teachers go insane.
Posted 2/5/2008 at 1:23 PM

Tuesday September 16, 2008

Ah... the chew... the Technical Communication class is typically known for that. Big wads of the crap stuffed in my students' mouths as they try to argue for more points on a project. Fun times. In my other classes, I sometimes just have to put up with a whiff of cigarette smoke from their clothes or breath as they talk to me right after a in-between-classes smoke break. If it's not that, it's the iPod buds hanging from their ears or the constant clicking away at another text message.
Posted 9/16/2008 at 9:44 AM

Sunday September 21, 2008

What would give students the idea that it's okay to deliver my pizza to me and then want to talk about how their paper is late? I forsee Brandon, pizza boy, and Sam, who he mentioned had told him that I don't like late work (this Sam is also the one who slept in class one day, then was on the computer the next day, and then asked me why he had zeros in the Gradebook), not doing well at all in this

course. Get your shit straight; this class is really not that tough.
Posted 9/21/2008 at 7:18 PM

Tuesday October 14, 2008

Pretty sure student C wanted to holler at me this morning. Mumbling about his short temper and telling me he was about to lash out at me. Asking me to just call his mom to get documentation on his illness. I just need proof & he doesn't know who to call to get it? I call BULLSHIT. And how he doesn't like English and how he knows someone who got a 200/200 on his portfolio and he didn't revise (well, maybe he didn't and still highlighted changes or maybe he did and he told you otherwise because you're a slackerass); I just love when they talk to each other about deductions.
"I have it done." Cool, just show me an excused absence. "You've been gone a lot." And so have YOU, Mr. Chew-in-the-mouth-makes-me-wanna-throw-up.
Looking back through his Gradebook, it's not just that one assignment that has fucked him over, so he can just SUCK IT. If you don't like English, fine, but do the fucking work so you don't end up hollering at me for your laziness at the end of the 8weeks you little [...].
Posted 10/14/2008 at 10:24 AM

Tuesday September 21, 2010

"No offense but I find it stupid to write an essay about an essay."

When students point out, vocally or textually, that an assignment is dumb... what are they truly saying?
Are they just blatantly disrespecting the teacher because that's the cool thing to do (and they are conformists)?

Or... are they fishing for attention?

Often, I ignore these comments and just assess the text as it is.
If it's a vocal response, combined with the rolling of the eyes, I usually look through the student at the floor - and sigh.

When one signs up for a class, a required one or not, aren't they supposed to TRY to learn?
I can't force them to "get" my assignments or to "see" the connections.
"You can lead a horse to water..." and sometimes when you lead a lot of horses, a few won't drink just because the others aren't.
They like to be stubborn and un-intelligent, when they aren't or don't have to be. If that makes sense.

Once again, for the gazillionth time, I need to focus in on those students who come to class willing to do something, to think about something.
They are my go-to-people, and they are still in the majority.
Posted 9/21/2010 at 11:50 AM

Monday December 17, 2012

For some reason last night, I started to think of all the students I've pissed off in the past. I don't think I have fully torked off a ton of people in my time, but I have upset a few students = over plagiarism issues, over ten points on a project they were earning an A on anyway, over the swear words in Carlin's book, over my late work policy, etc. I've even had one student say, "I'm about to get really upset here," and instead of backing off, I pushed him, "What does that mean?" I think he's been the only one to attempt to threaten me, and he was probably suffering from the Napolean complex. Oh wait, there was the student who accused me of being racist, and I said, "No, I'm prejudice against all students who aren't using their brains in my class."

What if any ONE of those students was just mentally-disturbed enough to find a gun and hunt me down? Would I have much of a chance to survive? It could happen at 2pm on a Tuesday, when I'm walking across the parking lot to the library. (So, I suppose this should teach me that whole "live each day as your last" lesson?)

And it sounds like there was absolutely no rhyme or reason for why those children had to die in Connecticut. The man was nuts-o and just wanted to take out some innocent lives? This scares me even further. I can kind of understand the revenge motive (and using the words "kind of" is pushing it), but when there is no reason ... what the heck do we do with that?
Posted 12/17/2012 at 10:9 AM

February 5, 2014

Firsts This Year.
Sometimes, when I start to create lists in my head, or say, "Guess what happened TODAY that has NEVER happened before?" I realize documentation has to occur. And, so, I think I should document these items.
I really, really hope that these are all situations that have just oddly happened in one school year...[...]
1. Student who logged into eCompanion & thought what I was showing them on there would magically pop up. No, um, you have to click on the "Projects" tab and ... yeah. Click around, duh?

2. Student who thought we'd meet in the same room we met for the fall semester... ?
3. Online student who asked when the first paper was due, where the guide was for it, and did I have a student example? Um, did you bother to look through the online shell? It's ALL THERE!
4. Student who has a disability and didn't go to the disabilities person on campus, yet gives me attitude when I don't help him/her out. Huh?
5. Student who leaves book bag in our room instead of taking it with him/her while he/she goes to lunch. Are we students' lockers now? Um, no.
6. Student who brought his/her mother to our advising time.
7. Student who used attractiveness to get my attention.
8. Student who didn't log into eCompanion to see his/her grade for fear of "jinxing" it. Yeah, he/she failed. CHECK YOUR GRADE!
9. Student who, instead of citing his/her source in the paper, just put a hypertext link stating: Click here. Um, no. That will not be happening on my watch.
10.

I hope that's it.

Remember when I had my first "crier." That was a long time ago. Now, if anything, I come across arrogance and anger. Yikes.

Posted at 1:22 PM

October 7, 2016.

God bless them, because I'm not going to.

Okay, so, I was just reading responses from Monday's videos that covered racism and sexism and weight. The 8am class, overall, was insightful and very open-minded and well-written. Then, I skip over my 1pm class because I'll read theirs while they are peer-reviewing today in class and go to my 3pm pile. Ugh. Beyond the women's legit and solid responses, the men – on average – didn't see what the big deal was with racism or sexism or weight. In fact, a few of them think that if you are "overweight," you should work at being "healthy." I simply asked how they knew someone was "overweight"? How could they tell someone was "healthy"? Why anyone would be obligated to be "healthy" for others? Like, to speak to the latter, my grandpa just had some chest pains this week and went in to check to see if it was a heart attack. It wasn't. He had one many years back, and I don't know if he is following the diet they gave him back then... you know, less saturated fat and butter and yummy things. And let's say he hasn't given up butter. Why should he just so he can live longer FOR ME when I see him like twice a year? How selfish is that of ME? Very.

I think a lot them live in this scrawny white male privileged world. [...]

They don't know what it's like to be on a diet, to starve themselves[32], to see magazine ad after magazine ad of a women with the "perfect bodies" that have been photo-shopped (much less the fact that the woman is already "thin" and has probably dieted for that ad). Sure, they'll say that commercials show the "perfect man," too, with six-pack abs and "perfect hair," and it's true, but the amount of time women have been subjected to these things and the number of images out there pushed upon women... is astronomical. And all this shit goes back in time to the generations before us. It's ugly.

+

[32] Yes, I've written one book about this, and I may write another one.

Miss Priebe,
I realize that you have a purpose in assigning a book[33] which tears down the moral fabric of our nation; however, I do not understand why you would take the unlawful stance of insisting that I read such filth, when I have already stated that I will not because of my religious beliefs. I am familiar enough with the Constitution to know that your reference to the seperation of church and state only gives me the right to study English without being insulted by being assigned reading which teaches poor grammar, spelling, and in general, destroys all that is good and moralistic. You may call me a fundamental extremist, though it would not be true, I don't really care. I do however take offense that you would think it alright to replace proper English studies with a program which has yet to address the obvious delinquency of the current English programs in the U.S. If you are willing, I would have no problem doing a book report on "Hans Brinker and the Silver Skates" which has the same ability which the "book" you chose has, but is completely devoid of profanity, explicit verbiage concerning carnal acts between the sexes, and references to the drug trade; all of which, from your description, make it sound as though it is alright to do the aforementioned, so long as you are poor, and unable to provide for yourself at the level that you would prefer.

I do not want to sound rude, but I must insist that you allow me to do a book report on a different book. Otherwise, I shall have to talk directly with whomever I must to point out that "making" a student read material which is unneccessary, and violates that students God given religious rights is unContitutional, and therefore, illegal. Please do not make me go beyond this e-mail. I do not like to stand against those who are suppposed to be in authority, it goes against the grain. However, I will not back down when I know I am in the right, and cannot lose.
J (Fall 2008)

+

[33] *Rule of the Bone* by Russell Banks.

Ms. Priebe,
I'm frustrated as a student that you want me to grade, check, critique other students' work on various assignments. You are the teacher-we are the students. Its your responsibility to teach us information and then check our work to make sure that we are getting the concepts. Why are you having your students check another students' work for errors and making sure they are doing their work and correctly at that?

I am not a babysitter. It's not my responsibility to hold other students accountable for the work you assign. I have more then enough work to add a "pier-babysitter review" to the list. If they choose not to come to class, not to pay attention, not to learn or to ask you questions for clarity, that is their choice. Let their grade suffer for it. Not mine.

You should not be putting me in a position of accountability where I have to ensure they are doing their work and then have my grade effected by it.

Additionally, I have barely enough time to research the P3 let alone make sure Tom, Dick and Harry are doing theirs.

To be honest with you, I hold absolutely no weight to anything a "student" pier review says and discard it right away. I would respect a teachers review before a student.

I prefer my work to be kept between my teacher and myself. It seems in your class privacy is not an option. I must show my work to other students and have them review it. Makes little sense to me.

That's the frustration you see in class...
Kind Regards,
J (Fall 2010)

+

J,
I appreciate your concern; however, peer review is a common practice in English courses in our courses here at NDSCS and around the nation. I required this activity at the high school level and when I taught at NDSU.

But that's not the only reason I assign it...

When students leave universities and community colleges, their work gets critiqued by others - colleagues and bosses - whether it's physical work or text-based. Not only does this activity prepare students to share their work, but it prepares them to give feedback to others in a constructive manner.

It's true - students are not babysitters; students should feel free to critique the work of those who have completed the assignment as well as they have - sort through & find someone who probably really wants to earn an "A" (in comparison to those who have slacked off).

You are not held accountable for their work, only your own. You have control over the quality of feedback you give; that is where you earn points. This activity basically "tests" students' ability to critically read another classmate's work, just as we would critically read anything else.

I'm attaching a sheet that's found in our [LMS]. I wrote it up a while ago when a few students took issue with this very topic. I hope it helps.
-Sybil

+

Sybil look im still having a hard time adjusting from high school to college where in high school i go to class EVERY DAY that the teacher is there hopefully and they ask for the assignment in class, im having troubles remembering to submit assingments online when we dont have class. Not to mention during the week of midterms and my mind is flustered by the five other classes i have other then yours so its hard to stay on top of everything. I put alot of work into that paper and i know you got alot to grade and throwing one out only benefits you but i demand FULL CREDIT. I have proof on my computer i was done with assingment six days before it was due, why i didn't submit i swear to god i did, then i go to look sunday morning and it was due friday and mine wasnt in yet. I am not asking for future second chances but really I spent a whole friday night doing this paper and i want the full credit i deserve. And not trying to be smart or anything but I know you werent waiting on my paper, so cut me a break and give me the credit i deserve.

It will never happen again and please read this in a good mood.

Thanks-
T (Fall 2011)

+

Hi there,
First, it's always intimidating to compose anything longer than a sentence to an English teacher. (Case in point, should I have capitalized the "E" in English or not??) ☺ But, I'm living dangerously and writing to you anyway.

I LOVE to read and believe I have a good sense of humor and an open mind. That being said.....considering the infinite amount of literature we have at our fingertips....really-good-stuff.....how, or rather why, was this book selected? Granted, I have not read it and I don't judge a book by it's cover nor title (which I think is catchy, by the way ☺. It did peek my curiosity enough to read reviews on Amazon and, for the most part, they weren't good.

I should say before I sign off, I have a young adult in your class and that is how I heard of this. I know it's good to think outside the box, expand horizons, read things you wouldn't normally read, read something that makes you uncomfortable, and it probably has something in it that may be good for debate and class discussion......but, why this one? I need someone to share with me what a student would get out of
reading this book when there are soooo many more important books.
Please read this email as light hearted as it was written. ☺

Thank you for your time!!
A Curious Parent (Spring 2015)

+

Hello there!
I require this book in my English 120 class for many reasons. Here are a few thatI mention to the students:

Chuck Klosterman is a local author. He grew up in Wyndmere, wrote for The Fargo Forum, and attended (and graduated from?) UND.
He is still a writer; there are chances for my students to read his current things which is a bonus... he also has many books out, fiction and nonfiction. I'm aware of the criticism he's received, but I think that leads us to more discussion on him. Many times, half of the class like him and half don't, so we argue (the focus of English 120) about that, too.

Chuck's style of arguing is very much from a nontraditional perspective. I start off by taking students through a very traditional (logical) way of arguing, and we use his essays to show the opposite (and tell them that sometimes arguing in a nontraditional way works!).

I already have many materials on how to write a traditional argument; Klosterman's book is inexpensive, and we only read half of his essays – yet that allows me to change up which ones we tackle every semester, too.

I was introduced to the book by colleagues in the English department at NDSU; they were using this book of his for the reasons I mentioned. I figured that since our English 120 transfers to that university, why not use a similar book (especially if I liked it)?

Those are the basic reasons.
Let me know if you have further questions!
-Sybil

+

My question to you is, why can't you just give a decent, kind, regular reply. I asked what it was, in return all I was wanting to know is, what page in our book, or if not that then just the name of it. Just be civil with me. I do not enjoy your class&your don't enjoy me, so why don't we just fake a smile and get through this with as little friction as can be, part ways, and never see or deal with each other again. Because if I fail, yeah that sucks for me, but then we get to do it all over again. Now I ask you, Sybil Priebe, do you really want to do this all over again? Let's just be kind, I'll ask you questions when I need to know, and in return you just please tell me what I'm asking. Now, will you please tell tell me what the name of MP#6 is.

L[34] (Spring 2017)

+

---

[34] There were many – MANY – email exchanges with this particular student that drove me up a wall.

Dear H (Fall 2018),
Due to you calling me a bitch in the hallway this afternoon, you've lost your eligibility to hand in the Shortfolio. You no longer need to worry about that project, nor do you need to attend class Friday.
My department chair heard you in the hallway and agrees that this consequence is minor - if you would've done this at the beginning of the semester, I would've dropped you from the class immediately.
Also, I haven't decided yet whether to allow you those 18 points on the Chuck Test. You were obviously checking the classmates' tests on either side of you, and that's cheating.
-Sybil

I was straight-up with one of my classes today. Told them I didn't want to be that a-hole teacher anymore. It felt good to confess, and I think it made them relax. I feel content and calm.
4:01 PM · Jan 22, 2020

+

I know I've complained about students (a lot) in the past, but this week - tonight especially - it hit me (yet again) how great they can be. And even when I haven't been at my best, they've still remembered me/my class with fondness. They are the #goodstuff.
9:30 PM · Jan 23, 2020

+

In embracing a few more nuggets of compassion when it comes to my Ss, I found a lovely sidenote: I've been kinder to myself. #winwin
8:19 AM · Jan 29, 2020

+

It's highly unnecessary to have a sign on your classroom door declaring that late students can't enter & take test. No matter the excuse, allow them to demonstrate their learning in the way YOU'VE decided. Jeez. Or don't give tests. I mean... wow.
3:36 PM · Mar 10, 2020

+

Here's the thing: I've been #teaching #fyw #online since 2006. It's different, but not worse than f2f. Sure, chucking your material online mid-semester is not ideal, but the key is to just start w/Ss. How will they learn? What choices can I give them? Find resources to help.
5:39 PM · Mar 11, 2020

+

I'm not saying having an #OER textbook is pretty awesome to have right about now, but I am saying it's pretty #awesome to have all the time. And I think I was able to calm the student down, which is a bonus. #onlinelearning #remotelearning #distancelearning
9:06 AM · Mar 23, 2020

+

Ditto. The #hyflex[35] allows for so much flexibility on their part. I think the piece that is funky is that I'm leading & not them. I could definitely send my typical Slides to them Monday morning & then say, "Hey, what do you want to talk about in class MW & who will lead that?"
3:55 PM · Oct 19, 2020

+

F2F attendance took a nosedive today, & I don't blame them: we got our first batch of snow last week & the high today isn't above freezing. Weirdly, I had no one pop in at 11am virtually or otherwise; on the Schedule, it clearly said I'd be introducing a big project. #hyflex
3:49 PM · Oct 26, 2020

---

[35] The Hyflex mode allows for flexibility in attendance for students: virtually, face-to-face, or they watch recordings after the fact.

Cliffy's Notes.

Mostly from February 11, 2021[36].

1.

When I started journaling about my life, after losing Mr. Wall in 2014, I never expected those journal entries to be anything but records of my daily/weekly life. I never expected to witness on paper, on the screen, a literal change in philosophy, in pedagogy, in attitude. I don't think the teacher who started the journaling was totally prepared for a mid-life epiphany. She wasn't thinking about how outrageously angry she got with students and their behaviors. She wasn't concerned about how this was affecting her; she relished in it and used them as jokes and storylines and lead-ins for reasons to drink. As her hanger wore off, as her drinking ceased, she calmed the Fuck down. She probably didn't like being upset with them, or maybe some inner other side of her was exhausted with keeping it up. That inner gangster died and gave way to the hippie who was waiting in the corner to say: Sybil you don't have to be a Dick.

And from that came the intrigue during the summer of 2019, seeing hashtags of blasphemous ideas ideas, all while I took two of my own online classes and really learned their content - the Creative Commons and OEP - as well as how to set up a structured, helpful online course (or MOOC).

"Trust students." Whoa. Why didn't I start with that in 1999?

2.

I also didn't foresee my physical body go through "the ringer." I've had body image issues my whole life, but I didn't think my love for bicycling would change. I didn't think the anorexia I

[36] Cliffy is the asshole squirrel who lives in our yard and throws branches (I have witnesses) and apples at me. He also steals bird seed.

had my freshman year of college would come back in a different form. I didn't plan on the deep dark diet post-breast reduction that would lead my partner to concern: "How far are we going down?" I obviously didn't think my physical body would come into play while teaching...

3.
Change (from February 2, 2016).

It just occurred to me – eating the other half of my egg salad sammie that I wasn't hungry for in the Diversity Council meeting at noon – that my lunch breaks used to be so different on this campus. Before I met the people who are now a combination of colleague and friend, I ate at the student center's café by myself or sat at the faculty table and hoped I didn't make a fool of myself either by getting shit stuck in my teeth or saying something "too liberal" (true story: Dr. B and I once had a chat about which one of us was the MOST liberal, after much of the conservative male faculty left the table, which means just Dr. P was left, probably). I would head over there – rarely with my officemate at the time or anyone from my department – and just take a gamble on who I'd end up sitting by and what the conversation would lead to. I rarely went off-campus, and before Cochise bought me a microwave and fridge, I rarely ate in my office.

Nowadays, I leave campus with colleagues to hit up the ECR[37] or El Toro, or I head with colleagues over to the student center's cafeteria, and we sit away from the "faculty" table. Usually, I eat at my desk after picking something up at home because I've had to let Sadie out. Things change, and I'm realizing that I always thought the changes would get better and better. I went from having not a lot of friends in town – not

[37] "East Conference Room." This is code for a pub in town.

a lot of events to attend either – to having almost too much going on weekly. I went from being involved on campus because I wanted to build up that tenure portfolio to being involved to make a difference.

I think the fact that we've lost two colleagues who were amazeballs is showing me that change sometimes really sucks, and while I'm always open to change – for good reasons – I do not like this change at all. There isn't a good reason behind it, and it has made me incredibly introspective. I've been a little down for all of fucking 2016, for crying out loud. This year has already been tough on my heart and my mind; sometimes, it just feels like it's not going to hit an upswing… perhaps I fear that having everyone around me all the time – even during a very chaotic year like last year – was the peak. That scares me to a certain extent, but I also know I have to walk through this dark time until I find the glitter at the end of the unhappy drag queen.

August 26, 2016.

A year ago, Lola[38] was teaching here. Brit[39] was in my office. I was optimistic about Bernie Sanders. Charlie[40] was teaching here. Dawn wasn't getting riffed[41]. It wasn't that long ago, and in another year, who knows what my surrounding world will contain…

---

38 Colleague turned friend.

39 The officemate I had after Camilla.

40 Colleague turned friend.

41 RIF stands for Reduction in Force; we have had to endure a few of those on our campus. It usually meant some staff member was about to get let go.

Pause (noun)[42]

- a temporary stop
- a break in a verse
- a brief suspension of the voice to indicate the limits and relations of sentences and their parts
- temporary inaction especially as caused by uncertainty
- a reason or cause for pausing (as to reconsider)

Pause (verb)

- to stop temporarily
- to linger for a time

[42] "Pause." Definition. *Merriam Webster*. https://www.merriam-webster.com/dictionary/pause

{This page intentionally left blank.}

Meditation

January 16, 2019.

[...]

Meditating...
"Your thoughts are not you."
"Picture your heart. What do you see anything that doesn't serve you, in your heart? Is there a hole there? Someone or something missing?"
"I release all negativity in my heart to the universe, for healing."
"We're forgiving them for us. When we stay angry, it's like a poison that we drink. Forgive."
"Forgive yourself for all the judgements you've had on yourself."
"I am enough."

[...]

Battle Lake Journals #2.

08.30.1999

We, new teachers, had our big meeting today and met up with Gary (Mr. Carr) and Rick (Mr. Belchner). It was interesting; I wore my corduroys and a simple top – Gary said that the outfit was okay for every day, too. This will at least be a comfortable school, clothing-wise.

I keep worrying that the students are all going to be little devils or something. I will just have to be firm and IN CONTROL. I will have to demand control from my students; it is my classroom.

08.31.1999

We have a football game at home this Friday, so that should be interesting. The Spanish teacher is also a recent graduate – she seems like the one I will probably "hang" out with; I think I'll ask her to go to the football game with me.

I need to go to the bank Friday after school for depositing my apartment (Fargo) check and also to apply for a car loan. I hope that goes well.

I hope tomorrow also goes well.

The other teachers said that they still get nervous. This calms me a bit. I will awaken at 6am, I think and go walk down to the lake and sit – maybe listen to a new tape or the waves.

I will choose my attitude every morning; I will do my very best!

I am following my path, my purpose at this time.

Sybil, you are fantastic and will do fine! Remember, it is your first year!

No one called me tonight. Perhaps they will call tomorrow night to see how it went.

Las Vegas High School.

Of all of my college memories, Dr. Kathy Cummings' classes (one being at 8am TR, of all time slots!) are in the top ten. Sure, sure, sure, college parties are smattered in there, too, but I can't recall them as specifically as I can her classes and content.

The auditorium wasn't lit particularly well, it was heated almost too well, and it could house one hundred students (I'm guessing) ... yet there I was, a few rows back, listening. Her stories captured my attention every time. Educational Psychology. She had taught at Las Vegas High School once upon a time, blocks from the strip. She used the stories from that experience – and others – to link course material to the terminology of the chapters we were learning.

I'm not the best test taker, but I recall flying through her tests because each question would bring up a story. "Oh, this is the story about how a student barfed on her; the answer is obviously cognitive dissonance" or whatever.

I suppose the only criticism I had at the time was that I had discovered how she'd been the wake-up call for a particular student. He admitted this to me when we were on a supposed date. At the time, I thought it seemed highly unfair that this student was potentially receiving preferential treatment. Who didn't want a wake-up call from a professor for an 8am class?

In the end, it's a story I tell quite often: that I rarely missed her 8am class. That I would look forward to that class. That I would then walk to my 9:30am British Literature class and promptly fall asleep listening to Dr. Bob dispense way too much information about dead white guys.

"You'd Just Have Them Read Blogs."

Every once in a while, I get a few student eyeballs to pop out on Day 1. Do you know what I tell them?

I don't like Shakespeare.

I never liked Shakespeare. Not for a second. I found him so damn boring. I don't care that he invented words or wrote a truck load. There isn't much anyone can do to convince me of his supposed "awesomeness." And recently, too, reading about how he engaged or encouraged – whatever the verb is – racist crud in his plays just adds to my general angst for the guy.

My jam was learning about Thoreau and Emerson and Whitman in Junior English (high school). I specifically remember highlighting TRANSCENDENTALISM in that classroom with Mrs. Morris. Before them it had been *Ramona Quimby*, the *Babysitter Club* books, and then a jump to Danielle Steele. That group of authors got my attention.

So, cut to me having to teach literature – when I'm really into composition and rhetoric and linguistics – and there were times I wanted to scream. The classroom in Battle Lake gave me piles upon piles of *The Great Gatsby* and *Fahrenheit 451*. The latter wasn't something I'd read before, but I threw it at the Juniors. There were also piles of textbooks that contained a lot of more dead white guys. Oh yay. The Minnesota Standards asked that Freshmen tackle *Romeo and Juliet* (how original) and that the Juniors (or maybe it was the Seniors) read something else by Shakespeare; I remember choosing *Othello* over *Hamlet* or *Macbeth* simply because it was similar to a soap opera (with its love triangle), and that format is easy to understand. Plus, in college, I had overdosed on *Hamlet*. It was difficult, to say the least, to lead the students through those plays when I was not a fan.

Once teaching at the college level, the freedom to choose my readings was beyond thrilling. I tried *Rule of the Bone* by Russell Banks, George Carlin's *Brain Droppings*, an actual textbook that might've lasted a semester, David Sedaris, and –

finally – my own Open Textbook (OER) with readings from all sorts of people, including students.

The quote attached to this chapter is one that still hits me. My first officemate was a kind older woman who had been teaching k-12 for a long time before popping over to a part-time teaching position at the college. She, and another colleague at the time in our department, definitely had FEELINGS about what we should ALL be teaching in our classes, and the old dead white guys were IT. We had many discussions about this; she felt they needed to read the sort of literature she was requiring because it was probably the last time they'd ever read "good literature." My perspective was that if they read something enjoyable – Carlin or Sedaris – they might CONTINUE to read ANYTHING later on in life. I didn't think that Greek tragedy was the key to reading for diesel technicians; I thought George Carlin was a better pick.

Either way, we're both technically right, but she didn't see it like that. I saw us as being different; she saw my path as wrong. And since my Master's research had been on blogging, she threw that in my face as a last resort.

"You'd just have them read blogs."

You're damn right I would.

This Is About Blogs.

Thursday August 29, 2002

[...]

I got into weblogs when a former student of mine e-mailed me his address. I was in the middle of a huge project last spring in my Electronic Communications class, and I suddenly dropped ALL of that crap and took up researching blogs. I have always kept a journal and these are easier for me. I can remind myself what happened on a particular day (so I don't have that syndrome where I can't remember what I ate an hour ago, etc), and the process of things.. relationships, projects for school, when I met cool people and what they said. I try to be humorous so my audience is entertained and, yet, enlightened even a little by my insight on daily stuff. It's made me, I think, not only a better writer, but more aware of my audience. :-)

Posted 8/29/2002 at 8:40 AM

Monday September 8, 2003

To Do September 9, 2003 in the computer lab: IACC 114--

1) Try out your own weblog on either Xanga.com or Blogger.com (if you have one already, please help others with questions they have)...
2) Your first entry should be what you think of weblogs thus far and anything else you want your first blog entry to say about YOU.
3) When you create your weblog, put the address on the board at the front of the class so others can read it in class and later on in the semester. I will take all the weblogs down on a piece of paper and make a list for everyone to have so you can meet others in this class and in my other class (8am or 12:30pm).

4) As you are doing all of this (creating your weblog and reading others'), I will come around and ask you to show me the weblog you found for Writing Assignment #5 and give you credit for finding one.
5) As it nears the end of class time, please go to the class weblog (by logging on with your username/password on blogger.com) and type in an entry about Meg's article that you had to read for today. Also: CHECK THIS OUT! and write about it in your class blog entry too.
6) Note= You do NOT have to write in the personal weblog for class. This is simply a way for you to meet others in the class. I will check them once in awhile, but you get your blogging grade from the class blog only!! So you can do whatever/say whatever on your own blogs. That's what they are for!!
7)Who hasn't gotten my e-mails OR hasn't gotten on the class weblog yet?? Let's figure that all out today too!!
[...]
Posted 9/8/2003 at 3:39 PM

Monday January 19, 2004

To my dear students. [Welcome to my personal blog devoted to teaching and researching.]

The "To Do" List for Tuesday, January 19 (and the night class' 6-7:30 slot on Thursday):
Hopefully, you read/skimmed heartily through Chapter 16 because pages 532-4 has a simple personal situation that points out how researching can be tough online. I know, from my point of view, that writing a paper is tough enough... so I hate when I can't find good, relevant research to back me up with. Erg.
[...]
Posted 1/19/2004 at 5:34 PM

Tuesday April 3, 2007

Abstract:

"But students don't know how to write IN the classroom." A positive approach to student writing using class blogs in the composition classroom.

... As they walk out of class, just what are they thinking about?
... What does that quiet student have to say?
... How can I post announcements or web sites that everyone will look at?
... Can peer review be conducted outside of the class?

These are just some of the questions I had before I started using class blogs (and even while I was in the middle of using them). While sometimes technology can be frustrating, I have found that the positives of using class blogs in my classroom have out-weighed the negatives. The biggest positive I've seen is getting students to write more often and to each other as an audience.

Since getting my job two years ago at the North Dakota State College of Science, I have put class blogs to the side while getting accustomed to the campus and students. Now, this coming fall I plan on returning to using class blogs via our LMS. My presentation will cover how I have used class blogs in the past, what I plan to do with class blogs in the future, and why I find them helpful in, and out of, the composition classroom.

Bio:

Sybil Priebe, an alumna of NDSU, currently teaches at the North Dakota State College of Science in Wahpeton, ND.

This fall, she'll teach Introduction to Poetry for the first time as well as 3-4 other courses she's been teaching the past two years: English 105: Technical Communication, English 110: College Composition I, English 120: College Composition II Online, and World Literature Online. Beyond blogging on her teaching blog [...]
Posted 4/3/2007 at 5:27 PM

Camaraderie (noun)[43]

- a spirit of friendly good-fellowship

Belonging (noun)[44]

- acceptance as a natural member or part.

[43] "Camaraderie." Definition. *Merriam Webster*. https://www.merriam-webster.com/dictionary/camaraderie
[44] From the American Heritage Dictionary.

{This page intentionally left blank.}

Corn Eating Contests.

*I think we need an explanation of the chapter title[45].

Monday October 17, 2005

I think I may have a great draft of my proposal for this conference all figured out:
I am about to embark on "letting go" of my classroom. That's right. After being handed a journal article on using the theories and themes of punk rock in the English classroom, I bought a skeleton ring and I decided to create a "D.I.Y" ("Do It Yourself") syllabus for my English 110 next spring - 2006. Teachers are leary of trying a "Do It Yourself" course; they want to maintain control. But since I am young and rebellious (part punk rock really), I knew I had to give it a shot. Hey, I gave blogging a try and it turned out pretty "kick ass" if you don't mind the punk language.

What I propose for this presentation is to cover what it is about punk rock (theories, themes, genres, attitudes, lessons) that needs to be in the English classroom (introductory or not), how I went about taking words from a journal article and putting them into action - the creation of a syllabus, and, finally, how the class is taking to having some of their very own say in what their English class does for them. So far, the syllabus: gives them say in 40% of the final points, allows them to determine when their deadlines are, and gives them choices as to what

---

[45] When I was in graduate school, I attended one of my first nerdy conferences way up in Edmonton, Alberta, Canada. I thought I had informed my family, but supposedly, when my parents came up to our "Fargo house" that weekend and noticed my absence, my brother shrugged and said, "I think she went to a corn eating contest?" So, it's now a family joke. And, I mean, I DO like corn on the cob. I WOULD win those contests. For the record.

projects/papers they will write.
I think I just need to put in the person who wrote the journal article (and title) and I'll be good to go. Maybe?
Posted 10/17/2005 at 9:51 PM

Wednesday September 29, 2010

I'm heading to TYCA (Two-Year College Association for English Teachers), the Midwest branch, this week. In some video recently, maybe it was "The 7 Habits of Highly Effective People" (shown to the FYE class?), one tip was to "sharpen your saw" or something like that. Basically, the story goes that some dude who's trying to cut a log has a dull blade... he needs a sharp saw. He's not going to get anywhere fast with a dull blade; he needs to stop and take the time to sharpen it. Same goes for those of us in education. We shouldn't be stubborn and consistently use the same process; we sometimes have to stop and sharpen even if we think it's going to waste time. I look at conferences like that. I don't like to be away from students because it disrupts what we're doing, but a teacher should sharpen every semester, if not every year.
(Everyone be good while I'm gone.)
Posted 9/29/2010 at 7:38 PM

October 12, 2016.

I am SO EXCITED to head to TYCAMW[46] tomorrow. YOU have NO idea. No, you DON'T.

As I'm getting the minutes and agenda for the executive committee meeting tomorrow, I'm seeing lots about budget cuts and trying to figure out how to get more attendance at our

---

[46] TYCAMW stands for Two-Year College English Association for the Midwest region. These regional conferences bring together two-year college English teachers for professional development, learning, and networking... and the occasional cocktail or karaoke or disco night.

fall conference, etc. Tomorrow's meeting will be fun and possibly a wee bit stressful, but from what I recall, they're always like that. What's nice is that since we don't all teach at the same colleges, and this is a meeting that happens once a year, we are nicer to each other. We are civil; we are like long-lost cousins who just want to wrap up the nitty-gritty so we can hit the hotel bar for conversations about saunas, bare-foot running, and crockpot recipes.

It's 3:45pm. I should just shut down everything and get the fuck out of here, but I wanted to stay until my 3pm class officially would've ended. Just to say I was here until 3:50pm, I guess. Which is a super stupid thing to give a rat's ass about... truly. But here I am. Contemplating what to pack for the conference; I really want to just have a purse and carry-on, so I'm thinking of going uber light with leggings and tunics and scarves. No one will care what I look like; many of my TYCAMW peeps dig my personality. I know this; it's not vain. They aren't going to care about my attire. I have noticed that I barely do anymore; it's like the weight shit... when you realize that people don't love you for your gravitational pull, you also realize they don't love you because your hair is always curled perfectly. They don't love that I wear something totally different everyday – that used to be a pressure I would put on myself as if I had the money of a famous person to do so.

Anyhow... I've thrown what I need from my campus office into a big tote (Target clearance – black and white herringbone pattern on the outside, yellow in), and I'm just allowing myself to write for a bit.

October 16, 2016: On a Plane.

So, I lost my pink pen. My favorite pink pen.

"Drunk Me" used it to pay my tab at the hotel bar, and then I left it there. And they didn't find it in the morning, so someone swiped my lucky, favorite, pink pen. Eh. It is what it is, I guess.

The conference was a blast, of course. I confessed early on to "sucking" the last two years but told both MG and MB I would be sucking no more. With that said, I think the wee bit of guilt that resided in me over the suckage of the last two years caused me to sign up to be the Web Manager and the possible Grant Writer. Yeah. I said yes, but I said yes to my people. My people. My posse. I even just write an Ode to them that perhaps J-Rich could put in the Messenger – our newsletter – or something?

Here it is:

So, maybe there's a reason I leave TYCAMW last when I do attend. Maybe I am meant to be the nonelected, unofficial reflector of the event. Maybe I've become that person because I travel the farthest, typically, to TYCAMW, being the North Dakota rep and all. Maybe it's because I love to write journal entries about my life anyhow. No matter the reason, here's my Ode to TYCA (post Midwest conference in St. Louis, 2016). To the nerdy family that exists within TYCAMW, who welcomed me with open arms in 2009 at the Madison, WI conference.

To the long-lost "sisters" I've found in J-Rich, MG, Kathy S., Sara J., Carrie F., Connie M., and MB.

To the long-lost "brothers" I've found in Rich, Paul, Alan, and BH.

To the conversations I've had with anyone at a TYCAMW who listened and possibly reframed advice I'd already gotten from my favorite colleagues back home.

To the ideas that congregate collectively in our minds when we are all together, and how they come out of us in articulate, silly, or blasphemous ways.

To the laughter that pours from liquor-lined mouths when we tell stories about past TYCAs, about students, and about ourselves.

To the joy I feel when I am around people who are like-minded, yet come in all shapes and colors and backgrounds.

To the happy exhaustion after the conference, trying to figure out what the hell to try in class - what ideas will work in 3 days, 3 months, or maybe in 3 years?

To the nerd love.

To the cocktails, and toasts to those who've come before us and reminded us to remain true to who we are: teachers of writing.

To the "small, practical, hands-on conference" this is and will continue to be (MB).

Yeah. I love that crew. I do. I got a little sad yesterday after everyone took off for the airport. I had a conversation with J-Rich about her health, about her pets, about her family... she's the bomb. I got to chat MG up at the airport before the conference even got rolling. She's amazing. Kathy S. hugged me more times than I can count. Rich and I talked shop about biking and his wife's triathlons. I joked with Paul about saunas (and the word's pronunciation) and told him that the advice he should give his beautiful daughter is that there are guys who will tell her whatever to get in her pants. He seemed to appreciate that bluntness.

That group of people understand me and really seem to want me to be me... the core of me shares their cores. It's just such an amazing feeling to be around people – who were once strangers all simply teaching English at two-year colleges like I am – who "get me" so quickly. They are all gems; I wish there was one big university where we could all be colleagues together... but maybe that would defeat the purpose of TYCAMW. We need that unique reconnection once a year (if not more due to the spring meeting or 4Cs). We reenergize one another. Easily.

Anyhow, I'm on my last flight of this year. It was bumpy for a bit, but I just remind myself of what Lola would say – that it's physics. Also, I just became an aunt for the fourth time today, so I'm pretty sure George Carlin and God want me to meet her – the 10 pounder who came out of my sister this morning.

[...] this conference constantly proves to me that the small things matter. At one point I can remember sitting at the post-conference meeting and listening to Jen's voice – it almost sounds kid like at times – and I just smiled. Everything needs to be put into perspective. Always. So, one has to retrain their brains to do so. Sometimes we need a reboot. Sometimes that reboot is reading something, sometimes it's a conversation, and sometimes it's a conference with a bunch of nerds. Truly.

4Cs[47] Notes from 2017 in Portland, OR.

THURSDAY.

The walk from the hotel to the conference center (at 7:30) was chilly, but okay. I got registered by three helpful ladies, got to hug Katie M. (former grad school classmate), and chat her up, and then I got a newcomer badge before going to the newcomer coffee session. I found a quiet table that didn't really say much to me, and at first, I was like "okay, ignore me; that's fine," but then when Jacob (random newbie) sat down by me, I thought "okay, finally someone wants to get to know me" but then I regretted that about 5min into our conversation. Why? Because after we exchanged basic lengths of college teaching, and I shared our newest budget shit show, he proceeded to um mansplain me... to tell me the solutions... to tell me to use contract grading (told him I did, but he said that he uses the contract grading system that some guy - Saul? going to be the chair of something soon?) ... to tell me how to get my students

---

[47] Conference on College Composition and Communication. It's the "big time" conference for Englishers.

to read (with a web site to look at) ... it wasn't a conversation; it was a lecture. I walked out with him, ditched him by the bathrooms, and then texted Suzie and BH about this dingleberry of a person.

Did he give me ideas? Kind of. But the delivery blew, and after being underwhelmed by the hotel room, I was like "really? This is my first 4Cs experience?" But hey, I sat by BH and one of his friends at the opening session, and that turned things around. The latter part of the session lent itself to this: "Because writing is never just about writing." (I retweeted a lot; I need to return to that after the conference.)

I decided against my first "normal" session (about Self-regulated learning; I looked it up online and I don't know if my students could handle it) and went to a session about "rigor"[48] at the two-year college. The panelists showed off amazingly rigorous projects. At the end, I jumped at the chance to ask about how I can keep my rigor (I gave them the ND shit show background) and not go insane. I also asked if I am doing too much at six projects. They felt that I was doing too much, and that rigor can remain by going deeper.

A panelist in that same session brought up an awesome metaphor. The bicycle. We are holding the back of the bike, but at some point, the students have to do things on their own. We have to let go and let them wobble and fall. Later, I added: "We can't run alongside them as they write their damn papers!"

After that session, I grabbed a Dragon burger (slaw with a juicy burger) & fries. At the table, I sat with some helpful people who listened and also concurred that I might be doing too much anyhow. Another woman who joined us at the end of lunch said that she tries to attend these with a goal in mind... it's not like she doesn't want to learn about Y, she just wants to focus on Z. BH said as much in the opening session; he's going to all medical ones because he is creating a new class about

---

[48] Just what is "rigor" anyway? How is it measured? Twitter has gotten wild with this topic, FYI.

medical writing. Very cool. So, I realized that I had done the same thing; I'm going to sessions that will help me be efficient in this upcoming stressful time. I love learning about multi-modal projects, but I don't need that information right now.

So, after lunch, I went to a session about keeping one's energy. It started off a bit vent-y, but we eventually came around to solutions. [...]

I told my table about the 75% story I heard about Donny Osmund; how he has horrible performance anxiety and that someone told him to just give 75% because his fans wouldn't know. I also told the story about the student who threw their paper away in front of my face; that's when I stopped giving a lot of feedback[49]. The ideas I got were to follow through on my sacred space – weekends: no email. I should use that "Out of Office" reply/notification more, too, and if it's over spring break, I should state that I will be deleting my inbox and starting over so they should just re-email me. In addition, I could try this kind of notification over weekends for the first month of each semester to get students used to asking questions during the week.

[...]

The best question: What is academic life worth when you have no time to read or think?

Another idea that popped up as we were chatting about feedback and assessing papers and using rubrics to ease the grading for one feedback-lover at the table... I thought about my pretty rubrics, and how I should make the students use them. As in:

[x] Organization: Evidence ____________

[x] Format: Evidence ____________

Also, peer review might be worth practically removing. Instead, perhaps I conduct grading conferences. A project is

[49] I would learn later that when feedback is attached to a grade, students don't look at the feedback.

due, the students hand in something on a Saturday, and then that following week, they meet with me in class with their rubrics to show what they've accomplished. OR perhaps the way I can get them to attend PR[50] and give great feedback is to state that if they show up and conduct PR well, they are exempt from the grading conference or something? If they show up with a legit draft, that means they are on it. They are good to go, probably. They help another classmate then, and then get help in return, and BAM, they have one less class to attend because they have their poop in a group[51].

[...]

The last session I attended before feeling my brain reach overload was about teaching online, f2f, and hybrid (plus some other things in that panel too). The first presenter was funny and spoke to PBL[52] which I've heard about and liked. The image he showed that hit me the most was about how 44% of class is the teacher lecturing (activity) and only 2% gives students their choice in activity. This overall just leads me to wondering how I rework my classes in general... can PBL help? Can scaffolding? I just have to really dive into the possibilities. This presenter brought up the site CompPile that I hadn't heard of (this is the thing I was concerned about on my walk over - I don't feel smart here among the name dropping or site dropping) and talked about having his students create podcasts (Stanford) for his class. Like 30-50min podcasts! Shit! Speaking of name dropping, Beth Hewett was dropped for OWI (online writing instruction).

[...]

The last presenter in that group spoke to peer review using social media research. What I thought would be interesting

---

[50] This acronym stands for Peer Review or Peer Response. This is the activity many English teachers use to have students review their classmates' work and give feedback.

[51] I use this phrase often, huh? For those unfamiliar with this euphemism, it means "to be organized" or to have one's life "in order."

[52] PBL stands for either Project Based Learning or Problem Based Learning, depending on who you are talking to or if the moon is full or not.

would be to ask students to share a screenshot of their writing on social media to get reactions that way... is their conclusion a total mic drop moment?

[...]

So, before I shut down the iPad and plug her in (my phone is low, too), I want to just throw around changes willy-nilly for a minute. In English 110, I'd keep contract grading and perhaps consider researching that other way – mentioned by Mr. Early Morning Solutions – and use concepts on the contract instead. Then each rubric for the projects would use concepts and they'd still have to hit those spots to earn the B contract.

Now, as for the projects in there... letters, human research, fake company project, visual, argument, and publishing. Hmmm... maybe I ditch the last one? Maybe the visual becomes hands-on? I don't have much more to say about 110 right now. So brain dead.

As for 120, I think that the foundation is the GBP[53] (just as the Fake Company[54] is for 110??), but I want to put a cool fake presidential campaign idea in there too or more writing for an audience. Ugh. So tired.

FRIDAY & SATURDAY.

I slept like a baby Thursday night into Friday morning; I even took my time getting ready and got the buffet breakfast at the hotel (which wasn't horrible – I definitely abuse buffets in that I pick at everything, taking like one bite of fifteen things). It was a rainy morning, but it felt good and smelled nice.

My first session at 11am was about engaging students with engaging assignments and how the layout of those assignments can be "blueprint" like in nature, not allowing a lot of choice or creativity, or they can be "sketch" like in nature that allow

---

[53] Global Blog Project. Students use blogs, and other genres, to answer a research question and then organize it in a multi-genre format.

[54] Students create a Fake Company, complete with: logo, motto, letterhead, mission statement, condensed business plan, progress report, income/expense charts, etc.

choice and creativity, yet still contain loose boundaries. Blueprint assignments use verbs like "avoid" and sketch assignments use "imagine" or "consider." Blueprint assignments contain regulations and commands; sketch assignments are balanced with choice and guidance. The blueprint assignments give students less of that authorship feeling; the sketch ones make them feel like they have more say in what they write as authors.

I also learned, in this 11am session, the term "mutt genres," which are kind of like my list essay? Not technically a genre that is well-known, but it's comprised of other genres.

Possible Assignments: Have students rewrite instructional guides and IKEA instructions, etc.

Other ideas I wrote down during this session: Asking students to print a chapter or article out, ask them to annotate it (I would model this, of course) finding "golden lines." Then in class, conduct a show and tell where they talk about their annotations and golden lines.

A participant who I chatted with at lunch has her students hand-write the first draft because it causes them to slow down and then they have to revise at LEAST once to type/print it. Suckers.

The session after this was about California's system's best practices, and I thought that was classroom related, but it wasn't. I did learn that their average salaries are similar to ours (but I bet the cost of living is very high), and they teach 4/4 or 5/5 unless they are on quarters (then it's 8 classes a year?).

The session I hit up – and last one, truly, for the whole conference – was about "flipped assessment." A few ideas that popped up: Use the Tao idea of "less is more" approach in order to be more effective, call the introduction a "creative opening," and how maybe I should have a few abstract formats to show that essays/letters all look differently: not all need a big intro and three body paragraphs... maybe there is a one-liner paragraph in there, maybe there are seven paragraphs of equal size purely by chance...

The questions I was going to ask at the end, but then had to jet to the Action Hub table (I put myself down to help from 3:15-40), were: Do we need student buy in? One participant brought that up about how she has her students mark up everything before they hand in their projects (they highlight the summary, analysis, wrap-up, etc.) ... then another guy stated that he couldn't figure out why not all students liked to do their own assessment[55]. Why? I'll tell you why = they detest responsibility. They want to declare what their grade should be, but then when it comes time to provide evidence for that grade, they are too lazy to do so. This is only SOME students, but still.

You know, I sound like my parents when I say, "Back when I was in college, my profs didn't try to get my fucking buy in," but the reason people mention the past like that – I think – is to demonstrate that not everything in the past was shit. People like to declare that lecturing is so over, and technology is the way to go, and all that, but it's not perfectly true. New things work and old things work; we need to label them as just fucking different.

While at the Action Hub, I met one of the TYCA-to-You reps (Alexi) who I hadn't met yet. She was delightful, and then after we chatted it up, Brian (Ohio buddy) and I vented and brainstormed about this conference vs. others, and it was just generally a good talk. He's good to dialogue with; does not try to mansplain me. Then his friend Niki came up and talked with us, too, and her synopsis of the 4Cs vs TYCA was that when you leave a TYCA, you feel like you can DO ALL THE THINGS. When you leave the 4Cs, you wonder what the hell you are doing with your life.

Sooo cut to a few hours later, and I was reunited with one of my bestest friends Fran. It was awesome. We talked and

---

[55] Foreshadowing?

drank and laughed. Her and her husband are sweet, and the conversation was needed after all this conference stuff.

I got home late that night, so Saturday had a rough start to it, but it's all good. I had a free coupon for the TYCA breakfast, the business meeting was interesting to observe, and then before we got rolling on our TYCA Executive meeting for the day, we listened to the Saturday Keynote which was by a guy who is Pilipino by birth with a Spanish name. He is probably the most famous, and most privileged, undocumented immigrant right now. It was one of those Keynotes where a person just wants to listen. I think I picked up my phone once to see what everyone was saying on Twitter.

Our TYCA Executive meeting was slow-going, but it was nice to finally attend one AND meet all of my reps who send me regional reports. I got hugs from most of them, and they were just so nice. I also met the editor of TETYC, Holly, and now we're FB friends. It was actually a nice end to the whole conference; they listened to me, I got to be involved in some complex discussions, and then after we took a selfie and had cocktails. By about 8pm, I had taken a bath and put myself into bed... I knew I had to head to the airport around 5am, so I figured I would try to get some sleep. Out of the four nights away, I slept fairly well 50% of the time. It was nice to not wake up to Sadie's urging to go outside, but I miss her. I was sent many updates on her this week.

[...]

October 10, 2017.

TYCA-MW has come and gone, and it was fun, but perhaps was missing the typical hangover after because I wasn't able to fully enjoy it. It wasn't my expectations or my female colleagues that put any damper on it; it was the male influence. But more on that later. [...] I didn't feel amazeballs, and that didn't help the whole trip either. Fucking sinuses. [...]

We rocked our presentation Friday morning; Zooey wins award at lunch! Yeah... but then Saturday hits.

After my solo session yesterday morning about contract grading, I was walking out of the room with Josie and this guy stops me and says, "I wanted you to know that I walked out of your session because of your use of profanity."

I was so shocked; all I could muster was: "Okay?" And we walked away.

I think I said "shat," as in: "My students were supposed to hand in their first projects last week, but then Blackboard shat on me."

What an asshole, right? What a total dick move! Walter wasn't upset with me, nor did he support my emotional crisis that followed (unlike my TYCA-MW family, who were pissed for me) ... instead, he observed later that that same guy was in another session where the presenter used the word "ass" as in "We did this half-assed" and the muthafucker didn't leave. I bet the presenter was a dude.

March 18, 2019.

As predicted, the 4Cs has sent me into another mental "tailspin" of emotions. Both positive and negative, but nevertheless the imposter phenomenon is full-on in my head and while I know I'm doing my best in everything I do, I question my motives and whether I am doing "any good" with all this. The first ever National TYCA[56] was amazing. Wednesday was the best. I got so many ideas just from MG's session – the last one of the day (before the Norton Party and dinner at The Commoner) – about graphic organizers. And then the rest of the week hit me like a bunch of bricks. I should not have attended as many sessions, perhaps. The one where

[56] The TYCA regional conferences have been around for a while, but a National TYCA conference got its own spot at the beginning of the 4Cs – finally! – in 2019.

the three generations of women teachers reflected on their backgrounds was the doozy now that I look back on it. And it was one of the sessions I had to sneak into because I was in the wrong room at the beginning. I should have stay in the one about drones and zombies, I guess. But I digress.

The slides showed various compositionists and lots of book covers. I knew a few people (Donald Murray, Peter Elbow, David Bartholomae), but not all of them. And I didn't recognize the book covers. Everyone in the audience nodded. It was dumped upon me – I didn't know what everyone knew. Imposter. It felt horrible. I almost wanted to leave the room and just cry, but instead I reached out to my support system. They reinforced my nerd-dom, but I still felt out of it. [...]

So, I pushed onward. I grabbed lunch (figured I should battle this mental anguish with physical fuel), and I went to a session about online teaching (got so involved in that session that I got invited to their SIG, Special Interest Group, Friday afternoon) and ended the day with an upper for my system – OER. While at dinner with MG and her co-presenter/colleague at Sienna Mercato, I brought up the downer of the day, and they understood. Oh, and MG informed me that Peer Review is now Peer Response. I think I had been told that day or Wednesday that our placement test (Accuplacer) was racist. Oh, the things you learn at conferences!

We spoke deeply at dinner about weight and sexual predators. And MG asked me why I never married Cochise. Sravani would ask me the same question Saturday evening[57].

Friday started with a meeting for *TETYC* Reviewers. Holly invited me, and I was a fish out of water (because I've only just reviewed TYCA National proposals), but they accepted me, and then I speed walked with Holly to her session afterwards and she mentioned I should consider being a reviewer. The session she chaired, about Feminist Theory, was very helpful. Then I found a session on Imposter Syndrome, right before sneaking

[57] Why do we ask people this question but never: Why DID you get married?

out to have tacos at an awesome nearby joint. The afternoon was filled with nap time before the SIG and dinner with the TYCA peeps at Ten Penny (the place I went to alone Tuesday night when I got into town).

Saturday was the TYCA-EC meeting; it went quickly and was full of silly and serious moments. I stated that I didn't like to swear before noon, and I also ranted about how our job isn't to educate the general public. At lunch, I got to sit by Cheryl and Stephanie and Leigh in the booth, and we enjoyed ourselves. Later that night, Stephanie, Suzanne, Leslie, Sravani, and I joined up for dinner and drinks at the hotel bar. It was a nice wrap-up ending.

Oddly, Suzanne threw a wrench into the whole should-I-go-to-doctoral-school-or-do-something-else when she asked me if I would ever want to be Chair of the 4Cs (I think she meant TYCA, but whatever). It wasn't something I thought anyone would ask me, but I wouldn't mind considering expanding my leadership skills... I mean, I've graduated from the Chair Academy and Leadership Academy... maybe that's another avenue to feel out?

[...]

November 10, 2020.

[...]

Speaking of the latter, I might get kicked out of the national TYCA group text after the convo last night. It was Alan's birthday, so Sarah shares a photo of her and him from some gathering with the caption (paraphrasing): We talked about Shakespeare[58] all night. Me, on the inside: "Oh jeezus." Then the thread was "I want to talk Shakespeare all night" and hearts and thumbs up and I was annoyed at it all. Sarah's comment about ALL of us being the kind she could gush about

[58] I could never wrap my head around why everyone things he's so damn awesome. He wrote some racist plays, yo. There are others who are better at telling stories.

Shakespeare with sent me over the edge. I texted back that I didn't dig him; they all could have him. The New Yorker of the bunch responds that his work teaches about gender-bending and racism and blahblahblah, and I respond that we could let the gender-benders and people of color speak for themselves.

Crickets.

The New Yorker agrees, I believe, and then I said that my intro to lit was white-washed with dudes. I top that off with another cricket inducer: "What would happen if our syllabi didn't have white cis male authors?"

Minutes later: "Would be cool."

More crickets. I comment about being deleted for my comments. A few hearts and two "Never!" comments. Then someone shared a picture of their puppy.

Discussion over.

In the meanwhile, I had been texting with J-Rich, MB, and MG about this very thread. They heard me. They understood. I bring up how that whole crowed LOVED Asao's speech at the 4Cs in Pittsburgh, yet they didn't want to really put any of that shit into action. Huh. Interesting. Is this where white supremacy sneaks into and overlaps with white privilege? Is Shakespeare "better" than others of his time or have we only been exposed to him as the best, just like Hannah Gadsby mentions about artists in her standup.

So, essentially, this year I've discovered how problematic certain historical figures are (Aristotle, Lincoln, Teddy Roosevelt, Obama) and now I know that the popular kids of the national TYCA realm are also sitting in their white privilege, and probably not going to budge.

Anyhow...

[...]

Tweets:

Everyday should be a #tycamw (#tyca) day! Presenter just said she uses her bitchface! First time I've heard it at a conference. :D
9:39 AM · Oct 13, 2012

+

#tycamw Less is more in the classroom? Work smarter not harder! I say that all the damn time.
9:07 AM · Oct 4, 2013

+

#tycamw Slow down! What's the rush? Why do I have so many projects? Do they all matter?
9:31 AM · Oct 4, 2013

+

#tycamw No more spendy textbooks![59]
9:39 AM · Oct 4, 2013

+

#tycamw Writing Spaces for free textbooks! Woot woot! http://writingspaces.org
10:02 AM · Oct 4, 2013

+

#tycamw Model pre-reading, during, post-reading strategies in the classroom... How do YOU read? What does it mean to read critically?
10:49 AM · Oct 4, 2013

[59] This was the first TYCAMW conference where I was turned onto the idea of using OER, Open Educational Resources. Thank you to whoever presented on the Writing Spaces books.

+

#tycamw Ticket In/Ticket Out. Students put ideas on ticket 2enter class; students reflect on what they learned in class for ticket out.
11:12 AM · Oct 4, 2013

+

#tycamw Fri lunch keynote: The best teaching methods will always trump the coolest tech out there. True story.
12:38 PM · Oct 4, 2013

+

#TYCAMidwest #tycamw *KISMIF keep it simple,make it fun.The Canadian presenter is wonderful! *Using music to notify students of new task...
9:58 AM · Oct 5, 2013

+

I like going to class & teaching; can my students see/feel that? Do I give off that vibe? #apathy #tyca #tycamw
11:42 AM · Oct 14, 2016

+

Their social lives affect the classroom. Are they being bullied? #tyca #tycamw
11:44 AM · Oct 14, 2016

+

How many students wouldn't like my class no matter what I assigned?How I graded/assessed?If I was a man?My skin tone?Why? #apathy #TYCAMW
11:52 AM · Oct 14, 2016

+

"We hold the back of the bike;but at some pt, students have 2do things on their own." Yup: can't run alongside them as they write #c39 #4c17
10:06 PM · Mar 16, 2017

+

Hey #4c17 let's not judge teaching ideas or research or food choices as good or bad; it's all just different. Okthnxluvu
4:14 PM · Mar 17, 2017

+

#TYCAMW17 In my session:quality vs quantity. "A" writers who don't show up earnCs; "C" writers who revise=As. Is this "ok"? #GreatQuestions
10:32 AM · Oct 7, 2017

+

Empathy is taught to medical students and business students; do we assume teachers – those in the humanities - have empathy? #TYCAMW18
8:55 AM · Oct 12, 2018

+

#WhyIWrite To record my life, to express myself authentically, to practice creativity, to vent about idiots #TYCAMW18 #FridayFeeling
9:34 AM · Oct 12, 2018

+

I just really want to give credit. I'm certain I got it from the crew who presented on hybrids at a #TYCAMW conference not that long ago. They covered #COI Community of Inquiry = teacher presence, cognitive presence, social presence.
8:56 PM · Jan 11, 2020

+

#TYCA is always a good idea (national or regional), and in the weeks leading up to it, I'm participating in a state-based #OER conference & an #ungrading webinar hosted by the #4Cs. #blasphemy #PD #conference @ncte_tyca #TYCA2020
9:50 AM · Feb 23, 2020

+

It's one thing to present #oer ideas to writing teachers via #tyca #tycamw @ncte_tyca, and it's WHOLE OTHER thing to present my #oer projects and ideas to OER experts at their national conferences. I dunno if I'll ever get the guts to do so. Intimidating... #opened #open #oep
1:11 PM · Feb 19, 2021

+

In scanning the on-demand #TYCA & #4c21 sessions, I see more #OER (since 2019) and hints of #ungrading (#gradingcontracts), so basically... Englishers are slowly moving to the dark side. Which is good for them because we have cookies. And less stress.
12:47 PM · Apr 5, 2021

Open.

Wednesday October 5, 2005

I think I am going to use this book[60] for my English 110 next semester. I still haven't decided on a book for the World Lit course. I think I'll have to just find something (not too spendy) that has a majority of what I want to cover and then copy off (from the web or other books) the other things I'd like to use - poems, etc. I am hoping that at least one of the books in these huge anthologies will work (like the 21st century - book F in most packs) ... then I could assign Sandra Cisneros's book of short stories along with the massive book. I am bound and determined not to have my students pay a ton of 'moola.'[61]
Posted[62] 10/5/2005 at 10:29 AM

Thursday December 11, 2008

Mini-Story & Mini-Lesson of the Day, Wednesday...

It started off as a good day. Oh sure, some students completely missed the boat on our month-long massive research project that I've been assessing this week, but that's nothing new. I had a Rockstar[63], got jittery, had yummy Thai noodles for lunch, etc. Then... just as my day was wrapping up, I head to the bookstore's 35% off sale. I'm thought, "I'm going to load up on sweatpants and a sweatshirt - my finals week attire for this year." Just as

---

[60] Links to *The College Writer*. It's nice to see I was thinking about students' textbook costs as far back as '05.
[61] Slang for money.
[62] Posts with two time stamps are blog posts; some were public posts and some were private.
[63] Energy drink.

I'm about to leave, I remember to pick up a copy of *Sex, Drugs, and Cocoa Puffs* for next semester's class.

As I walk over to the wall o books, I see THEM. THEY are BLUE and not ORANGE. "SON OF A..." The bookstore had stocked up on the most recent edition of my English 120 book, *everything's an argument*. Immediately, I'm upset. I have the class built around the previous edition[64]. I attempt to not freak out on the bookstore people; I find out that Walter had okay'd it or whatever. No matter what has happened or who caused it, I feel overwhelmed. And somewhat lucky I caught it NOW and not after break.

So, I have two books to integrate into the English 120 course, not one. Yikes.

Then, after trying not to holler/bitch at Walter, I leave campus for food. My sugar levels are low, and I need comfort food. McDonald's. While in the drive-through, I recall that my parents were going to celebrate my dad's birthday a second time in Fargo last night. I call my sister to vent, mostly, about the book situation. She asks almost immediately, "Why aren't you up here? Are you coming up?" Yea. That was pretty much the straw that broke my tired/hungry back. I could heard dad in the background say it was his fault for not calling me. Errrg. Once again, kept out of the loop. I tell my sister that it's too bad - I already have fast food for my belly and get off the phone so I can scream in the interior of the bug.

I don't always have to BE at all the places and know all the inside jokes, but when I'm left out of the loop on matters

[64] One of the many reasons to use Open Educational Resources (OER).

that pertain to my sanity, I get pissy. There's no one person to blame in particular, but yesterday TWO incidents were all about me not knowing what the heck was going on.
Posted 12/11/2008 at 11:37 AM

April 8, 2016.

I've been elbow-deep in planning my Online World Lit class for the summer. I've found so many free PDFs online – because I refuse to have my students buy a $50+ book that we won't entirely read anyhow – that I've been geeking out hardcore.

[...]

June 4, 2016.

I'm thoroughly enjoying putting this open-source textbook together. Too much, probably. It's given me a reason to go back into ALL of my teaching documents, all of my old files, to see what I've created that we could use in the book as text to explain an idea, as an activity, as an exercise, as a sample. With that searching, however, comes the possibility of running into old situations. Like the ones I had with Ersula[65].

July 28, 2016.

[...]

A day before Zooey's birthday – which is today – we finished up DRAFT #2 of the open-source textbook. Zooey and I frantically pulled together two chapters that had been assigned to Cecila; she just wasn't able to get us what we were thinking... for example, the Argument chapter content she sent

---

[65] Ersula was one of two colleagues who didn't exactly make my first years on campus "easy." They had ideas on how and what I should be teaching. My methods were "wrong." In order to focus on MY pedagogy in this book, and not theirs, I'll keep their "voices" to a minimum.

Zooey was from a site that wasn't an open-source one, so ya know, we did what we had to do.

I've learned a lot about group work throughout the making of this textbook. We aren't quite done, but we are very, very close. I think we will have a bunch of tiny tweaks to figure out in a week or so (the Copy Center is overwhelmed this week, so we might not get our physical copies until Monday – we decided to print off five: Walter, Maggie, Cecila, Zooey, and I will give it a first or second once-over), and then it's fall semester, and we will be able to try out the sucker on our classes! I think we'll need to tidy up our pre and post surveys of assessment (asking the students if they've ever used open-source before or how they feel about not having a textbook-textbook, etc.).

August 8, 2016.

Boom. Drop the mic. The final draft is done. Holy fucking shitballs. I was so happy to be done, I got home and let Sadie out, ate Taco Johns, and fell into a nap coma from about 2-4pm! I woke up, thinking about going kayaking for about two seconds, but then realized I wanted to shop online (to celebrate?), I wanted to write, and I wanted to brag on Facebook. [...]

This morning's meeting went better than expected. Every so often Cecila would slow us down a bit with rewording a sentence or saying "sorry" before she even had anything to be sorry for, but it was all good. Zooey had a doc's appointment to leave us for, but I took over her computer, and Cecila and I tweaked the rest. Just as Zooey got back, we had found the small errors. She inserted the images that I had changed, she fixed the typefaces that were weird in a few spots, and then we made a plan for what was last to take care of. We'll go through our last digital copy this week once she color-codes certain infographics, and that will be that. Super cool. I'm so happy to have that completed. It's a good feeling. Now I can "play" the rest of the week – I literally have no plans beyond a possible lunch with Johansson and others Wednesday – and I love that feeling.

January 10, 2017.

I just dropped off two OER textbooks (*Writing Unleashed* and *Write or Left*[66]) with our college president. He seemed impressed, asked how long it took us to create them, how much their paper cost was, and I told him how we've made them more accessible (and plan to create audio versions eventually).

I woke up with a migraine and some sinus issues that kind of subsided but found a friend – stomachache. Now that I'm at work, the whole bodily system feels better.

Just had lunch with Josie after finishing the first draft of our mini-grant proposal to create an English 120 OER textbook. It was a happy chat, an awesome burger and fries, and a former online student tracked me down to tell me that she liked my class. I thanked her for thinking so and telling me, too. I like when things like that happen. Going to lunch over[67] there wasn't really on the agenda, but I'm glad we trekked over there in the blowing snow.

[...]

September 29, 2017.

Well, I took a dive and now I'm in too deep. Surrounded by the deep blue chaos of NaNoWriMo[68]. All it took was that one video on Facebook, and I'm fucked. Fucked in a good way. Fucked in a way that doesn't let my brain shut off. Fucked in a way that I want to print off ALL THE THINGS about NaNoWriMo. Fucked in a way that makes me ponder if there

---

[66] This is the title of my Creative Writing textbook; it was given to me, I believe, by my creative friend James Wateland. Thanks, man.

[67] Yes, our campus has its own restaurant, separate from the dining hall for students with meal plans.

[68] National Novel Writing Month. It usually occurs in November.

is a college packet of lessons out there, and if not, maybe I should fucking create it! Because I don't have ENOUGH SHIT GOING ON RIGHT NOW.

Jeezus.

I've started a Piktochart, a schedule, a new Medium Project booklet, and I just now emailed Lyle to ask him to print off the high school text (plus the PDF of curriculum ideas) that is shared on the NaNoWriMo site.

This was bound to happen. I've been thinking about having them write a book for a while now. It's popped up in countless semesters, in countless prep hours... yeah. So, maybe that's what happens this coming spring. Maybe it's time to take that leap? And perhaps a smaller version of it gets plopped into the creative writing class? I don't know about that yet, but Jaxton said in class that he would've loved to write a book in English 110 and would like the opportunity in Creative Writing.

It's a lot to take in, and I'm unsure if I have the energy today. I didn't sleep well – could be multiple reasons – and I know I'm going to need to crash this afternoon.

So, that was a nice walk around campus. The sweet little lady at the library wants us to sign the OER *Writing Unleashed* textbooks I gave her, I freaked out Barry and Lyle at the Copy Center with my NaNoWriMo idea, and then I grabbed grilled cheese and fries at the Wildcat Grounds[69].

I asked Lyle: "If you walked into my class on Day 1, and I said you were going to write a novel that semester, would you shit bricks?" His eyes got big: "YES!" And Barry added: "Gold bricks. Gold bricks." But then I used Barry's discipline, and said, "You know, I can see Diesel students having an issue, but what do they want to write about? A guy who parties all the time? Go for it? A guy who fixes things and the climax is he ends up with something that CAN'T be fixed?" They nodded. I should definitely include that one guy who wrote about parties...

[69] Campus café.

Aaron Karo and Tucker Max[70]. I should look through all my things to find examples of nonfiction, humor (George Carlin), fiction… and examples by women!

May 8, 2019.

What a helpful webinar last night from the "digital northeast."

My notes: OER is a Legacy concept & leads to a digital reputation. I was chastised for saying that teachers steal from each other (that's not OER, and yeah, I should've used the word "share"), and before that, I answered a question in the chat and was told that some moderator would share questions with the presenter (I'm learning all sorts of webinar etiquette these days). At the end, I asked about OEP ideas (what could I do beyond having students remix a chapter into their own voice and add samples; she mentioned audio and multimedia), and we chatted about accessibility - Torrey stated that too much text can become inaccessible, yet I'm still concerned for those who have hearing/sight disabilities (or even are just prone to seizures). Anyhow, I asked about how my CW211 book has an overarching CC license but then the two passages by Maggie and Travis are more restricted; the way I have it set up (calling out the restricted licenses on the page and at the beginning) seems to work well, according to Torrey and Gaby. Cool beans.

[…]

September 12, 2019.

Okay, so our first OER textbook is/was a beast. And complex, too. But I am oddly liking the tweaking of it. I've taken out pieces that are unnecessary – why have images with text on them when we can write it out? – and added parts to the research unit (CRAAP test) that Zooey requested; I added

---

[70] I'm sure these guys aren't the only ones who write about partying. I should've looked up writers who were people of color, writing goofy stories.

the annotated bib genre to the genre unit, changed the student names in one section from "white" ones to "non-white" as a means to be more inclusive. I've added readings from the *88 Open Essays* OER I found recently via Twitter, and I'm revising/deleting those as I go through them (do students want to read about how walking is a great American pastime? Or that old people have sex?), so yeah, it's shaping up to becoming even better than what it was, especially when it comes to accessibility and inclusivity.

[...]

October 9, 2019.

[...]

Before my 3pm class – which went swimmingly, thanks for asking – I tuned into a Zoom webinar from the Rebus people about their OER Textbook Program. They sent me some very helpful shit, and the ladies were VERY sweet. But unfortunately, it just TURNED UP my urge to create YET ANOTHER FUCKING OER textbook. Yeah, only this time, it's not like a newborn... no no... it's another revision – the *Writing Unleashed: The Very Best Nuggets*. This will be JUST FOR ME. Less Strategies, more Genres. More funk. Weird images.

I AM SO FUCKING EXCITED to take that textbook and take it to a WHOLE OTHER LEVEL of awesomeness. I've already found more pieces on *WikiHow*, like how to write a commentary, how to write a movie review, how to write a manifesto, etc. Amazeballs. So pumped.

Part of me is like, "Wait, weren't you going to edit Book 2 of those teaching journals," and yeah, I should get to that, but I love projects. I love them.

The day I don't want to give myself another project is the day I die. End of story. Amen.

And now as excited as I am, I'm going to head home and eat my yummy white chicken chili and wait for the storm to hit. I shall resume excitement tomorrow... okay, we know I'll research more shit tonight to put into the Nugget book, but yeah. Pajamas are calling me.

October 22, 2019.

[...]

I did possibly come up with a partnership idea today. Well, I told Walter about it today; I came up with it like last week and told Johansson then.

Those of us who use OER could ask alumni and community members to sponsor printings of our textbooks. They wouldn't be necessarily "sponsoring" the content, just the paper. Boom! Then I have physical books for my students, and we can use them in class for reference. Ditto for everyone else who uses OER. So, hopefully the Alumni Director thinks it's do-able (and super cool!), as does the Partnership Taskforce Team.

[...]

December 11, 2019.

Well, Past Me helps Present Me once again. As it turns out, I have quite a few of the audio versions of my chapters already in Blackboard for the English 120 course and the Intro to Creative Writing course. Yep. Go me! I'd like to have audio of the other readings in those courses as well, so those items will have to go onto my holiday break prep list, along with embedding my version of *Writing Unleashed* (the very best nuggets) into Bb and creating audio chapters of that beast, too. BUT it's nice to know that some of the pieces I thought I needed to create ARE already FINISHED. Boom.

[...]

And in nerdy news:

Dear Sybil Priebe,

Thank you for your presentation submission for the 2020 TYCA Conference in Milwaukee, WI, March 25, 2020.

We are happy to inform you that the following presentation has been approved: You down with OEP? Yeah, you know me. (TYCA-80)

Please accept or decline your invitation in your speaker zone, and check your presentation description and biographical information. Use the link above to upload your presentation file prior to the conference.

You may notice that your session type has been changed by the TYCA planning committee. This was intentional to accommodate as many presentations on the program as possible. If you have any questions, please email cccc2020@ncte.org.

March 7, 2020.

Yesterday's OER conference was refreshing at points and frustrating at others. [...]

Firstly, the drive up and back with Trish[71] was wonderful. I talked her ears off, but it was a good conversation about what we didn't read in high school/college (history, Native authors). [...]

Once there, we sat in the back... we said hi to Lee, and Cecila found us eventually. The morning was filled with lots of speeches and data, but it wasn't totally dull stuff. At some point, a woman from a particular university bookstore said we have to make sure faculty have what they want – tests and worksheets – but my immediate response was NO. Start with students. Always start with them and you can do no wrong. Then this same woman didn't think she needed to use the mic at the front of the room later. UGH. No, use the mic. Be accessible.

[...]

Okay, and then our session after lunch went well. I carried us, mostly, and I guess Lee was concerned beforehand and

[71] Our lovely librarian, and possibly the only other person on our campus who knows almost EVERYTHING about OER.

Cecila was like, "Sybil's got this." I'm amazing at presenting shit from my ass. Freeballing[72]. Winging it. It's my expertise. We had very few questions and wrapped up early. I got two ideas from two ladies in the back in using the internet archives (flips like *Issuu*?) and the state library to produce material for the blind/deaf. One dude asked why we didn't have an index... I didn't know why we didn't include that, but later I thought: Wait, we offer our book digitally, so the page numbers change AND you can typically search using Adobe or Word...

In the next session, Tanya showed our book on the *Open Textbook Library* (through the U of M); there was a review... yeah. It was half criticism that made sense and half pissy picky shit.

June 10, 2020.

[...]

Just now, I gave feedback to a person in the NDUS[73] regarding an OER fellowship form and OER textbook stipend; I felt honored she'd asked for my feedback, really. I think I might apply for both, unless I can use our campus OER money for the ideas I have. One would be promotion of OER courses to students and OER textbooks to faculty. Another idea: Look into how close we are to a Z-Degree[74]. Then, with a certain sane colleague as the interim Marketing Director, we could market that Z-Degree to future students. I feel like the first idea would include social media and posters, but also one-on-one interviews with faculty.

[...]

September 21, 2020.

[...]

---

[72] Yes, I know I don't have the anatomy for this, but it's a wonderful synonym for "winging it."

[73] North Dakota University System.

[74] This term applies to degrees that a student can earn with ZERO textbook costs.

Um, what else? I did A LOT of work on the Z-Degree Fellowship project. I'm in the process right now of finding materials for those who don't have ZTC (zero textbook cost) courses, so when I email them this Thursday – my third email to faculty this semester regarding this project – I can say HERE IS SOME FREE SHIT YOU SHOULD BE USING INSTEAD PLEASE AND THANK YOU. Essentially. Some of them are using digital access codes upwards of $100, and that means the students don't even get a goddamn BOOK for $100. Jeezus. At least with me, you have a choice. Digital is free, and the Amazon people are charging like $5 for my physical book. Students are basically paying for some really fucking cheap paper when it comes to my class. It shouldn't cost them THAT much beyond tuition, should it? And it kills me that some of these classes are filled with content from the public domain. Like my discipline – rhetoric hasn't changed much. Nor has chemistry, physics, etc. Has economics? And when it comes to the PRESENT, why not use current articles in your Political Science course? I don't know. This project is interesting and frustrating all at once, and I have no idea what will really happen in the end. Lisa Johnson (Vice Chancellor) said that the governor, or his people, are interested in what I'm looking into, so we'll see if it goes anywhere beyond my brain, mouth, and Google Slides.

October 21, 2020.

[...]

I might never get recognition for all the cool [OER] shit I'm doing at this level, and I have to be okay with that. Maybe? I mean, what good will it do to point out that those two[75] MIGHT NOT be the epitome of OER knowledge? I'd just look – as sexist as it is – jealous. Huh.

[75] Two people at a particular conference who are bowed down to as OER gurus.

And WEIRDLY enough, as I pointed out to Maggie yesterday, using OER at the freshman level is probably MUCH more important than at the fucking senior level. Just tweeted:

I'd argue until the cows come home that #OER is important at any level, in any class, but is it particularly helpful in retaining freshman? Has anyone looked into that? Like: Yay, saving seniors $50-150 is great, but if we can start off freshmen w/#ZTC, wouldn't that be AWESOME?!

Yeah. I poke bears for a living.

[...]

December 1, 2020.

My email to a co-worker regarding the Student Satisfaction Survey results we just got to review this week:

Is it just me or could most of our challenges be "fixed" with some good old OER and ungrading practices by faculty?

Hint: I bet it's not just me.

I do have a meeting with our college president December 11 to discuss review monies for those who still may consider OER for their courses, which could push us closer to a Z-Degree!

Tweets:

I've probably tweeted this before, or maybe someone else has, but you can't really have an anti-racist class by ONLY un-whitening the materials & content. Your policies shouldn't be racist. Your "grading" processes shouldn't be racist. #TYCA21 #4C21 #ungrading meets #OER
3:12 PM · Apr 8, 2021

+

It'd be intriguing, too, to attempt an #OEP project where Ss write abt the bad ideas ingrained in them. I'd also still like to try an #OER that is "about writing, written by 'non-writers'"... #FutureIdeas
8:19 AM · Apr 11, 2021

+

Cynical Me / Tired Me: "Well, if students aren't going to read the textbook, it might as well BE FREE. Amiright?" Deep sigh. #OER
10:00 AM · Apr 22, 2021

+

I, too, started off thinking #OER as an affordability& accessibility "thing," but I should've started w/the lens of social justice. I agree w/ @ProfJasmine that my Qs would've been SO DIFFERENT w/that approach! And I would've un-whitened the content earlier instead of later.
9:32 AM · Apr 26, 2021

+

Also, to speak to the consequences of being #open... what I've learned is that my obsession w/#OER #OEP is translating into extra work to convert/convince faculty (w/o the leadership role label) WHILE, unfortunately, NOT seeing it considered legit work in tenure portfolios.
4:22 AM · Apr 30, 2021

+

Yep. Yet, when I feel undervalued, it is something I remind myself of. That this is my legacy to leave behind. This #OER stuff makes me happy. If they want to look at $$$s, okay, but I'm looking at how a S didn't have to choose my book over 5 lunches.
2:55 PM · Apr 30, 2021

+

The moment I was sucked - happily - into the #Open Ed vortex, I began wondering HOW to open up EVERYTHING. Just like Heather, #OEP projects brought me to "god, how do I grade stuff like THIS?" Add in how #OER = inclusivity & #ungrading was the logical next step in both cases.
7:52 PM · May 1, 2021

+

I'd EVENTUALLY like to say: Okay. Blank slate. What does a textbook for writers by "nonwriters" look like? Go. What chapters would they create? What topics would they want covered? That's my end goal... probably. #OEP #OER
8:35 PM · May 4, 2021

+

I tripped and fell into the #ungrading rabbit hole back in the summer of 2019; I've been embraced by ungraders (and the #open #OER community) in a way I never thought could happen on social media.
9:08 PM · May 8, 2021

Poetry Break

Sunday October 3, 2010

She wanted to do a project on anarchy
and my eyes widened.
He wanted to show me a poem he wrote
and his hands were normally groping car parts.
Rarely, I come across them.
Them.
Those students who have ideas.
And I want to turn vampire on them; I want to clone them.
It's like an idea monster met another idea monster and had babies.
That's the demented viewpoint I have on my classes and students.
Posted 10/3/2010 at 6:28 PM

I'll Call This Chapter: Pedagogy.

Wednesday October 2, 2002

Ok. Been thinking a lot about these "stretch projects", and I have various ideas...

MAINLY, I want you to take YOURSELF, stretch something YOU LIKE, into how it can increase your literacy skills or knowledge with something.. then later you will write a paper on how it helped you, how it could help others, and why it was useful (or not).

Some ideas: Creating your own webpage (on Yahoo! or Tripod, etc) since you'll need to use one later in this class with Dreamweaver and putting a hypertext creative writing on it... OR collaborating with others to write up a multi-vocal piece of writing (so that will concentrate on your collaboration skills AND writing skills!) about college life... OR putting together a little movie (see ITS lab for checking out and editing camcorders, etc) about life.. being a literate person... being human.. being online now.. OR write your own Blog Novel, like Mark Amerika , in a creative format... OR research something you are really, really into and doing a survey with it regarding what others think- then write up a paper on what you found OR put together a powerpoint presentation of it all...

THERE ARE MANY POSSIBILITIES.

Come up with five possible stretch projects for yourself by Tuesday. Be ready to tell us what they are!! And be ready to share your "Be Funny" Minute Paper as well.

Today in the Lab: Play with some programs, search the

internet for project ideas, write up your Be Funny Minute Paper, hand in your Paper #1, (e-mail me an electronic copy SOON), check your e-mail to see if you got my most recent message, and read Mark Amerika's Blog Novel for Tuesday.. found on the reading list I think.
Posted 10/2/2002 at 2:40 PM

Wednesday November 15, 2006

I love surprises. I should clarify - GOOD surprises.
After talking to Walter yesterday, I realized that I want to add into my syllabus for next spring (English 110 and maybe English 120) the possibility of a Minute Paper that follows the Major Papers. I'll hand back Papers 1-3, and only circle "mistakes." Students then have to write up a short, one-pager (single-spaced) identifying why I circled what I did. Was it a run-on? Comma splice? A misspelling? This way, I don't write as much, they have to learn what those sentence problems are, and they use the paper more after it's written (instead of chucking it after viewing the grade). I think we also talked about paperless writing conferences... which would be something to try. He mentioned adding more reflection in his classroom, and I think that's a great idea. Asking students to write extensively and read critically is great and all, but if we can get them to go beyond - ask themselves why they wrote how they did, or how they came to the conclusion they did with the reading... How = Process. This adds a whole other level of critical thinking... Bloom would be proud.
[...]
Posted 11/15/2006 at 10:30 AM

Wednesday March 28, 2007

Today, I realized that when a teacher assigns great, well-thought out projects (ones that both teachers and students can enjoy/appreciate), that particular teacher has less

complaining to deal with in the classroom, AND the students use class time much more efficiently. I haven't had many problems in class since we came back from Spring Break. And students have even stated (to me) how much they are enjoying the project. In addition, for a few of these work days on the PPT MusicVideo, I have had a majority of students staying past the :50 mark. Some in my 11am class come early and barge in on the 10am students, too! If only they looked at papers this way. I think I need to survey them next week about this project and get more input from them.
> How can this energy be placed onto paper writing, the type of composition required? Is it possible?
> What is it about this project that enthralled them so much? What "sold" them?

I think I am also getting better and better at explaining any and all of my assignments. Having a handout for everything (designed well with grading criteria) really, really helps them, and I am able to refer back to it instead of saying and repeating, "Well, when I introduced I said you had to ___."
Posted 3/28/2007 at 11:17 PM

Wednesday September 26, 2007

Things I am reminded of (whenever I grade papers or see the papers post-writing conferences):
= Most students write well.
= Most students revise.
= Some students don't look at my rubric that's in the syllabus; they have no title to their paper.
= Students shouldn't meet with me if they aren't even going to revise afterward.
= Students will try all sorts of ways to lengthen their

papers; now that I used eCompanion & they submit them electronically, I can see that they've added pts in the spacing, or used a font that has spacing that looks triple-spaced.
= Students don't know what I mean when I say, in conference, "This needs to be heavily proofread by you or someone."
= Students like to concoct their own version of what the top of the first page should look like; MLA isn't creative enough (and, really, I have no problem with creative headings to their paper, but adding a 24pt font isn't going to help the situation).

There's got to be better assignments out there than "the essay" that I can implement into the classroom to lessen the "uh, we have to write a paper" syndrome. *I'm really tired of that attitude*. Perhaps I need to switch to 6 smaller papers/projects/assignments?
Posted 9/26/2007 at 12:36 PM

Wednesday August 27, 2008

"Write a bad argument for Friday," I said to my English 120 class at about 1:35pm.
"Write a bad essay for Friday," I said to my English 110 class at about 2:35pm.
Jaws dropped in both classes. *WHAT* do you want us to *DO*?
I gave this as an example to the English 120 class:
"Well, how do you know when an argument has gone badly? Someone starts swearing, right? Or it turns into 'You suck' 'No, you suck'."
And I gave this to the English 110 class as an example:
"If you've been told you write like crap, just do that. If you've been told you write well, do the opposite."

I've confused them and challenged them all at once; I'm awesome.
From confusion comes critical thinking? I hope?
Two new assignments... we'll see how it all turns out come Friday.
Posted 8/27/2008 at 3:54 PM

Thursday February 3, 2011

I've wondered a lot of things lately...
--- Who To Challenge?: One would be that I fear I'm catering my classes to those who "clearly don't care" rather than those who "somewhat care and want to be challenged." Oddly, the first group, right now, is typically males making the latter female. And, during this semester, I've noticed 2/3 of my on-campus classes contain talkative females = another oddity.
--- Spoon-Feeding: Do I somehow give students the option to not think? When they email me questions, am I giving away too much? Should they be trying to figure out more of it on their own? I mean, I give a lot of details - some students have said my handouts are too detailed. So, essentially, the information is there, man. Read it. Read it again. Then read it to your parrot.
--- Spicing It Up: I've been really using up those Reading Activities I created[76], and I'd like to think they are working. I think my students are reading the material more than students have in the past when I've just said, "Read X" and not given them an accompanying reading activity. I think. It's only a hunch. Since I didn't quiz everyone before, I have no statistics to compare the current reading activity grades to.
Posted 2/3/2011 at 9:58 PM

---

[76] I'm putting these into an OER textbook someday, by the way.

Monday October 24, 2011

So, using the site *ThoughtCatalog* as my guide, I assigned a new paper this semester called the "List Essay." I introduced it before I left for TYCA-Midwest (Monday, October 10); it was due last Friday - they had two weeks to complete it. Part of the assessment will include classmates voting for their top 5 in the class (so that the audience would be more than the instructor), in addition to me going through them looking for length issues (it had to be 1000+ words), etc. Thus far, in scanning the ones that are uploaded to the correct spot, a lot of students missed the mark on the length requirement. And a few didn't even employ the "list" idea... *Hmph*. I might ask for feedback on all this, yet I know they'll say they didn't get enough direction... when I *think* they did. I covered it, there was a sample from me they could've mimicked, and there were 5 samples on ThoughtCatalog they were supposed to look at while I was gone (which, yes, 10% of them did - but that's not "on me" technically).

It makes me think that they struggle to just have a few parameters sometimes. The list essay needed to be humorous and 1000+ words in length; they even had samples to view. What more did they need? I'm kind of unsure. And, many of these students are Liberal Arts/Transfer students = they will potentially not get a lot of direction at a four-year university OR on the job in "the real world." Same goes, actually, for my trade/tech students - like a boss is going to sit there and go through exactly what needs to be a in a letter to a customer or in an incident report? Maybe this is what needs to be brought to their attention?

My guesses right now = 50% didn't hit the correct word requirement & 40% didn't put the essay in a list format. They had samples for the latter, and the requirement is in the Project Catalog (that maybe some

have lost, yet it's online in our Doc Sharing area) - I did say it aloud in class. But probably only once, and that's not enough (even though it should be? They had long samples in front of them...).
Overall, I'm a bit frustrated, but I'm not going to not use it next time. It was bound to happen; it happens with each project. And this was a guinea pig project = brand-new.
Posted 10/24/2011 at 9:36 AM

Wednesday September 5, 2012

Why is is that I like watching students at work?
Right now, I've assigned them their 10 min writing prompt = read the website of *101 George Carlin Quotes* & respond to one.
Some are reading; some are writing. It's like I want to see the imaginary neurons bouncing all over the place.
Next on our agenda: creating double entendres. Last semester I did these for the first time, and the students liked them. Sure, they can end up "perverted" but it shows them how language works in strange ways. I think we'll put them up on the board like I did last time, too, so we can laugh at them.
Posted 9/5/2012 at 9:11 AM

Friday October 26, 2012

On Wednesday, I assigned the Racial Experiment prompt. I maybe shouldn't have been shocked that it was pretty split down the middle; some thought their life would be VERY different, some thought nothing would change. There were also some sprinklings of racist comments. I don't know what to do with those; I'm thinking of just reading aloud (in the 1pm and 3pm classes = they seemed to be the most opinionated) the most intriguing responses where students thought critically about how A LOT would change. And how they would be looked at differently.

I guess it shows me how some students, whether they are "racist" or not, can't wrap their heads about what it is like to BE in others' shoes!
Yes, they might have the same faith, but they would've had parents with different backgrounds, too, so they might have pushed them to do other things. Sure, there aren't "black farmers," so what else would your parents be doing for work/career then? Think think think... it's complex, for sure.

And a handful used the term "colored." This saddens me to no end. I mean, really, guys? Let's get with the program & if we must label people, let's label them appropriately by their backgrounds. Plus, there were a few who claimed they'd use the "race card" or whatever. Jeeeezus. So disappointed with how they think.
shakes head
I know I can't change minds, but what can my course of action be with this? Maybe by just having it as a prompt, that will help the neurons in their stale melons to make some noise? I should look through the prompts I had them create to see what they threw at me after we responded to this one. (Yes, I had them create prompts after responding to the race one. So, those could be interesting, to say the least.)

Last thought: Many just figured that WHITE covered everything. Many were okay with lumping German with French and Norwegian when really those cultures are VERY different... different histories, etc. Yeah.
Posted 10/26/2012 at 10:55 AM

February 25, 2013

insert swear words
How on earth am I supposed to change my students?
Not ONLY am I attempting to improve their reading and writing skills, but today I realized I have yet ANOTHER "challenge" or "task" or "something like those words." Changing their racist & homophobic attitudes and ideas. Yes, racist and homophobic remarks have always popped up my classrooms verbally. Like ugly bubbles in a glass of Diet Coke.
But now they are showing up in student papers.
I guess I should put a clause into every projects' instructional guide? = "No homophobic language or racist language allowed. Don't even try it." Because YA KNOW WHAT? Sure, George Carlin is vulgar. He's got F-bombs shooting out of him like fireworks on July 4th, but swear words don't mean much when they are just thrown into the air.
Example: If I walked into a classroom, and just said the f-word. That's it. Just "F**k." Students might giggle, but that's it. If I said "F*g" or the n-word. By itself. Nothing else. Someone could easily get hurt by that, and I know some students would say that PEOPLE GET OFFENDED by everything, but they have a REASON to get offended by the latter words I brought up and not the former. I guess this is my opinion, but no one is set apart from another with the f-word. In a classroom of mixed religions and races and backgrounds, the f-word could offend the uber religious, maybe, but only because they don't like it not because they identify with the word, like the other words I've mentioned.
So, yeah, I'm a weirdo. I don't care if I hear the f-bomb in class (as long as it's not used WITH other derogatory words, of course), but I can not deal with the n-word or anything derogatory towards other races and sexualities.

Ugh ugh ugh.
Posted 12:47 PM

September 25, 2015.

My first response, upon seeing Johansson[77] this morning, was to make a fart sound with my mouth in his general direction. And then we laughed about it.

So, apparently, some students don't know how to address envelopes? And apparently, it's totally cool to consistently come to class 15 minutes late, not hear the teacher say your name when she wants to do a journal check because... well, the student has ear buds in and is feverishly writing in his journal because he didn't do his seven entries in the last five weeks. Yeah, you read that right, kids.

Ugh. Then I go and make the mistake of posting on Facebook about addressing envelopes. I say "mistake" because a former person (I can't even say friend) from grad school – Landon – decides to argue that we shouldn't be teaching students these types of things because they are the "old ways" and that makes them pointless. Before placing him on a high privacy setting, I argued that people still do write letters. They do matter (www.moreloveletters.com), and I could've gone off about how I show the video connected to that web site, but I just posted the URL which I'm sure he didn't look at. Smug ass. I called him out on being a know-it-all, I told him that these "digital creatures" don't have a fucking clue how to take a screenshot or use our online platform, etc. etc. etc. I finally asked if he was teaching, if he was in the trenches like Connie (another poster & fellow teacher) and me... well, the obvious answer was "no," but instead of just saying that he gave me a guilt trip about using the word "trenches" because teaching isn't a war. I'm being insensitive by using that word. OMG. Yes, please give me a guilt trip. Tell me I'm being insensitive when

---

[77] He is a colleague of mine who doesn't teach in my discipline, but "lives" down the hall and always has coffee brewing.

you haven't been doing what I have been doing for OVER FIFTEEN YEARS now. Jeezus H. Christ.

He just messaged me, asking why I censored him and that he's going to write a letter about it. Smug ass. I just sent him this: "Write a letter to these people: www.moreloveletters.com" because YOU HAVE NO IDEA WHAT I AM DOING IN CLASS. Hey, by looking that web site, one might realize that people – people who aren't doing so hot or have lost loved ones or whatever – want letters. In the mail. Not discussion board comments. Not fucking text messages. Not a stupid email. A FUCKING LETTER.

Deep breath.

[...]

October 2, 2015.

I was just chatting this lovely Homecoming Friday with Brit and Zooey about what our students will remember in class, because Zooey feels like she's battling something she shouldn't have to by teaching and re-teaching them how to create thesis statements as well as dissect papers and find those elements, etc. I say that I'm sure Mason might only remember my mini-lecture about double entendres because on Wednesday of this week, he connected it to the show he watches, *The League*; there's a character who goes by Double EntANDRE... or something like that. I state how my diesel guys love talking about those crazy double entendres, euphemisms, etc. Well, judgment came down from the officemate on that, basically saying: "Oh, sure, it's fun to talk about those things, but we have real things to cover." And I shut down because her comments insinuate that I'm not doing what I'm supposed to and that these "fun" things can't lead to real learning, and that a teacher can't mix "fun" with "skills." Which is just plain false, right? I know she's smart enough to critically think about how to take something they'd be interested to learn about – euphemisms – and add it to something skill-based. Here, I'll do it right now: What if we asked them to create a one-page essay on any topic, but they had to use X amount of euphemism, X amount of double Entendres, and then within that essay, they also had to underline the thesis, the topic sentences for each paragraph, etc. Sounds fun AND complex, doesn't it? FUCK YES IT DOES.

Think smart, people. Add creativity. Boom. Done.

[...]

October 7, 2015.

If you were a student of mine who saw a sign on the door that said we didn't have class, wouldn't you seek out information on what to do in my absence? I sent out an email Monday and put my instructions in our Announcements page, but a few students – good students, even – didn't bother to check those things?

Also, I took my own advice and mixed the "fun" elements that were kind of looked down upon by my officemate last Friday and added them to an assignment. Project 12 – assigned via email to my students Monday when I was sick – asked the students to compose a 250+ worded 5-paragraph essay that contained 3 euphemisms and 3 double-entendres. A few had fun reading them aloud, actually! Yes, they were on the perverted side, but oh well; this is college – time to have fun with writing! Anyhow, before handing them in, I asked them to dissect their essays by underlining the thesis and topic sentences. I shuffled through my 1pm class' and reported to Zooey that it appeared they were able to identify those things in their own writing. I told Brit the same, and her response was a quiet one.

August 9, 2016.

[...]

And I'm oddly grateful I just turned this day into productivity because now I just have odds and ends for next week; I don't have to really worry about my classes all that much – just my presentations which won't really take a lot of prep because I already have a Tenure infographic, and for the Show and Tell, I'm starting off the session with the contract shit I just tweaked the hell out of.

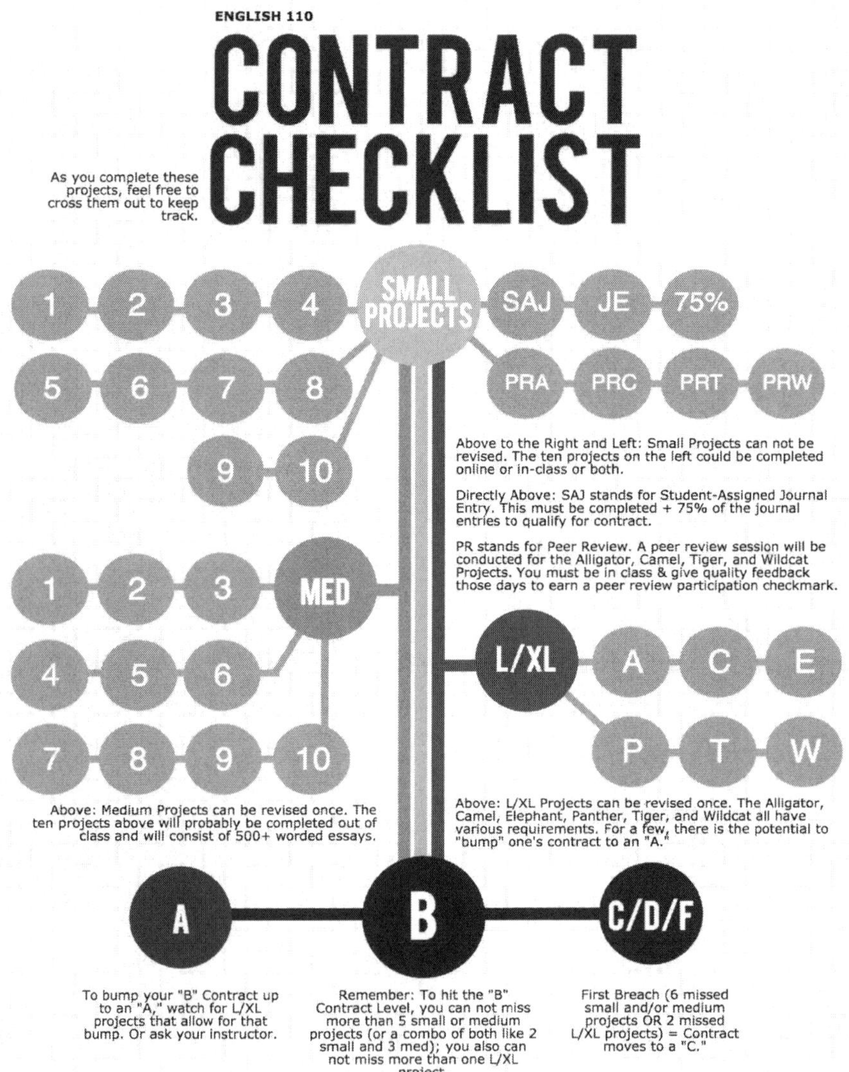

Isn't that the prettiest contract you've ever seen? I love love love Piktochart.

Okay, I really didn't do that much... I love deleting things apparently. Brevity is my new love? And with the contract check-off list, I had to figure out what to do with the student-assigned journal entries that I am trying this semester. I've been wanting to, but they aren't "Journal Checks" like I was doing last year. So, instead, I just put in the contract that students can't miss more than 75% of the total journal entries. This way, no matter if the class is 15 students or 22, they are responsible for a ratio instead of a set number like 20.

So, speaking of those student-assigned journal entries... I don't know if I have mentioned them before, but a handout about them has been sitting in a folder of mine for years now. The teacher who created the handout has the students take over that part of the class period. A student picks a day to assign a prompt and then everyone writes to that prompt. I don't know if I added the rest or if the person who made the handout did, but I'm going to have the student who assigns the prompt collect the entries. Within a week's time, they have to read through them and evaluate them based on content (I don't want this to be about grammar since they are spur-of-the-moment pieces), comment on them if they wish, and then report back their top five to the entire class (with an explanation, of course) and hand in the batch to me for me to then record.

I honestly don't know if this will sink or swim in every section. I have a "back-up plan" for those who don't have a prompt ready, and I have a plan for those who don't show on the day they signed up for, etc. I just really think this is a way for them to see other classmates' writing, for them to take ownership of something in the class daily, and for them to use their oral skills (and critical thinking skills) when they report back to the group. It'll probably need to be tinkered with, but everything does. And even when it doesn't need to be tinkered with, I do anyway.

Yeah.

[...]

September 7, 2016.

[...]

I'm introducing a new thing in my English 110 classes today: Student-Assigned Journal Entries/Prompts. [...] So, the 8am class took to the new idea very well. Students jumped at the chance to assign a prompt today! Yes! Two! They even did rock-paper-scissors to see who could assign the prompt today. I was shocked. I think I still am, actually. It was a good class, and the rest of it went smoothly. I think having to say their names more in class will help me remember them; today I had to recall names to put down who the assigners would be on my sign-up sheet and then I got to repeat that task when handing back the Medium Project #1s.

I'm hoping the other classes go as well. We'll see.

September 28, 2016.

During another conversation with Josie, I realized how much I need to focus on the "goodies" in my classes. I have only a few who really, truly, drive me batty. I told Josie that that 20% shouldn't get so much attention, and she agreed – in a class of about twenty-two students, it typically is about four of them who are going to push buttons or not have their poop in a group 85% of the time, etc. I cherish so many of my students, and this semester it's hitting me the most. I'm continuing to push myself to be present, and after my 8am class went well – they appeared to like having most of the class time to interview a classmate and practice on paper the art of integrating quotes and summary from that little interview – and after I assessed more Alligator projects today, I'm narrowing in on those who care. I noticed myself opening up their letters and reading them and appreciating the time MOST of them took in writing to people. Sure, some didn't do well. Some didn't bother to care or to proofread or to write to people in the three different categories [...] but most of them wrote nice letters. I knew this was possible, I have seen it before, and this time I appreciated it. And at certain moments, I found myself saying, “Oh, that’s so nice what [Molly] wrote to Obama; she’s such a gem,” etc.

These letters and these feelings have existed before this semester, and I might have missed them a little because I didn’t “get present” in the moment or I didn’t write a book about the whole goddamn school year, but I know they exist. I need to sit with them each year. I need to allow myself time to really read their “good” stuff, and those who don’t shoot me “good” stuff... well, they’ll get their shit assessed and that might be about it. I can’t worry about the intellectually lazy ones. I can’t focus on the ones who are absent so much. I can’t allow myself too much anger over a student who likes to constantly skip because she’s “not feeling well” and wants to just email me her homework. Um, if I allowed that, who would come to class? Oh, right, the ones who WANT to come to class.

So, yes, I’m trying not to focus on the ones who are going to be upset about their late Alligators... the ones who apparently didn’t hear me say, last Wednesday, that if they were done, they should put them in the Dropbox basket NOW... the ones who uploaded shitty drafts and have to revise big time... the one who didn’t do the assignment correctly at all and likes to have conversations with me on the regular about his work. He’ll probably be belligerent again, and I can firmly state that it’s belligerence because I’ve seen him put together okay work now within the parameters of my fucking assignment. Essentially, he can do the work, but chooses not to. I don’t know if this laziness or if he likes to just throw shit at me to see what I’ll do with it, but it’s really annoying. Don’t poke the bear, dude. Don’t.

Just don’t.

December 9, 2016.

I’m sure I say this at the end of every semester, but man, I’m so happy to almost be finished. I didn’t sleep well last night knowing that Martin might come to class today without his goddamn Wildcat draft… and then I can just see him waiting for the end of class so he can beg again, when I've already said no.

I was thinking last night – or maybe this morning – about how the bumps in the contract ARE "extra credit." It's their opportunity to bump up their contract grade JUST LIKE regular extra credit in a points system, only it's not called that, and it's not separate from the projects. I can't wrap my head around why students think it's totally fine to ask teachers to assign them extra work when the teacher is going to have to assess that extra work and the student should have just done the regular work in the first place.

If he remotely gets on my nerves today, I'm telling him to email Walter or talk to Dr. Holy. I'm done. I've said NO. For someone who has not only bothered me on a WEEKLY basis about his grade (Hi, how about we write shit down? OR don't lose that one list I gave you of what you needed to accomplish?) but interrupts me when he talks to me, has missed four big projects now, and has been late to class multiple times – if not full out skipping them – he has got some strange bravery to continue to push my buttons.

[…]

The one rule from yesterday: Don't make a change to your class unless it helps you be MORE efficient. Josie was going to implement some "email them when they haven't handed in something and give them a 12-hour warning" guideline, and I said that that's not going to help her, and probably not the students either. They have her schedule. They know when things are due. Don't hand-hold.

Then, today, another rule was to not allow recycling of papers/projects. In addition, Josie and Zooey don't want to allow late work. Another idea was to respond to on-campus student emails with: "Please see me in class," because then we don't type up some major response only to have them ask in class: "Did you get my email?" and we have to repeat ourselves. No more of that shit.

So, I went to my 1 o'clock class, and no one had a draft for the Wildcat project… yep, no one. I sighed one of my deep sighs[78], told them that small project #10 was due over the weekend, and then wished them well on their finals before semi-storming out back to my office.

I didn't think that was going to be how my semester ended, but oh well. I'm not going to worry about it; the activity was thrown in the schedule to help out students…

And, with that, I'm done. Practically.

I told Zooey what had happened on the way back to my office, and she said she wished the campus holiday party was tonight because we could so use a drink the size of our faces. I agreed. But tomorrow will be fun. I want to dance, drink, and be fucking merry.

December 13, 2018.

[…]

And in the midst of her own stuff, Zooey helped me form my purpose for the doctoral program[79]. I might keep teaching, I might use this education to move up in rank, but I also might just use it to become a leader on campus in the instructional design arena. I want to give myself options for the future, while meeting other doctoral students with difference interests and backgrounds.

My teaching philosophy is not as rose-colored as it used to be. Now it's much more practical, and it starts with the acknowledgement that teaching anything can be done in so many different ways. In my opinion, no particular "old way" is

---

[78] Apparently, I'm really good at these sighs, and you know what, they prevent me from losing my cool. Fight or flight? Nope. Just a long, deep sigh!

[79] Yes, at some point, I decided to attempt to "cheer myself up" by applying to a Doctoral Program at my alma mater.

off the table; the "lecture" can still be done so very well. The way education is going – with the integrating of an online component with hybrid courses, etc. – knowing a variety of classroom strategies that work face-to-face or online are essential. I could bring that to our campus; we are lacking that expertise, whether that became a part of my job or not.

[...]

January 8, 2019.

Oh, no, another "this is what is happening, and this is how you should respond" mini-lecture from Josie. I thought maybe they would disperse this semester, for no other reason than she had gotten them out of her system. But when I told her about a student – Jackie (the one with the apostrophe obsession) – who is in my Online 120 now and definitely wants some hand-holding, she stated that it's because Jackie's never taken a risk. She has fear. I state that it could just be dependence. She's always had people help her, so that's where she's been working within. Josie says she doesn't believe there are lazy students, and so, no, it must be because she needs the encouragement to take a risk blahblahblah. Ugh. All this after I just mentioned yesterday that I was thinking of taking the Instructional Technology route with the Doctorate – should I get in – because I think our campus needs an expert to say, "Here are the ways you could do X in your class" without judgment. She obviously doesn't see her own judgment of what I'm doing. She just appears to stamp each situation with some culturally responsive tagline and thinks that that is the cure.

There is NO ONE WAY to deal with humans. That's all I'm saying.

[...]

Ah, and Josie strikes again as I tell Zooey that I've been thinking of giving a certain class control over the first project.

Like – here are the outcomes[80], now write a proposal for a project that covers a majority of them. Zooey says it's a good crew to try it out on. Josie asked what the structure would be, and all I could muster was: "I'll just fly by the seat of my pants." I mean, the structure would be that they'd write the proposal and I'd give them a few parameters, but then we'd just go from there. I couldn't quite understand what she wanted as an answer, and she definitely didn't think our students could handle that kind of plan – especially as the first activity. I would like to try it.

She left to go get her child, and Zooey and I continued our chat. She looked at the class roster and confirmed that I'd have good eggs in there. We discussed how different we all are, and I just really dislike constantly having to prove myself to Josie. I do good work. I'm not you. It's okay if I don't follow the pedagogy you adore. Different is alright. I feel like we've had the conversations before – in regard to how she'd handle certain students – and it's like her brain can't remember: "Oh, right, how I do it is just ONE way to do it."

[...]

What I do know is that I want to BE ME in the classroom, and I wish my own officemate would respect that. I'd wonder if her need to "school" me comes from insecurity or jealousy or whatever, but I don't school her, and I have insecurities at times. I'm not exactly jealous of how she goes about her teaching because experience tell me that it's just different and it's not me and that's okay. I didn't want to teach like Camilla or Erusla, but they wanted me to. Perhaps I should ask her if she thinks I should just follow her ways. How can I open her to this bit of wisdom I've gained from being in a department where my teaching was questioned much more harshly?

January 9, 2019.

---

[80] It's called "Backwards Design." This is the process of starting with course outcomes and working backwards; what projects could one complete to fulfill the outcomes, etc.

Yet another mini-lecture from Josie about how when she tells students to get off their phones, they just do it. Or when they are on their phones (the 1 or 2 in each class a semester), she tells them she won't answer their questions, and that's the end of it. I simply say that's great for her because they will still try to push my buttons after; they don't learn the lesson from that one time. My resting bitch face is not enough of a deterrent. But, hey, she's got it all figured out. Seems like she was a lot more unsure of herself when she was first teaching here, and then suddenly, in this last year, she just knows what's up now, and it's apparent that I do not. Another shutdown on my end. Oh well. I hope she's gone when I wrap up my 3pm today because I don't want to summarize it for her whether it goes well or not.

And it's sad... because I keep starting these conversations thinking they will just be that, and I won't feel like crud when they conclude. [...]

Speaking of jerks, a few of her students have come by to ask about their grades from last semester. It appears a few failed, and it makes me question the pedagogy. Isn't it supposed to "catch" everyone? Those students weren't lazy, huh? Yes, they were, Josie. You just said they didn't come to class and didn't know when things were due. How does the pedagogy explain that? They feared your class and couldn't be bothered to show up and take a risk? Well, then that strategy/pedagogy doesn't work for all students.

I was thinking last night about all the pedagogies I learned of in grad school: expressivism, cognitive theory, social something... there were so many ways to approach the teaching of composition. [...]

March 22, 2019.

[...]

Meanwhile, I've been rethinking my classes AGAIN. Always evolving over here, kids. Yeah, fuck me. But it's a good kind of fucking around because I might bring back my punk theory of composition idea. Before break, I found the binder I kept ALL this punk theory research in. Yep, in 2005, I dove head-first into a *TETYC*[81] article about it all. It basically adds a DIY twist to the course – students choose projects and deadlines. It's got a little bit of feminist theory in it, too, in that students should use their true voices and say what they mean, etc. etc. In looking at the schedules I used for Spring 2006 and Fall 2006, I was extremely rigorous. Maybe more than now? But I also had a publisher's textbook, and it looks like the students read each chapter. I might have shown a punk documentary, too, and they all worked on the C2P2 (Creative Class Punk Project: a collection of poems and short pieces of writing by each member of the class). I barely recall giving the students the final days to work on this, and Camilla having an issue with these so-called workdays.

The changes I might make to the idea this time around would include giving them deadlines to choose from for each project and not just a massive list of potential deadlines (saying here are three deadlines for project 1 vs what I did before: here are 8 deadlines, pick four for your four projects). I'll keep my all-or-nothing grading, the Redos, and the Late Passes (the last two are very rooted in feminist theory, I think), and I don't plan on ditching the hybrid pieces (weekend journal entries and small projects). I just need to keep it all relatively EASY for me to keep track of. I think I can just change my folders in the Large Project Tab of our LMS[82] shells to Project 1, Project 2, etc. and then place the deadlines in those folders (Third Sunday of March, Fourth Sunday of March, etc.) and then they'll have to make sure to use those correct spots. The only project that will remain the same for everyone will be the Fake Company.

---

[81] This is in reference to a journal that two-year college English teachers subscribe to: *Teaching English in the Two-Year College*.

[82] Learning Management System. We've used Pearson and Blackboard; there is also Canvas and Google Classroom, etc.

The only other wrench in all this – if I do choose to use those punk theory ideas again – is that I'm teaching a TR 8am hybrid and a MW 11am hybrid, which means I see the TR students a few more days than the MW ones. I wish I could create one fucking schedule and call it good, but that might not work super well. I was thinking of reframing my schedule to just have weekly goals, and if we achieve them in one day, cool, but they might take two, and if I only see them once, that means things leak into the weekends.

A smaller wrench is to begin pondering how to scaffold the writing process for all of these options by using graphic organizers. Certain pieces should be due each class time for these projects, and I could create or seek out small activities that improve the piece each time.

I just worked on that punk theory stuff for too many minutes or hours or whatever. My brain hurts, but happily. I love ideas. But I have to nap now. Or at least just sit and think without a screen for a wee bit. Will take my punk binder home. Yes. Clean up the place a bit for the Sunday Funday with the nieces and nephew on Sunday. But that is it. Nothing too crazy, of course.

April 24, 2019.

[...]

So... there are ideas bumping into each other in my head. Can Open Pedagogy play nicely with my Punk Theory?

Well, let's start at the beginning, perhaps. Apparently, open pedagogy might have roots as far back as the late 60s according to Canadian Claude Paquette[83] who created "three sets of foundational values of Open Pedagogy, namely:

[83] Morgan, Tannis Dr. "Open pedagogy and a very brief history of the concept." *Exploration in the EdTech World*. 21 Dec 2016. https://homonym.ca/uncategorized/open-pedagogy-and-a-very-brief-history-of-the-concept/

autonomy and interdependence; freedom and responsibility; democracy and participation." Huh. With those values in mind, it does sound like it coincides with punk theory easily.

Should my students build their own textbook[84] or... try any of these ideas[85]:

1. *Adapt or remix current OERs.*
2. *Edit Wikipedia articles.*
3. *Facilitate student-created and student-controlled learning environments (Blackboard is a closed environment).*
4. *Encourage students to apply their expertise to serve their community.*
5. *Engage students in public chats with authors and experts... (Twitter).*
6. *Build course policies, outcomes, assignments, rubrics, and schedules of work collaboratively with students.*
7. *Let students curate course content.*

So, thinking aloud... if I am giving them a choice in project and deadline in English 110, maybe the open pedagogy part is that they have choices where they remix OER pieces or whatever. In the face-to-face English 120, I'd like to have them tweeting about something – or gathering tweets – related to a topic that turns into their research. I like the idea of them using Twitter in English 110 as well to talk to experts in their field (might work for the Interview Project) and then I'm also thinking about students curating content in English 120 for those Friday Fundays. Like, I put down a topic list, they choose the topic they want to cover and how (video, etc.) and then the Fridays are open to them.

---

[84] DeRosa, Robin. "Student-Created Open 'Textbooks' as Course Communities." *Open Pedagogy Notebook*. 18 March 2018. http://openpedagogy.org/course-level/student-created-open-textbooks-as-course-communities/

[85] DeRosa, Robin and Rajiv Jhangiani. "Open Pedagogy." *Open Pedagogy Notebook*. http://openpedagogy.org/open-pedagogy/

Lots to think on here. Holy shit. And I think I've run out of brain cells for right now. More tomorrow, I'm sure.

April 30, 2019.

I haven't kept track, but I get the feeling that I've "lost" more creative writing students since implementing the novel/novella idea. It's just a hunch. And while I only have two failing right now, it's out of ten... which was a larger number at the beginning of the semester (but under 20; did I start with 15-17?). That thought was followed by: what does it look like to put the spell of punk theory and PBL[86] and OEP[87] on a creative writing course?

If I like the idea of giving them a MASSIVE chunk of time to work on a BIG PROJECT, why not give them options for that project and then have check-in dates where they have to give us a holler as to what they are up to? Honestly, I like that they have to tackle something as substantial as a novella, but perhaps that's just one option, and there could be others like a creative shortfolio – where the requirements as them to dive into what they already created and revise (I have an instructional guide of this already) – and a combo package where they attempt YA[88] and horror and children's lit – the genres I don't cover specifically in class, but that are explained in the last chapter of the textbook. This way, I just ADD to the last unit instead of redo the whole thing. So, I rename it and then add new options. I shall put these ideas now in my Idea Booklet.

Post 1pm class, all finished meeting with them face-to-face, I wonder if I will ever have a semester where I feel like everything went well? Will I ever stop looking ahead to the next

[86] Project Based Learning or Problem Based Learning.
[87] Open-Education Pedagogy.
[88] Young Adult Literature. See *Twilight*.

semester and just enjoy wrapping up the current one? These are the things I could shame myself for, but I think they're common questions among teachers. Zooey confirmed that she too looks ahead and plans for the "next time." But, hey, we want to evolve. We're allowed to question what we're doing.

Sigh.

[...]

May 3, 2019.

So, I watched a webinar last night about this three-step process to get students talking in class. Essentially, the webinar was to promote these two brothers' (twins) course, but overall, the idea is that you start with a quote that is related to the content of the unit or lesson or whatever. Sum up the quote in your own words, then find the counterpoint of that quote. Let all that lead into the essential question. Basically, if I could find a quote that was about how writing is supposed to be hard – like bleeding on the paper, as Hemingway has said – and then realize that the opposite could be true, then let the students argue it out. The essential question is: Does writing have to be difficult? OR what is writing for you, easy or hard; when? And in what circumstances is it one or the other or both?

At some point, before or during or after the webinar, I started to think about what I wanted to do each day in class. What do I WANT to do, DAMN IT – after looking at all these pedagogies and approaches: What is my vision of the classroom? What are we doing that brings them joy? What are we doing that brings me joy? I want to write with my students, I want to read to them, I want to have discussions. I think all these things are possible, and this 3-step process might be the perfect way to jump-start certain lessons about writing, time management, revision, editing, workplace scenarios, etc. I have the artifacts in order to do all the "new" things within the punk theory idea; I know that I could implement OEP easily (asking the students to remix Wikibooks pieces, for instance), and PBL seems to be more of a culture of learning than anything, and that might take a lot of frontloading of habits at the beginning of the semester – like no more "before I let you go" but more of a "you need to complete X in groups then Y by yourself and then have a quick chat with me where you are with it all" and/or "please fill out the Exit Slip before you disperse."

[...]

June 28, 2019.

I started blogging on Blogger.com again. Yeah. I don't know if it will last, but it's a nice place to link to my/our OER shit... and why not openly chat about all this homework I've given myself?

With how messy my head has been lately with acronyms and pedagogies and webinar chatroom comments, you'd think I'd lost what my teaching style IS, but I think all of these Twitter-induced rabbit holes have only reaffirmed what I'm doing in the classroom and why.

- *Student voice and choice. Yep.*
- *Empathy built in. Yes.*
- *Creativity everywhere. Hells yeah.*
- *Real-world applications. Mm hm.*

\+

- *PBL asks students to create their own projects and create their own daily tasks.*
- *OEP asks students to write for the open movement, the creative network of the world. It demands: "Get rid of disposable assignments!"*
- *TFT*[89] *asks students to transfer what they are learning in one area to another.*
- *Punk theory says, "Give students voice and choice."*
- *OWI*[90] *is all about access and inclusivity.*

Some tweet the other day said that we should shy away from recipe assignments (14 slides, 7 sources, 4 transitions, 2

---

[89] Teaching to Transfer.

[90] Online Writing Instruction.

memes) because that's bad, and <insert their pedagogy here> says that we should give them the outcomes instead (I'm butchering the paraphrasing here). What I got out of that whole deal was this: Start assigning projects like this CC course assigns projects.

What do I mean? Well, here's a screenshot of a current project of mine (the goal is to argue whether you are a stereotype/birth order or not):

START HERE > Decide on Your Topic
Nerd, jock, first-born leader, spoiled baby of the family, bitch, gearhead, hippie,...

NEXT > Find Three Pieces of Evidence
Evidence 1: I recycle.
Evidence 2: I give money to Greenpeace.
Evidence 3: I use organic products most of the time.

*Can you identify the stereotype and argument by just reading the evidence?

LASTLY > Compose the Paper
Requirements: 1000+ words total, plus one valid source (dictionary definition, interview with friend / family member, article on birth order...).

How Will This Paper Be Assessed? Click Here.

And then here is a CC project:

Due Jul 14 by 10:59pm **Points** 10
Submitting a text entry box, a website url, or a file upload

Create a video, slide presentation, or infographic (or choose another medium) in which you describe the Creative Commons licenses as well as how and when they might be useful to your institutions' work. At a minimum, include a description of:

1. the three layers of the CC licenses,
2. the four license elements and the icons that represent them
3. the six Creative Commons licenses,
4. how the CC licenses affect exceptions and limitations to copyright, and
5. how the CC licenses affect works in the public domain.

Post your video, slide presentation, infographic, or other work online. License it with a Creative Commons license. Please also provide references and attribution, if applicable (more information on referencing and attribution can be found in the course syllabus). Then provide the link to your work. Alternately, you can upload your work.

Notice the difference? And why shouldn't I just list the minimum pieces that should pop up and let the students determine how many sources and how many words? It sounds very hippie-dippy to me, but it also sounds like less stress on my end. The products that students could create are endless.

September 4, 2019.

It's mid-week of Week 2, and I haven't assessed much. Feels weird. This new system. And the students are putting good ideas into the Backward Design[91] Activity, so I see good things ahead. Especially for the face-to-face English 120. I'm hoping to implement the design aspects we use in that class INTO the online class for spring. Spice things up.

I'm not worried about word counts as much; sure, I'm still using them in the online class for now, but I see that changing. I'm liking using the first weeks WITH the students TO PLAN. At this point, I'd have asked for Medium Project 1 already, and it would have been a mixture of good and bad writing. The Metacognition and Student Preparation Survey needs to be minimized and then analyzed – maybe by the students for bonus? I could try that perhaps? Seems a shame to use it and then not try to use parts for something.

Yeah. What else? I do feel a little isolated in my office, plus I'm removed from hearing chatter in the hallway even, and it's weird. Zooey said, though, that Walter mentioned the Haverty 210 project was okay'd, so probably by next fall, we'll all be in the same building again?

Okay, I'm going to go teach this 3pm. Godspeed to me and all that jazz.

---

[91] This is the process of starting with course outcomes and working backwards; what projects could one complete to fulfill the outcomes, etc.

Well, that went WAY better than I expected. [...] I commented that the Backward Design Activity is a way for them to give their input (just added Cards Against Humanity as a Medium Project because someone wrote that they wanted to play games but didn't think it fit the outcomes) and that if they wanted to write about hunting and fishing or horror movies for EVERY project, let's figure out a way for them to do so.

So, yeah. A good day was had by all. The end.

Oh, I should record this: someone wrote in the Metacognition (and Student Preparation) Survey that answered the "Do you have any further questions?" with:

No. You have done such a wonderful job making me feel at home in your class. I know we have only had a day at class, but first impressions mean so much! I staggered into English (after struggling through Micro and Bio) almost in tears... And I felt so loved. Thank you for being so friendly and considerate!

[...]

September 9, 2019.

Things were going so swimmingly until I saw the items I had to assess in the online class. And the face-to-face items are piling up, too, so I need to reframe assessment with my classes. I need to figure out what really needs to be gathered and assessed and all that. I need to organize activities into "effort" and "feedback needed" and all that jazz. Right now, I want to give credit for the BDA (Backward Design Activity) and Scavenger Hunt since we were working on them yet keeping track of contributions by students has been a little tedious.

I'll tweak it all. No doubt.

[...]

October 2, 2019.

I think the difference between being a hard-ass teacher and less of a hard-ass is maybe not that less students will fail my classes (one can hope), but that I can reassure myself that I placed more student choice and agency in the course. That I gave them a better shot at doing well instead of nickel and diming them[92].

[...]

August 31, 2020.

After Day 1 (August 26) this semester:

I want to like the #HyFlex design, but boy, I was more exhausted yesterday than I have ever been after a day of teaching... it feels like the content took a backseat to the tech, but maybe I will find my groove with it? Or maybe it will evolve into something better.

Sidebar: So, I was just thinking about some article that went around after almost everyone went remote: It was about how we SHOULDN'T do this too well because then admin sees that and thinks we can handle more than we can; case in point: juggling what the HyFlex model calls for - virtual & f2f at the same time. I can see how me getting "too good" at this may cause an administrator to say - "Huh, if she can teach 20 writing students in this way, let's add more students" - and that freaks me out. I might be making a mountain of a molehill, but we've struggled with keeping class enrollments manageable, ESPECIALLY writing-intensive ones. Basically, I should probably fall flat on my face with this HyFlex plan and tweak it to something MUCH more manageable for me - as long as the students don't "suffer" from the tweaks.

Side bar: New song alert – "Deep End." It's techno and very much about diving down into depression. It suits this whole year, basically. "I've been trying not to go off the deep end."

[...]

Anyhow... school feels weird. I can't see my students' facial expressions, just eyeballs so I don't know who says what, and I won't really recognize them after this semester if we ever run

[92] Bingo!

into each other post-mask times... I'm getting the hang of recording myself; I hope to build up some good recordings and explanations of shit. All the English 110 classes chose[93] the Fake Company as their #1, so we'll be creating those first.

We are urged to stay home on days we don't teach to feel safe, and we're probably getting new computer setups with the college's COVID19 money, I guess.

September 6, 2020.

[...]

Okay, beyond that, the writing samples looked good from most students. I'm asking them to fill out an anonymous check-in this week to make sure anxiety levels are low in regard to my class (even if Covid has them heightened). I'll use the responses in that poll to determine what to do in class Wednesday. I was told by two students who stayed after that my layout was confusing. I'm unsure how, but sometimes that is a cop-out for students. So, I sent out a bunch of slides Friday with an email to hopefully relieve the stress of my "Choose Your Own Adventure" class.

[...]

September 13, 2020.

[...]

As for classes, I'll prep the students for peer review Wednesday (all f2f classes) as well as writing conferences (conducted by video, phone, or text) next week. I won't be in the same room as them for a while, but that's okay. They'll hopefully use that time to seek me out, and it will give me time to give them individual attention. I normally would feel like I was slacking off in having this sort of lineup, but the pandemic has enlightened many of us to what truly matters: choice for

---

[93] This was the semester I implemented a "Choose Your Own Adventure" type path for students. As a class, they chose the topics of their large projects. As individuals, they chose the smaller projects they'd work on.

students, individual attention, flexibility, feedback feedback feedback, and the idea that just because I'm not IN the classroom doesn't mean I'm NOT teaching. Yeah. At the end of next week, Large Project 1 is due in all classes; in English 110, we'll use a March Madness chart to assess those projects so that makes it "fun" and takes pressure off of me.

September 29, 2020.

[...] I can't get in their heads all the time, but I'm pretty sure I appreciated a student's annoyance because it was a nice distraction from Uncle John's passing and covid and the world.

Yep, I'm now gladly taking annoying student problems because I want distractions. WOW.

In deeper school news, I've been feeling like this new-ish plan in English 110 (the Choose Your Own Adventure) hasn't been as awesome as I wanted, but I have to give myself some goddamn grace. It's been difficult to teach with students in masks, with students gone, and with students who have their own anxieties. Plus, add in Black Lives Matter and the fucking politics of the universe, and it's all insane. Are they able to learn ANYTHING? I definitely think I need to tweak how I explain it all. I think I need a better flow to it all – a better step-by-step process. They need to play with Blackboard earlier, I need a syllabus quiz maybe, and even though I know they are all overwhelmed by their ability to choose so much, I want to add in more choice with the Large Projects. These are things I could do come spring.

November 3, 2020.

[...]

Okay, on Friday, our county bumped up a level to orange for covid, and that meant my classroom capacity fell to 25%. I emailed students that we'd tweak the hyflex model to include just the virtual/recorded pieces. A student emails me that they learn best face-to-face. I reminded the student before logging off email for the weekend (started using the out-of-office automatic replies again) that I had stated in the email that I would be up for tiny f2f chats. I don't think they really READ email. Hell, I don't think anyone READS email like I do. My comprehension level is fucking ridiculous based on the amount of skimming I do; anyhow… I thought about it over the weekend, and I created a weird new hyflex model: 20/20. The first twenty minutes, I would be in my office virtually meeting with students. Then I would allow the last twenty minutes for drop-in students; I even created an editable Google Doc for this. Thus far, no one has signed up. We have workdays for projects, so in an alternate universe, they would be ditching class anyhow to work on the thing elsewhere. I get it.

At first, I thought this concerned student was in my English 110. If it was that student, I thought, they never came to class… so, um, why the concern? I told Walter as much yesterday. Then, as I was assessing this morning, I see that another student with the same first name is in English 120. He's the one who needs f2f, yet if I recall class times he came, he was on his phone while the talkative Caleb asked me questions. Was he learning from our interaction? He wasn't completing the online discussions IN CLASS from what I could see, and yet he is completing them in general, so where's the disconnect?

I read somewhere that students come to us from rigid high school schedules, and then when we give them anywhere from a little flexibility to a LOT of flexibility, things fall apart? I loved college because of that, but I could pace myself. I was also smart enough to guess well enough on tests I hadn't prepped for. And I loved writing, yet I did write a few papers at 4am in the IACC[94], so there's that. Yeah.

Maybe they think that by osmosis, if they are in class next to me and classmates, they'll remember shit? I don't know.

Yeah.

[…]

---

[94] NDSU's computer center. I think it has a new name now.

November 30, 2020.

I've got the holiday tunes cranked, and I've officially chatted with two virtual students this morning in one class (9am) and no one popped into the 11am. So, it is what it is, you know. I think 1pm will be quiet, too, [...]

Since I'm "saving" assessment (of LP4 in English 120, among other things) for tomorrow – which is my typical routine – I jumped into some prep for spring this morning. I think the inching towards a completely OER/Ungrading semester (Fall 2021) will work out okay. And I should gather some interesting data from it all, too. I have an exit ticket for that.

Yeah. I also have to rethink Creative Writing a wee bit yet, and luckily, I think I'll keep English 120 as is... except for the layout? Or maybe I should hold off on that until Summer? I want to reduce the clicking in that course layout by A LOT. Too much clicking, man. And eventually, I would like to give students more choice by using those Google Docs I started a few semesters back – did I call that a scavenger hunt[95]?

[...]

January 14, 2021.

My two f2f classes went alright yesterday. I find myself getting winded because I am fat, or I talk too fast, or the masks cause the first two to be compounded... either way, it's annoying. The new office computer set-up is annoying, too; we have docking stations, so the monitor is just a reflection of the MacBook Pro screen – no dimming, no speakers, and no webcam. I also learned I can't go from sitting at the big table in Haverty 205 (using wifi to beam virtual students to my laptop) to plugging into the system at the teacher station. It's one or

---

[95] I created editable Google Docs on a variety of topics and then students added videos, podcasts, articles (etc.) on the topic. They found very interesting things! I still use the TED Talk on Addiction that some student discovered.

the other. Annoying. In Haverty 204, we're packed in there (21 students signed up; at 50% capacity, we can have 18 humans in there, including me), and I can't sit at the big table, so that's fine, but it feels packed. And germy. I weirdly hope students skip to keep us somewhat safe for every 30-40 minute class session.

The "early bird" online students jumped to it earlier this week, and now yesterday and today have been quiet in the discussion boards. They all seem concerned about the virtual sessions, and yet I have this feeling that the two I conduct today (noon and 7pm) for the English 120 crowd will barely be attended. Maybe I'm wrong. I feel similarly about tomorrow's 2pm session for the creative writers. They want them available, they want me to know they can't make them, and then they want them recorded... so they want me to pop into a screen by myself and record it, I guess? I don't know. I think the "Get Stuff Done" Session idea I got from Twitter could be fun, but the majority of students wanted me to "lecture." They are a tough bunch of humans to understand, sometimes, let me tell you.

[...]

Once in my office, and full of pizza, I was fatigued. I needed to rest. I wanted to take off my bra. So, since I didn't teach until 3pm, I went home for an hour and completely undressed into cozy shit... I don't think I actually napped, but it was nice to rest. I think I need more rest. I need more water. I need more magnesium. I need to go for walks perhaps, and I need to get on my bikes more. I think I need to be gentle about all this shit since the world is going down the gutter, but why not just focus on my system? A happy & well-rested me can do more "good trouble" than a tired me.

Also, I bought a large coffee this morning. I had like 5 sips. Jeezus. I haven't had liquor in at least a week. You'd think those two things alone would make my system fairly happy.

[...]

March 14, 2021.

[...] At some point, I called Maggie to bounce ideas off of her that had come to me during a Twitter Chat. There are quite a few activities or things I think most teachers do because we've always done then, but they aren't necessarily conducive to LEARNING or to prepping them for the WORKPLACE. For instance, I have questioned group work for years (because in my workplace, I am still doing almost ALL the work anyhow – what does that teach anyone?). I have now questioned discussion boards, too, insofar as why we ask students to respond to a classmate. I am now wondering about peer-to-peer feedback.

How does working with a group improve MY learning of something? I might just learn that they are lazy and will abuse my productivity. Whoopie. What does me responding to a classmate do for learning? It just forces me to do something for the points or whatever because unless the classmate has brought up something interesting and I WANT to respond, I'm just going through the motions. I need to utilize how the Creative Commons course was set up in that fashion because it was "start a new thread of thoughts OR contribute to your classmate's thread" not both. Yeah. And I liked that. I still read what they posted in case I wanted to contribute, and sometimes I learned and sometimes I didn't (from them).

As for this peer-to-peer feedback, I do think using it 1-3 times in a semester is fine. I say 1-3 because I have three large projects now in English 110, and one of our course outcomes IS peer evaluation participation. The discussion board thing and the group work thing are in NONE of the course outcomes! NOT that I adore those course outcomes, but hey, if they are going to be in my goddamn syllabus, I might as well refer to them for backwards design.

I wonder if ANY of these pieces could be or SHOULD be implemented immediately? Especially the discussion board/classmate response. I could work backward from the end of the semester in English 120 and revise; this would give me less to revise for the summer shell?

I'll think on it.

[...]

Tweets:

"What is academic life worth when you have no time to read or think?" #sacredspace #4c17
10:09 PM · Mar 16, 2017

+

summers with a saint
outside we ain't
instead, I'm writing a grant
so, no, this isn't a rant
#NEH #PoemToWelcomeSummer
8:27 AM · May 29, 2018

+

"...I have learned that anyone promising answers to #teaching is almost surely full of shit." & "I hereby suggest that all strategies are either equally bullshit or equally valuable."
I'm totally digging this book already. #ItWontBeEasy
@MrTomRad
8:58 PM · Jan 27, 2020

+

I know it's not a perfect teaching model, but if you embrace the #hyflex idea, then you can ethically "kick Ss out of class" who don't want to wear masks & it's not like they are sentenced to "fail" just bc of their "mask idiocracy." #justsayin #teachinginapandemic
2:09 PM · Jan 27, 2021

+

AMEN! I was thinking the other day how I did so horribly on that teacher certification test I had to take after student-teaching. It cost me $400, told me I wasn't bright, and now out of all of the soon-to-be Ts I took classes next to, I'm the last one standing. Happily.
10:16 AM · Feb 3, 2021

+

“Empowering the Community College First-Year Composition Teacher” #TYCA21 Our job is the most intimate on campus. Teaching writing is intimate.
12:36 PM · Apr 7, 2021

+

Or maybe I should embrace my love for Google & use Docs like many of you do for collaborative annotation or they could edit a Doc with their thoughts. That might be easier on me & Ss. More accessible for both parties. This part of teaching shouldn't be so frustrating.
8:29 AM · Apr 15, 2021

+

All this leads me to this question or pondering: What else is “teaching folklore” that I’ve/we’ve believed... or currently believe? Ex: A former officemate once told me she HAD to teach them Author X bc they’d never read him otherwise. Me: So what? #TeachingFolklore
5:23 AM · Apr 17, 2021

Facebook Posts:

March 21, 2011.
is officially tenured & has been bumped up to "Associate Professor" status. She knows that tenure doesn't mean a lot to many people, but this feels pretty cool for her especially after being "let go" from her first teaching job. Validation, kids.

+

December 7, 2012.
I just had a student make sure to tell me, face-to-face, how much she liked my class. It means so much more when it's unsolicited; I'm going to miss the crazy crews I've had in each class this fall. They kept me sane when things outside the classroom were going haywire.

+

March 5, 2012.
I want to remember this: A student said aloud in class today, "Well, if they can't remember that, then it's their problem, not yours." I thanked him for saying that on a Monday. No, he wasn't an older-than-average student.

+

November 19, 2012.
I'm very contradictory; I give to charities like it's my job - like I'm on a freakin' mission ... but the minute a student gives me some sob story, the bitch switch is ON.
So, I'm the nicest mean person I know?

+

February 13, 2013.
The mentally exhausted teacher, who had just assessed way too many papers in one day, went to her 3pm class. They are a fun bunch of misfits, she thought - a combination of transfer &

technical students. And, oddly, they gave her a small bolt of energy. This is why she is where she is & does what she does.

+

June 1, 2013.
I might have to rethink how I'm doing this teaching thing, huh?
"To be willing to give up some control is to avoid getting too invested in the amazing course you designed. Strive to take pleasure and pride from how you help students to learn and become excited about learning, not just from the curriculum itself. Even the most thoughtful lesson, the cleverest assignment, the richest reading list is much less likely to goose students and engage them and help them to think more subtly, if you came up with it on your own and imposed it ON them. What matters is not what we teach; it's what they learn, and the probability of real learning is far higher when the students have a lot to say about both the content and the process."
---Alfie Kohn, "How to Create Nonreaders"

+

April 3, 2014.
"If all of them love you, you aren't challenging them; if all if them hate you, you're doing something wrong. There needs to be a balance." – Walter said this about my student evals many years ago & it works for other people in my life, too. Thanks, Dude.

+

November 12, 2014
For the first time ever, as a teacher, I said the following sentences aloud in class: "What the hell is this?" & "This is pathetic."
The student laughed through both comments, by the way. His response was, "Hey, now, that resume was good enough for _____ class." I said, "Um, just to clarify, but THIS project, THIS resume, is for MY class. NOT theirs."
Why do they try to mess with me?

+

January 21, 2015.
"So, I haven't figured out what makes one food good for you and another food bad. Like, when did food become morally good or bad? Does the good food go to church? And the bad food sleeps around?"
Only a few students laughed, but it was one of my best little commentaries to date. By the time I retire, I hope to make a student pee his/her pants.

+

September 15, 2015.
What if... Everything you've been told about teaching and learning and how education was "supposed" to look was A LIE? What could education look like if you started from scratch? What would be the "perfect" classroom or experience for both teachers & students?

+

April 20, 2017.
I remember when I first learned of this day's meaning. While teaching high school in MN, my publication students wanted to put a funny ad for "Free Visine" in our student newspaper. They giggled, I shrugged, and later I got called into the principal's office. It's kind of funny that the 60+ year old principal had to clue in his youngest teacher about this "marijuana holiday." I was completely clueless.
[Oddly enough, too, I was called into the principal's office more as a teacher than I ever was as a student. Huh.]
#IVoteForVodka

+

September 7, 2017.
Okay, so my college students are going to start a multi-genre research paper next week, and I'm creating a sample for them to look at. The research revolves around the media (I'm showing the _Miss Representation_ documentary as well as its male counterpart _The Mask You Live In_ before they dive into

research). Anyhow, the sample I'm creating is all about diets, of course. Please help me fill out a particular category in my research by answering: What are the lies that the media tells us about diets? Thanks in advance.

+

June 8, 2018.
I'm guilty of having judged students, and not been curious instead...
//And that's why I'm writing this piece. I'm hoping to awaken my fellow educators — of all levels — to the fact that if a student is struggling, they probably aren't choosing to. They probably want to do well. They probably are trying. More broadly, I want all people to take a curious and empathic approach to individuals whom they initially want to judge as "lazy" or irresponsible.// Quote[96].

+

April 18, 2019.
It's a damn good feeling when you see/read student projects that are so well-done. A few students obviously chose research questions they were passionate about, and it made for some awesome end products. (Faith in humanity restored.)

+

October 30, 2019.
I wasn't sure how good of an idea it was that Sadie was accidentally in many of my teaching videos, but today - a year after we said goodbye to her - I am grateful to be updating my Creative Writing course and seeing her face.

+

November 1, 2019.
If academic blasphemy is a pool, I often try to just dip my toe in.

---

[96] Price, Devin. "Laziness Does Not Exist." *Medium*. https://humanparts.medium.com/laziness-does-not-exist-3af27e312d01 23 Mar 18.

But then I lose my fucking balance and fall in head first. Now, I'm treading in the deep end, gleefully af. #FWordFriday

+

December 16, 2019.
I will not complain about my students.
I will not complain about my students.
I will not complain about my students.
AAAAGGGGGUUUUUHHHHHHHH.

+

March 22, 2020.
I'm going to try to type this without crying, but I just sent an email to all of my students. I asked how they were, what academic worries they have, how much should I email them, etc. as we move to distant learning for the rest of the semester... and many of them responded that they were okay and asked HOW WAS I DOING? This is the first semester in a long time that I don't have one jerk in class, and... I won't get to see them.

+

March 28, 2020.
{Preface: I know there are "pandemic pedagogy" groups on the Facepage, and I belong to a few, but I want to ask this of MY teacher friends since they know I was a "harsh points monkey" at one point, and recently I've been moving towards a more compassionate #Ungrading process...}

Okay, so this is probably "too academic" for a Saturday, but I've been following lots of educators on the Twitter who don't think Ds and Fs should be "given out" this semester. I'm torn... I had a few students with very low %s before we went remote... should they "earn" Cs when I haven't received much of anything from them? (I had urged those before Spring Break to drop with a W.) How are all of you approaching grading/assessment in the middle of a pandemic? And if you want to DM me for a more private convo, I completely understand.

*Student perspectives are appreciated, too!

+

March 31, 2020.
This pandemic is scary and overwhelming; however, at the end of it all, I hope it shakes us up in a good way. I hope we realize what's important. I hope we realize what education needs to be for our students. I hope we realize that certain jobs should be paid livable wages. I hope we realize what is wrong and what is right and shove everything into the latter.

+

May 3, 2020.
Eons ago, I started saying "people are stupid" as an explanation for everything. It still works. What's unfortunate is that some stupid people are making decisions that will get my family, friends, and students sick, so now - more than ever - I wish people were educated and compassionate.

+

December 2, 2020.
I'm going to go out on a limb here and state that I probably shouldn't feel pressured (internally or externally) to meet with students face-to-face when North Dakota just reached a horrific covid milestone: 1 out of every 800 dead.

+

March 8, 2021.
I don't know about the rest of you, but this time last year will be the week it all went screwy for me. On the Monday before Spring Break, we said goodbye to a beloved colleague. I believe on that same day, I had a chat with a certain chemistry teacher about this "coronavirus," and we decided it was being "blown out of proportion." Yeah.

At various times that Tuesday or Wednesday, students said: "Priebe, we aren't coming back after break," and I attempted to calm them down. But of course, it hit me Wednesday evening when the NBA canceled March Madness. "WTH? OMG. This is real." My mind changed instantly. Then we got an email Thursday from campus stating we wouldn't return until April 6 - my second 8-weeks students had only been "in class" with me 3x.

It was the longest week. It was the most surreal. It was sad and weird, and it ended on Friday the 13th with the last party I've attended since...

+

May 12, 2021.
"Many of us may agree with what a friend said to me recently: 'this is the worst teaching I have ever done, even though I've never worked so hard at it.'"[97]

[97] Holdren, Nate. "Faculty Moral Distress about Pandemic Teaching." *AcademeBlog.org*. https://academeblog.org/2021/05/11/faculty-moral-distress-about-pandemic-teaching/ 11 May 21.

Battle Lake Journals #5.

09.01.1999

The first day was not so bad at all. My expectations were not on; these students are well-behaved compared to the West Fargo ones which is a nice change of pace.

[...]

I wonder where I will go in this life. Maybe I'll move out to Duluth or Portland. I love Battle Lake so dearly right now that I can't imagine moving away for at least five years (until I pay off my loans at least).

09.02.1999

Another good day! I must be jinxed or something. I found out that one of the girls I would deem the most beautiful and kind is very depressed. I want to reach out to her in some way, shape, or form.

Battle Lake Journals #6.

09.09.1999

More and more, I have come to realize that maybe I won't marry. It is such a commitment; I have so much I want to accomplish yet. After a couple, five, years here in Battle; I may take off a year to get my Master's at Duluth or maybe I could do that during the summers out there. I could drive my bug out to my Superior lake cabin and live and breathe Duluth air for a few months and study. It sounds great now. Plus, I want to travel to Europe. There is this brochure I received in the mail today; it had free trips for teachers that take six students with them. There was one for all around Europe for around $2000. There was also one to China, one to Australia, too.

That would be so fun. Too bad I'd have to take students ☺. What else – oh – I'd like to be published whether everyone reads it or only a few; whether it is poems and short stories or a whole novel on teaching fails; I want to get my voice "out there."

04.22.2000

M&Ms for dinner again. I spent more than I am worth shopping this weekend and just got done washing my baby. No, not a human – my car. Hopefully, I won't flip it like I did the Bronco. But that seems ages ago when I used to dine on Twix bars and scream to Mariah Carey hits. Which brings us back to chocolate. If only the kids knew.

I've been teaching now for... um... well, not long enough to complain. I used to play house and school all the time with my siblings. First-borns are designated the "teacher" or "mom" in these situations. The rest fight for the lesser roles. At the time, I liked the control, the power. Hell, I was always president of our silly clubs. As I teach now, though, it is more about relating and inspiring them. Maybe I am secretly a psychologist and am plotting to figure out myself through them. Or, and this is my favorite of the two, I know that while on my journey, my path, I need to be beside those who also need someone to question... and question with.

Already, at the young age of 23, I have been tossed into paths that have thrown me for a loop – screwed me up a bit. Take for instance the scary fact that every four years now (since becoming an adolescent and therefore questioning life to its core) I have gone through hell basically. Either my more personal mental one, or one imposed upon me by someone else. My freshman year of high school, I suffered through some major self-esteem issues, wanted to commit suicide, couldn't figure out "me," and how/where I fit in, if I did at all. I think I was angry. Angry at my geeky social status, angry that my mom gave me her body images issues, angry for living in my head and thinking faster and deeper than I could write. I turned to reading and writing poetry. At first, for therapeutic reasons, slowly for my own personal expression. My next dip occurred beautifully after my "peak" of high school. My senior year was fabulous! Tennis season – went to State and beat a school record; Friends – many of them, and I graduated. I got away from people who were inadvertently crushing my creative spirit. But my freshman year of college tested me once again. I loved the freedom but had to get over my "first love" and once again couldn't decide who I was. So, I drank, starved myself, and cried. I took Vivarin one night (the birthday of my next boyfriend, actually) and drank along with that crap still in my stomach. Once back in the dorms, I shook the whole night from the combo. I cried for the two days following and did not want to be on earth anymore. Thankfully, I got lots of support from friends and stumbled through all that.

Like in high school, I was probably angry again. For having a tough time with my classes, for a high school boyfriend leaving, for suddenly being the girl whose future was again uncertain.

By the end of that school year, however, I was dating a new person, and all went pretty smoothly. I was writing about love, had found a path marked for me (English Education), and began to grow into my spirit, my body, and my mind.

With every peak, there is a valley. Another one happened in Dent, MN last summer when my college boyfriend decided to break up with me for another woman. And, after all the dumping that he had jolted on me before, you'd THINK I could have done well with this one. Maybe it's the hardest times that really, truly test who you are. Every time now, they (the valleys) have gotten tougher, I have gotten tougher.

Unlike men, women always seem to flourish after a relationship drowns. I have probably needed to exit from my past ones because of the changes that need to take place within me. I used to think that I had lost something when I would fail, get broken up with, but in all actuality, I am gaining so much! Past friends and boyfriends see me now and are amazed – want me back in their lives. I am proud of myself for that, but I don't return to them. I don't want to walk backward. I must continue forward toward my destination of simply being in the process of life, not looking for any end product to satisfy me. When I am pondering and questioning and thinking and reading, I am the happiest. I don't want all the answers to come to me. I know they won't at 23 anyway. That is perhaps the "meaning of life," that life's meaning changes. Every minute of every day. There is no specific meaning.

Epiphany (noun)[98]

- an appearance or manifestation especially of a divine being
- a usually sudden manifestation or perception of the essential nature or meaning of something
- an intuitive grasp of reality through something (such as an event) usually simple and striking
- an illuminating discovery, realization, or disclosure
- a revealing scene or moment

[98] "Epiphany." Definition. *Merriam Webster*. https://www.merriam-webster.com/dictionary/epiphany

{This page intentionally left blank.}

#Ungrading.

Once upon a time[99], I was a teacher who had a zillion policies. I was harsh with my students; I demanded a lot from them. I had extremely strict deadlines, and I didn't allow redos. I'm unsure where this approach came from, but I assume it was ingrained in me while I was learning about education and through student-teaching. That's my guess. I wasn't subjected to any sort of approach that was somewhat compassionate until grad school.

So, in the spring of 2019, I hadn't heard if I was admitted to the doctorate program at my alma mater. I took it upon myself to shrug off the inevitable denial and jump into whatever interests "floated my boat." Which happened to be OER (Open Educational Resources). This led to taking the Creative Commons Certification course last summer, as well as a free Wikiversity course on OEP (Open Educational Pedagogy/Practices).

Well, in that time span, it was all over my Twitter timeline. #NOGRADES! The hashtags #ungrading and #gradeless were in my face, taunting me. I had this constant conversation with myself: *These people are crazy; we need to grade students.*

I asked students about it this fall, and since they were as uneducated as I was on the topic as I was, their responses weren't helpful. I hemmed and hawed about it in my own melon, eventually, yes, dipping my toes into the blasphemous waters.

My previous knowledge of the topic of assessment is pretty typical. As I was learning how to become a secondary English teacher way back when, we learned about lesson planning and using rubrics. I'm unsure if we really truly dove into assessment. We might've talked about what an "A" paper

---

[99] This summary/reflection was written during the fall of 2019.

looked like, but we never really questioned the current system of POINTS and LETTER GRADES.

And this is a wee bit weird to me now because in the past (after I went to NCTE a few years ago), I found out that Peter Elbow was one of the humans behind CONTRACT GRADING. I hadn't really heard of that term until then - years into teaching! Isn't that odd? And we weren't required to take an assessment course in grad school either when I was earning my Master's. So, when it comes to previous research and knowledge, I guess I can say that it's sketchy at best. I don't know why I was taught what I was taught. Why is our educational system built around POINTS?

+

Here are my final thoughts about much of this: Even if students are trying to do the bare minimum or cheat or plagiarize or whatever - because, sure, there will always be a small percentage of those humans around - I would much rather approach my classroom with kindness and compassion and creativity and humor because it's good for MY mental health. Yes, ungrading is supposed to take the stress off of students, but what I selfishly love about the idea is that MY mental health is improving. It comes down to that **win-win** attitude that some famous guy once wrote about (Stephen Covey?).

Mic drop. Boom.

+

Wednesday August 16, 2006

I came across something yesterday in another free book... it was a conversation between teachers and the leader of the discussion about a student's paper. It was organized,

but boring (from what I gathered - they didn't show the student's paper), and the one teacher then decided that because it was boring, it wasn't organized. But it was just boring. And the leader tried to get across that that's not the same thing. I found that intriguing because I have probably been guilty of doing that - giving a student less credit for a paper because I found it boring. What's boring to me, may not be boring to them, and beyond that, whether I find it interesting or not is not the goal of writing a paper for any class. What matters is that they are writing, organizing their thoughts, and revising their writing to make it better.
[...]
Posted 8/16/2006 at 10:6 AM

Wednesday October 11, 2006

I am exhausted. Who knew that giving out grades could cause me to stress out?
Posted 10/11/2006 at 4:41 PM

Tuesday October 17, 2006

I just commented on X's site about being more lenient this year. Picking and choosing my battles. Making students laugh or feel silly about not handing in something rather then feeding them the rath of hell with my voice.
I don't think, then, that I have become a pushover or "easy," but rather, my reaction to it all is more: "Well, you have to suffer the consequences, but I am not going to freak out about it because life is too short to care." I have noticed that since going to The Great Teacher conference, I am more accepting that, yes, students are going to forget stuff and I may have to repeat myself. And I am accepting my shortcomings like having to talk louder with some classes who don't like to quiet down right away. And if they want to IM in class, oh well. If they miss something, I

just won't repeat it. Or maybe they can do it all because they have grown up able to do so. Multi-taskers.
Some things are just not worth the worry.
Posted 10/17/2006 at 2:21 PM

Monday October 30, 2006

Someday, I'd like to create a top ten list of things said by students that irritate me the most. Today it was: "When are you going to have those papers graded?" Ugh. They just handed in the papers a week ago. I think I have graded like 30 or 40 of them... so that leaves around 60 to go. I am no robot and I do have a life. Somewhat. Eeek.
And then when they say: "Well, my ____ is/are a teacher and she/he is always grading." That's nice. How much do they really get done? I mean, I am not going to grade for 3 hours every night. Sorry. That was what I did at the high school level, and I burnt out quick, fast, and in hurry.
I take my job seriously, but there are other ways to "grade" or assess if a student is learning. And I don't believe marking up an entire paper works for either side = the teacher takes up valuable time & then the student doesn't even look at it... or if they do, they just see the correct answers and don't learn why or how they wrote incorrectly in the first place.
Posted 10/30/2006 at 4:59 PM

Thursday April 5, 2007

From *Strategies for Teaching First-Year Composition*: "And teachers can change the way they think only by changing what they believe about what they know and how they know it" (35). I have to remind myself that while I do love writing, students usually do not. And that what worked for me (as far as learning to write), may not work for them.

[...]
Posted 4/5/2007 at 9:38 PM

Saturday October 20, 2007

What if...
... Students graded their own papers? [There'd be a rubric that they'd have to fill out & the instructor, obviously, could disagree.]
... I had a complete paperless classroom? [No more running to the Copy Center?]
... I took assignments from other classes (World Lit & Creative Writing) & used them in basic Composition classes? [Expose them to ALL that various writing/literature classes have to offer.]
[...]
Posted 10/20/2007 at 10:33 PM

Thursday January 31, 2008

Lately, I've been REALLY REALLY REALLY trying to focus on those students who "get it" and "show up" and listen and all that basic stuff (I mean, I had lunch with Richard yesterday; he's one of those students who has to have a 115% or he's in my office all flustered). But once in awhile, I have to *rant. Vent. Get it out*. This morning happens to be one of those moments:
After I assess/grade the online sections, I've always gotten students' emails asking why they got a certain grade, etc. Now, typically, I leave a comment in the Gradebook (which shows up in blue to them) that explains it (This was late, etc.), but sometimes I forget or *assume*. Yea, that last one is a bugger. I assume they've read the rubric or the syllabus or the directions. My Class Blog grading is rather simple: make sure you have the posts you should (is it three this week or two, which is explained), make sure to

comment/respond on what you are supposed to respond too (this article, not that one, etc.), and make sure to at least have 10+ sentences of quality thought in the response. Oh, and they can't be late (Saturday at midnight is the deadline, except for Finals Week). I understand why more of them have questions when it comes to the papers & their grading system because my rubric (yes, I even give them the rubric I'm going to use - How many of my teachers did that? *Um, none.*) is complex. But it's all there. Chopped up into a table. Yet, some students don't print it off when it's on the "stuff to print off this week" part of our semester's chart.

I really don't think I have a lot of mystery to my assessment.

Heck, I had teachers who never handed back ANYTHING. {I wonder if Steve Ward still has my World Literature papers shoved in some folder; I adored his classes, so it's even tough to critique that aspect of his grading system.}

--- End rant. ---

And... while talking to Richard yesterday, I realized that the fact that I am a wee bit different sometimes doesn't help me or my students. I like to think it does, but when they've had teachers who were mysterious about their grading or about what they wanted from students, students start to not only think English classes "suck," but they start to think that writing is a mystery. A mystery they'll never solve. Then, they take my class. I throw all sorts of possibility at them, and they probably think, *"No way. She wants what every other teacher has wanted. She truly does not want me to write what I want to write. She's full of it."* But I am not. Not when it comes to student writing. I KNOW they have something to say, but they are the ones who have to figure out how to say it. How to write it so it works for them. Sure, I want the darn thing to be

organized, but I want it to be interesting to THEM and to the reader(s).
I feel like I am constantly trying to tear down the statue that states, "Writing is punishment." It's a statue that's been built up by students ever since they got a red-inked essay back or got Fs in spelling or didn't know what a comma was even after weeks of grammar practice worksheets.
Posted 1/31/2008 at 10:50 AM

Thursday February 7, 2008
What the worst day in a college teacher's semester?
The day he/she hands back the first paper (or test).
Suddenly, students think he/she is out to get *them*.
When, all along, they were shown the rubric. Shown examples.
They were told what was expected, too. Repeatedly.
It's not *fun* for us. To hand back a paper with a not-so-great-grade on it.
To see those sad eyes.
So disappointed in themselves or me or the class or the smashing their grade just got.
Yet, to put it in perspective, it's 50 or 100 points out of 1000.
And... there have to be cut-off points:
Not every paper will receive an A whether it comes in on time or not,
an "A" doesn't go to those papers that aren't the required length, and
someone who cites his/herself has a better paper
than someone who's "forgotten" to put in-text citations.
Students look at these items and think they are petty.
But, are they? They aren't secrets; they're in the rubric.
p.s. Did anyone see US on T.V. last night? NDSCS = Highest spring enrollment in 5 years!

Posted 2/7/2008 at 12:32 PM

Tuesday March 2, 2010

[...]

The writing of most of MY incoming students is NOT appalling.

They produce quality, and it's not like I'm an idiot and can't tell good writing from bad.

Their vocabulary is not limited; it's just different.

Their paragraphs and papers and essays simply try to do too much; I see paragraphs covering more than one topic and sentences so long that I have to inhale deeply more than once to get through them - those are not hard things to point out and revise. Jeeez.

The reading issue I understand, but they don't read for various reasons... and they read differently than 'we' do. They're reading millions of webpages and texts a month, deciphering them and analyzing them. That's not reading? No, I guess it isn't in the traditional sense... but still. It IS reading. Ugh.

"The object is to engage students and to introduce them to the skill, and pleasure, of thoughtful reading." I do agree with her here... yet.

[...]

Posted 3/2/2010 at 3:27 PM

Monday November 1, 2010

Okay, so as it turns out, I'm not all about torturing my students. I kind of knew that, but then it became true when the assignment fairy sprinkled me with fairy dust this morning when I thought, "Yeah, I don't want to create a quiz." Instead, the assignment fairy's (man, I have to find

a Flickr image for him/her, don't I?) powder - not to be confused with the powder Dave Chappelle jokes about, mind you - magically revised that thought into, "You know, I won't quiz them; I'll give them some way to show their genius. They all read what I asked them to *cough cough cough* so this will allow for their creativity and knowledge to shine." A quiz would almost be too easy for them and for me. I mean, sure, I could "allow" them to fail and "allow" me to pass of the quizzes to my work study to assess. This way, they have to re-read the material *cough cough cough* and learn something. Quizzes don't always cause learning; I think that option has a 15% rating of knowledge-induced activity. Anyhow, if you weren't in class, you missed the lil' half page sheet detailing what to do with P4 Doc Sharing readings for Wednesday. Too bad, Chad. If you're nice, I may give you one pre-Wednesday classes. Stop by my office or just ask a classmate what the options were.
Posted 11/1/2010 at 2:23 PM

Wednesday May 4, 2011

I wrote recently, in an email to a friend, that I couldn't wait to be done grading after next week. Because then, like, I'll have 2-3 weeks of non-grading bliss before... yeah... before summer school. But I cherish those weeks of non-grading-ness. I'll have to pack and run instead, but still. A brain break, people. A break for the brain - no evaluations, no charts, no points to add up or delete. And, yes, once again, I think I'll revise my grading strategies with some assignments (if not all) so that it's a win-win situation. Easy for students to understand, easy for me to complete. Yay.

I'm always super hopeful pre-summer time. I'm going to do

this and this and this and this. Ah, I'm such an optimist.
[...]
Posted 5/4/2011 at 1:39 PM

Monday August 1, 2011

Grade, grade, grade, and then grade some more. Until my head falls off my neck. Yep.
[...]
Posted 8/1/2011 at 1:59 PM

Wednesday September 14, 2011

[...]
One annoyance: I have found that even thought I gave my students "Penguin Freebie Homework Pass," they don't want to use them up too quickly. Yeah.
"Well, the homework is late, but you could use your Penguin."
"I don't want to use it already." Um...? Then don't, man. I didn't skip class, so don't put the guilt trip on me.
Posted 9/14/2011 at 12:21 PM

Monday October 10, 2011

Sometime in the future, I should just NOT assess things as quickly as I do. To see how students handle it.
Because I just got asked when the P2 Presentations would be graded... and we JUST FINISHED THEM IN CLASS. Sheesh almighty.

Or I could just tell them they'll be assessed next year. Yeah. Humor/sarcasm...?
Posted 10/10/2011 at 2:58 PM

Friday November 4, 2011

Other Recent Thoughts On Life and Learning:

1.When students take our courses, we assess them. Now, are we really TECHNICALLY assessing what they've learned in our classes? Not really... I mean, if they knew how to write before they took my English 110, and they score well, then DUH, it wasn't really me. However, if they can't write, and they take my English 110 and are assessed (and "can't write"), then who is really to blame? My semester-long class or the 12 years of schooling they had before me? I'm just saying... and what bugs me the most is that many people on campus will say, "Our students can't write." Sure, some of them can't. But it's not like I can turn them around in 16 weeks ESPECIALLY if they skip class.

2.I'd like good sample papers from other teachers who don't teach English.
3.I'd like the writing instructions they use, too. How are they assigning the paper? What are the guidelines?

[...]
14."Just because you don't have a plan, doesn't mean you don't have a plan."

"You have to evolve no matter what you teach."
Posted 11/4/2011 at 10:44 AM

Tuesday September 4, 2012

What if everything in my classes, all the assignments that is, was worth 10 points?
Why would I do that? Because students seem less worried about something worth that much.
How could it work? The papers and projects would be graded as normal, but it would be tougher to get 10 full

points out of the deal. So, those daily assignments would REALLY be helpful & uber necessary to pass... Huh.
Posted 9/4/2012 at 9:55 AM

Wednesday January 30, 2013

I like to play the "What If" Game a lot... in a positive way, that is, in regards to my classes.
This week, I'm thinking:
---What if I didn't assign & grade these small assignments so much & we focused just on bigger projects (kind of like how some classes only focus on tests?)? It would be less maintenance on my part, less paper work, perhaps. I think I'd keep my daily prompts, in this hypothetical, and we'd build off of them or something. Or maybe I shouldn't feel the pressure to grade EVERYTHING and just give effort points more often, especially on 10 point things. I really like focusing in on their prompts; I kind of like going through them to circle errors & see what they generally wrote about the prompt that day. Since it's fun for me, I should keep that around, right? Right.
[...]
---What if...
Posted 1/30/2013 at 12:52 PM

Friday February 1, 2013

What if I didn't use word counts? Would the papers be better, the same, or worse from students?
Huh. I have no idea, but I would guess I'd get a lot of questions similar to, "Is this enough?" Ugh.
Posted 2/1/2013 at 1:43 PM

September 22, 2017.

[...]

I had to revise how the Wildcat would be assessed in English 110; I was originally going to try the grading conference process with them, but since I had to back up the deadline, I changed it to a self-assessment. Yes, I'm going to have them assess themselves, and then I'll check to see how correct their assessments are. I have veto power, essentially. But when I think about how they will compose the research paper, and then have to identify whether they completed each section or not, I think that process is chuck full of critical thinking. Sure, they could just be dishonest and give themselves credit for shit they don't do, and some of them will, but those who are okay with having responsibility over what they hand in... they might appreciate that I'm not assessing them without their input. If they know what they are putting together and why, they'll do well. Creating something is one thing; understanding what parts are in that creation is another level. Sooooo, we'll see how it goes. It could blow up in my face, or it could be a new way for me to assess that isn't torture. And since assessment/grading is the crummy part of my job most of the time, it'll be fucking wonderful not to have to avoid it like the plague.

December 3, 2017.

On Friday, I tried looking for a segment of a syllabus (through all of my files) I thought I had – stolen from Carrie. It started with "You have chosen to take this class at this time in your life..." basically stating that there are going to be outside factors that will attempt to interfere. Anyhow, in seeking out that nugget, I found old syllabus after old syllabus, and it dawned on me how much I change – how much we change, as teacher mostly, but also as people. I found my punk syllabus, I found this list of ways to improve verbal skills (read alouds) and then written skills (retype paragraphs), and I just sat there... seeing the years: a syllabus from 2009 (8 years ago), a useful handout from 2007, etc. It was a history lesson; it was a blast from the past.

So, here I am, on a Sunday morning (our dad's birthday and Cochise's niece's too), looking at the week ahead but also looking at the next semester. There are so many ways to lay out a semester! There are so many ways to go about teaching writing, and every time I take that in fully, I get incredibly overwhelmed. I've used punk theory and George Carlin and Mark Manson, and it's nuts. Now I'm using self-publishing and book creations in my next semester.

Should they be reading aloud in class weekly? Should they be reading from more diverse authors? How can I incorporate them reading snippets of literature and chapters from the book (easiest solution: have them read samples of those genres like memoirs and profiles and letters) without me having to assess more than I am? How much should they be reading and how can I asses that when I am having them writing a lot and I assess that as best I can? How can they do more but the assessment stress[100] on me remains low? Perhaps I assign things that never get put into the gradebook? Have I really tried that tactic? I tell them that ten medium projects go into the Contract Grading, but they won't know which ten and I could assign 15? Same with the small projects, perhaps? Or journal entries... how can I make them digital but difficult to cheat on?

November 9, 2019.

The Professional Development (PD) day went better than I expected. [...]

What I tweeted:

Rage on the Stage. Crush apathy. Trust Ss. Authentic discussions. We need to model excellence. We need to improve. Student agency and advocacy. #ndscs #teachingandlearningday #gradeless #nogrades Thnx

What I posted on FB:

---

[100] Obviously, I was looking for ways to lower my stress and increase/improve the student learning process all along.

#whatilearnedatPDday
I want a t-shirt that says: "Rage on the Stage" & I want #gradeless classes.

My notes: we need to have open and authentic discussions, we bring our own energy to our classes, we need to improve ourselves, and we model excellence for each other and our students. We need to refrain from saying "that won't work with my students" or saying, "Everything's fine." "Nothing's gonna change if nothing changes." On one chart displaying the skills people use in the workplace, non-routine analytical and non-routine interpersonal were going up. "If your students can Google the answers, you are asking the wrong questions." Mental health is getting worse for students, and that plus classism is potentially causing the poor diets and trauma (has the median income gone up at all?); students need to take initiative, ask more questions, and gain student agency/advocacy.

[...]

When Walter came to our table, and Zooey said we should go gradeless, he seemed on board. But what happens when we really want to implement it? He said at the table that he still wanted to hear another department member's Italy trip stuff, so it's either good that he thinks it should be a dept meeting topic or bad that he thinks it's Italy or the other (when it isn't).

It was the universe talking when they put Cory – superintendent or principal from Northern Cass – at our table; they've gone gradeless recently! His presence and ideas really drove home the idea that grades are not helpful to our table (me, Cecila, Erin, Zooey, Josie, and Bryan).

[...]

Ideas: Ask them what they know and what they don't know, ask them how they like to learn, and then go from there. Make sure that the things they want to do cover the outcomes. Ask students to create the rubric/criteria used for the self-assessment quizzes. Constantly ask "Are the students learning?" Allow them time to reflect. Allow yourself time to reflect.

November 13, 2019.

[...]

I walked over for our department lunch today, and we ended the conversation with the gradeless idea; I completely understand everyone's struggle with the concept. Hell, I just screenshotted my online students discussing it. It can't work, they say, and I want to throw piles of data that I've read at them. OH, BUT IT DOES WORK, KIDS! Na. Instead, I'm using a self-assessment quiz this week, and that will demonstrate to them how this works.

You can't blame people for being stuck in the brainwashing of letter grades and points and all that. It's just like diet culture.[101] We're not sure where it came from, we don't like it, but it's been the way of the land, and in order to change it, we'll give ourselves headaches. But in both cases, there is data to prove it all wrong. What is the goal of education? What is the goal of my own little classroom? Learning, right? How can they learn best? If I've always asked that administration keep students in mind with their decisions, our decisions need to constantly go back to DOES THIS HELP STUDENTS LEARN? If not, why are we doing it?[102]

So, I had used a self-assessment quiz for Week 11's class discussion in the face-to-face English 120 course, and I have my first "liar." Chris went and clicked on true for all of them, but he did not upload a selfie, nor did he follow length requirements on the posts. And it was late, but that wasn't asked in the self-assessment quiz, from what I recall. Do you suppose I might have to "threaten" to do discrepancy tests with

[101] Yes, as I've mentioned, I could write a separate book about this. And I might.
[102] Boom! Bingo!

students? How many will just lie their way through the self-assessments whether they are on paper or digital? Is the same amount that lie and plagiarize, etc. now? Perhaps.

I'll have to think on all this. For now, I've sent the following to him, and I have not taken away any points:

As the self-assessment states: "Please be truthful when completing this self-assessment; if there is a discrepancy between what you completed and what you claim on the quiz, you may lose points."

You assessed yourself as having uploaded a selfie and written 10+ sentences/100 words for each post.
???

I know a certain Twitter person mentioned that lying was not allowed, so perhaps that'll be something I'll have to reinforce constantly.

November 18, 2019.

What's my deal with them handing in things "late" after "ditching" class? Why do I want to punish them for skipping? Is that the issue? Was I punished for skipping class? I don't think I did skip a lot, but when I did, I had compassionate teachers – Cindy, Kevin, Betsy, Amy, Kathy Cummings – fill me in on what I missed. Why do I place such a massive power on attendance? "YOU WERE HERE; YOU WIN THE POINTS TODAY." What the fuck? I hadn't assessed the reflection handouts from Friday, or the Frayers we did in class yet, so it's not like I had to go back into the dark hole of Blackboard to update anything. What's my problem? Well, I'll tell you – not only have my students been brainwashed by the points-point-points system, but I have been too! I've been the keeper of the points for too long – only wanting to "give them" to the students who show up. I would tell myself I was rewarding those who showed up on those random Fridays, but it was also a way to "get" those skippers. But who cares. Is it important for me to see – in the reflection handout – whether they doing okay or not? Isn't that why I handed out the reflection? YES IT IS, DAMN IT. UGH. MUTHATRUCKER.

[...]

December 2, 2019.

From the notepad, last night:

I'm definitely appreciating my newfound approach to the classroom. My newfound attitude adjustment. The additions of OEP and ungrading and kindness and trust. And I want to tell everyone AND not tell everyone all at once, too. Some will not get it, some will frown, and some will openly wonder if I can keep it up. Or if I'm just becoming soft, or that I want to give myself less to do. I can hear the criticisms. But I don't care much. I brushed off criticisms when I bought the bug, I could hear potential criticisms from people regarding the Jeep, and in general, I hear the "why are you like that / why do you do what you do" pissed off whispers of those who've done what's expected of them 24/7. Anyhow... yeah. So, I think I'll keep myself to myself on this as much as possible. The change benefits me and my students, and that's all I need to be consumed with.

[...]

December 10, 2019.

[...]

Yesterday went alright. That 11am class is fairly amazeballs; the women are on top of things, and I basically make fun of Phillip. They all had good questions about how to send their presentations to people, they handed in redos, and they created a rubric regarding the differences between As, Bs, and Cs (etc.) in record time.

The 1pm class was emotional; we almost finished the documentary *13*. It reminds us of such a deep ugly history and present. Those students have also been legit awesome this semester.

Then the 3pm class went okay, too. Even after I saw a student's paper response to the last piece of Hybrid Homework; he claimed he didn't learn anything of value. That Walter's class (that he's never taken – confirmed with Walter after) is more helpful, etc. I let it get to me a little; I even chatted with Josie about it in the middle of my students working. But in the end, I detached. I can't reach them all, whether I am a jerk with a zillion policies or a hippie dippy with multiple deadlines and late passes and redos. I can only plug progressive ideas in, watch my attitude change from harsh to light, and hope for the best.

[...]

February 5, 2020.

[...]

Well, I have an hour until lunch, and I think I'm caught up on most things. Allowing students the ability to go back and redo assignments and not being a strict ass when it comes to deadlines hasn't really backfired. I feel like I'm doing the same amount of work, but it's focused on feedback and not just throwing points into Blackboard.

I do want to rethink (and rethink and rethink) how I can streamline my use of Google and Blackboard. Could I get to the point where Bb is just for the Gradebook and major projects? Maybe. I used to be an overachieving user of that damn interface, and now I detest it most days.

Oh, I know what I can do: Send in Starfish alerts for online students.

[...]

February 10, 2020.

[...]

I'm thinking that since Starfish isn't required (the use of the attendance feature, etc. etc.) that I shall use it to what I see fit. And that means NOT attendance, but rather, to alert students to the fact that whether they've been in class or not, I do not have their STUFF.

AND, speaking of their STUFF, I just took a peek at a Large Project #1 in the 3pm class by a girl named Aubrey. It's a list of artifacts (supposed to have screenshots, images, etc.) and no CASH document (**C**riteria **As**sessment **H**andout[103]) or screenshots of usage on the Grammarly or Hemingway apps. Yeah. In the traditional grading system, this would be a bombed project, possibly. But now, I can throw a REDO on it and shoot it back to her. "Hey, you need to showcase your artifacts. And you're missing the CASH and app screenshots, doll. Get this all to me a.s.a.p. Gracias."

I've noticed that this ungrading process replaces certain types of "work" with others. Now, when I go to the "Needs Grading" area of Blackboard, I decide how much feedback to give. I read their discussion boards, looking for any missing things, but mostly just read for reading's sake. In Creative Writing, I give loads of feedback on the mini-projects and simply follow their lead in the Homework discussion posts. I should probably create an "Exit Ticket" for the online classes... perhaps I could shoot those out on Wednesday? (Okay, I created them and called them Check-Ins.)

Off to the 3pm class; I hope I can explain the LP2 a wee bit better this time. Sometimes, I feel like I'm reading off a screen – off the list – when my freestyle is better. Yeah. After that class is a damn meeting. A meeting I hope goes swiftly without me rolling my eyes too much.

February 19, 2020.

---

[103] I tend to create my own acronyms for activities. The CASH activity – Criteria Assessment Handout – was designed as a rubric that is filled out by the student before they hand in the project. There is a column for the criteria – typically chosen by the class – and then a column for evidence where students declare where the criteria is completed.

I've officially been recruited to speak on ungrading via a CCCC[104] webinar. Yep. I might gain some haters for it, but oh well. I get this feeling that the kind of Englishers who attend the 4cs LOVE to grade and grade and grade. They're obsessed with judgment and ranking students, aren't they? Or am I generalizing?

So, I just went through and did a quick shot of how many Fs I've got in my classes... the Online 120 has 7 which is 28%; I also have 7 in the 9am class, which is probably close to 30% because I have less students in there; over half of the 3pm class is failing (12/22), and just 3 are struggling in the Creative Writing course. Yeah. Maybe after I catch up on assessing things this week (should wrap up the LP1s in English 120 by Friday, as well as all the English 110 stuff), I'll send out "alerts" to those with Fs. The list keeps growing, and I'm unsure what could be the cause. Would they be failing even more with my "old system"?[105] I have no idea. I don't think the deadlines matter; they are not handing in stuff at all... Huh. I'll maybe dig into it all tomorrow; are these Fs like BAD ones (way below 50%) or are they able to "come back" easily from these percentages. Man, even in a super progressive system – like where they would assess themselves – how could they manage that and say they are doing C work even with NOTHING handed into me? Is it me, the new system, or just them? I mean, if we try to blame the hybrid formula, then the 9am would be doing shitty, too... but they aren't. Is it the time of day? Type of student? I have no clue. Perhaps giving them that speech about not wanting to be a dick did me in?

Today felt weird in there; some of them chat while I'm talking, and it's just rude. Eh. I'm going to chalk it up to a weird

---

[104] The Conference on College Composition and Communication. If TYCA is the two-year college arena; the 4Cs is for the big wigs/the universities. That leaves NCTE – the National Conference for Teachers of English – for k-12 people.

[105] Yes, they would have. And they did.

class period; I hadn't seen them since last Monday, and one girl who is typically cool asked what the project was, and I got a bit flustered – like is it that hard to keep my shit straight? Maybe it is. Maybe we need a refresher every class period. Maybe that needs to be on the slides: Hey kids, we're working on X, REMEMBER?

April 9, 2020.

This week has been tougher than usual. I mean, yes, March and April are going to be chaotic and weird and uncomfortable, but I had an emotional chat with a student... and Bernie suspended his campaign. And recently - in various tiny forms - some faculty members have been hinting at, or downright saying, that the way other teachers are "teaching" right now isn't quite right. Ugh.

My first thought on this was that if you are offering students choice and agency, you're doing alright. If you are considering their "new" situations – homeless, jobless, no device, no wifi, living with too many people in a small space – and you are working with them to help them learn, you're good to go.

So, don't go telling anyone how to do anything right now. You probably shouldn't be doing it in non-pandemic situations anyway, but yeah – we're all doing our best. Trust each other and keep your nose in your own business.

April 13, 2020.

Easter is not a favorite holiday of mine (for reasons); however, this Easter is the one year "anniversary" of when I took a deep dive into Twitter, and realized I needed to take my ego out of the classroom and put more of my heart into it.

[...]

April 14, 2020.

I just sent out my bi-weekly email messages to students. At any other time in my life, I'm sure doing this wouldn't be riddled with emotions and worry. I am truly worried that they are all okay. I'm worried that they are consumed with classes and are pouring a lot of energy into them... which maybe for some, that's a distraction, but for others, I can see it adding to mental health issues.

What also bugs me about this worry I have is that pre-pandemic, I'm sure I had students who needed a dollop of compassion. And I wasn't about to give that out. I was a jerk. My department members told me last week – during our virtual lunch when I ranted about how much of a dick I was – that I am being too hard on myself, but I disagree. This evolution in me should've happened early on. Imagine all the students who turned in an assignment a wee bit too late, and I was ultra-harsh about it? Or those who didn't hit some random word count. Gross. Who did I think I was? Where did that harshness come from?

Luckily, I can now spend the next 25 years NOT being that person. She was necessary, I suppose, because she brought me to this space where I care less about deadlines and more about feedback. I care so much more about them as humans than my own excuse that "deadlines are everywhere in the real world." That was BULLSHIT.

February 18, 2021.

An apparent hobby of mine is getting into fights with random people on Facebook before 8am. I guess I like to test my argumentation skills out on the masses. #ungrading #YesThePandemicPedagogyGroupAgain

I have to tell myself, "Some people aren't ready, Sybil. Some people don't get it."

Tweets:

What I've learned: I do things differently than others in my dept & that's ok. What I want to learn next: #OEP! #PBL #GoogleDoc usage #metacognition #ungrading Student voice & student choice & #accessibility & writing with my Ss. A lot more one-on-one time w/Ss.
5:21 PM · May 25, 2019

+

Old Me-hard ass with late work(etc); New Me-infusing more kindness-based policies. Q for #EDUcators #AcademicTwitter #AcademicChatter #ungrading #opened #edutech How do/did you reconcile the switch? Meaning, Ss in my past classes might've done better with New Me... #inclusion
8:36 AM · Sep 8, 2019

+

Qs: Has anyone meshed #OEP + #ungrading & what does that look like? Also, I have #OER textbooks, so the OEP could be 1) asking the Ss to remix w/other oer they find;2) skimming down txtbk in2 a template & ask Ss 2create original material; 3)...? #edutwitter #teaching Many THNX!
5:10 PM · Oct 20, 2019

+

I once was the teacher w/strict deadlines; I had reasons(etc)& I understand that angle. But I now see the other viewpoints,&I'm trying to find my way to something that works for my Ss' workload, as well as mine. Ditto for grades. #deadlines #balance #ungrading
10:25 AM · Oct 27, 2019

+

My Ss are points addicts. They are consumed w/grades, & how can I be mad when it's part of the system? And I'm part of the

system; I'm providing the "drugs." I'm a "points monkey," & I want to get off the ride. #ungrading
8:59 AM · Oct 29, 2019

+

A bad grade on a test shows that the S can't demonstrate knowledge in that way. A bad grade on a paper: ditto. Give Ss choice in demonstrating learning, let them fail and struggle w/the content,& then assess the process&improvmnt. #trustSs #nogrades #ungrading #tg2chat #gradeless
6:30 PM · Nov 11, 2019

+

Dipping my toe into #gradeless #ungrading #nogrades by using self-assessment quizzes in LMS (idea from
@OnlineCrsLady
); recently had a S lie in said quiz. I emailed wondering why S said S completed X when S hadn't. This can be a teachable moment, yes? Hoping this is rare. Thots?
6:36 PM · Nov 13, 2019

+

What's my deal w/Ss handing in things"late"after "ditching"class?What's my problem?Well, I'll tell U-not only have my Ss been brainwashed by the pts-pts-pts system,but I have2! I've been the"keeper"of the pts-only wanting to "give them" 2the Ss who show up. #ungrading #epiphany
2:10 PM · Nov 18, 2019

+

It was at the #NCTE in #Minneapolis that I was introduced to #contractgrading... which brought me to the recent realization: I wasn't taught why we use pts&letter grades. It wasn't covered during undergrad or grad school. Weird. And now I'm all abt #gradeless #ungrading #nogrades
8:01 PM · Nov 18, 2019

+

And the #gradeless #ungrading crew will tell you not to grade behaviors anyhow. IF I am preparing them for the workplace, in additional improving their writing skills - at a #tyc - then let's look at workplaces: no one cares when I skip mtgs or when ppl are late. So... yeah.
11:57 AM · Nov 23, 2019

+

#ungrading is this idea that grades don't help Ss learn & improve, feedback does, so Ts should focus on giving lots of feedback & allow Ss the opportunity/freedom to assess themselves in a variety of ways. I'm still learning abt it. Ppl to follow:
@OnlineCrsLady
@Jessifer
9:48 AM · Dec 6, 2019

+

I will not end this semester #complaining about #students. I know they mean well. I know they are addicted to #POINTS, which is y they fight 4every last one. #ungrading #gradeless I will #reflect, instead, on my changed #attitude & how well the #multipledeadlines went. #Winwin
5:10 PM · Dec 16, 2019

+

I thought I was headed towards burnout.{Even applied for PhD program last yr so I could maybe jump into admin.}But #oer & #ungrading & other Ts/ideas have created a spark. I think I'll be okay.
5:27 AM · Jan 4, 2020

+

What if... you didn't have to "grade-grade" them? What if they came self-assessed to you? Maybe in the form of a reflection letter? Or a S-created/S-filled-in rubric? What if you only had to leave helpful feedback in the margins and... that's it? #ungrading #nogrades #gradeless

+

I'm ready to leave the crabby professor behind. She was useful to me for awhile & for reasons & I appreciate her service & protection of my time/energy. But I don't want to be her anymore. I want to be the kind professor. It's better for my heart & stress. #evolve #ungrading #OER
7:23 PM · Jan 11, 2020

+

From "sorry, it's late" to "when can you get me your stuff?" From throwing zeros down on 100 point papers to allowing redos on an incomplete 10 point one (that is self-assessed). From spending hours being an exhausted "points monkey" to a happy lil "feedback junkie." #ungrading
7:37 PM · Feb 6, 2020

+

#ungrading doesn't mean Ss won't "fail." It's just that you think you failed them. And sometimes, you did.
4:41 PM · Feb 19, 2020

+

Dearest #ungrading posse: I need words of encouragement. I'm feeling alone in a sea of strict policies & deadlines, even during this crisis. It's been insinuated that I'm the one who needs to be harder.
4:01 PM · Apr 28, 2020

+

What is your goal? Student learning or student sorting? And why aren't you starting with kindness? #realcollege #ungrading #teaching
8:32 AM · Apr 29, 2020

+

I'm reading the process letters I assigned in a class that has been fully online all semester, and they are helpful, constructive, and sweet. Great idea from the #ungrading concept.
9:32 AM · May 4, 2020

+

I'm almost always revising my classes in my head. Tweak here, tweak there. It would truly be amazing to spend time in class w/Ss just giving feedback & reflecting on their writing. Why didn't this occur to me before? Maybe it's #ungrading meets #flippedclassroom & #OEP? Whoa.
2:19 PM · Oct 5, 2020

+

What if - and hear me out on this blasphemy - I didn't "grade" those last projects like I have in the past, but instead, I gave feedback & encouragement & passed whatever Ss could get to me during this time? Grades are arbitrary. #ungrading
3:35 PM · Dec 4, 2020

+

I mean, 1) what S is going to read all of your evaluative info? 2) it's a pandemic! 3) is there truly a perfect separation of A-B-C? To all writing Ts w/piles of papers: you aren't paid to grade; you're paid to help Ss learn... & there's so many ways that can happen! #ungrading
4:58 PM · Dec 4, 2020

+

Is student participation or engagement more important than student learning? And if we can't objectively "count" (in points, etc.) the latter, how can we do the same with the former? #ungrading

7:54 PM · Dec 5, 2020

+

Ever since I started assigning a Process Letter at the end of the semester, I have felt better about their learning and writing bc that letter forces me to see the class from their perspective; so even if you think they haven't improved, they might feel differently. #ungrading
11:22 AM · Dec 10, 2020

+

After putting final "grades" into the "system" this morning, I'm more convinced than ever that they are just a nuisance. I'm more than ready to jump into #ungrading fully & put all the anxiety and worry behind me. I don't want to be the judge & jury in a simple writing class.
10:23 AM · Dec 19, 2020

+

Our #ungrading book club will be tweeting up a storm later (noon CST?), but I wanted to ask this before I forget: How does one get passed the "this S didn't 'deserve' X grade" feeling? I have to refocus on what they learned, not my perceptions of their labor, right? #MyUnlearning
10:26 AM · Dec 19, 2020

+

Even if a S comes into my class w/angst, & might constantly self-assess themselves higher than what there is evidence for, I need to come back to - In their mind, did they learn? What other mantras do I need to plug into my own brain about this. Has anyone else used #ungrading...
10:28 AM · Dec 19, 2020

+

they have their own #unlearning to do when I offer up this approach on Day1. They might see it as refreshing; they might think they can fill self-assessments w/o doing the labor & think they can "cheat" this "system." I'm a tiny bit conflicted, but still going w/ #ungrading!
10:32 AM · Dec 19, 2020

+

This semester, I did hear tiny bits of "I did want you to tell me what you wanted on X Project." It was the only project w/o a S sample to view. It makes them uncomfortable, but it's good for them to imagine what that project might look like or be comprised of, etc. #ungrading
12:46 PM · Dec 19, 2020

+

And what's wonderful abt that is my soul feels better knowing I've extended grace. Plus, very few Ss need that extra time... & if I've done everything in my power to help them in that way, the "Fs" feel less "gross" (if that's the word to use). #ungrading
12:16 PM · Dec 20, 2020

+

It's such a tiny thing, but I just sent out my #LiquidSyllabus email to my Ss. With EVERYTHING going on, it's nice to feel like I have a bit of control over the start of the semester. The quicker they understand my #ungrading #OER courses, the easier learning should be for them.
12:20 PM · Jan 7, 2021

+

Speaking of judgment, this is slightly related to A2... I'd like to get rid of the "martyrdom" writing teachers use? Like the whole I HAVE SO MANY PAPERS TO GRADE AND THESE STUDENTS DONT GET IT SO THESE PAPERS ARE THE WORST. I was there. I did that. It's ridiculous. #ungrading
11:36 AM · Jan 9, 2021

+

Completely understand that. Many of my Ss hand in things by the “flexible” deadline set in schedule. Others need hours or days or weeks and I’m happy to say, “Hey, no worries. Please get it to me when you can. I want to see what you created.” #ungrading
11:53 AM · Jan 9, 2021

+

The gradebook is filling up w/their self-assessments, & I could not be happier. They have control. I'm literally just a guide for once. I have very little to do but check in & type up feedback. It's the only cool thing abt #teachinginapandemic rn, but I'll take it. #ungrading
12:18 PM · Jan 19, 2021

+

Thus far, #ungrading has really encouraged me to "up" my feedback game. I've been used to not really giving fdbck (due to Ss not reading it, etc) or constructive criticism on organization or spelling/punctuation. Now, I respond as a reader. Maybe the latter if they ask for it.
10:21 AM · Jan 24, 2021

+

I've been fumbling around w/this idea for a while, & I dunno if I'll say it correctly, yet I also know I'm not the first to say it: when we tell Ss to write "professionally" or use "appropriate language/grammar/spelling," we're saying, "You should sound like a white person." T/F?
2:33 PM · Feb 3, 2021

+

Want to know ANOTHER cool thing about #ungrading? Of course you do. I gave out oodles of feedback this morning & looked over homework. Did I miss a “requirement” by a S? It’s possible but if

it's about learning, it's not necessary for me to check every period or comma.
2:47 PM · Feb 9, 2021

+

When I think back on the Ts I adored, they kind of had an underlying #ungrading feel to them. They were heavy on work, & yet, the work was useful/I learned so much & I can barely recall my grades. Counter that w/hard Ts whose paper grading was so subjective,& I remember my grade.
9:37 AM · Feb 12, 2021

+

And that "grading" process still affects me now as a T. The Ts w/flexible deadlines & empathy: those courses are the ones I feel most comfortable teaching or speaking to... the Ts who were harsh & subjective - Critical Theory & Hippie Lit - turned me off to those topics. :(
9:40 AM · Feb 12, 2021

+

A2 = My stress is DIFFERENT now, & it's a BETTER kind of stress if that makes sense? I don't dread "grading" anymore, bc I'm NOT; it's been changed to FEEDBACK TIME YAY. Ss have also expressed that they are "excited" to try this out; they want lower stress, too. #ungrading
11:23 AM · Feb 13, 2021

+

A3: It happened yesterday! A colleague had met w/her Ss for writing conferences; she was procrastinating the "grading" part. I said, "Data shows they aren't going to look at the feedback if a grade is attached." Her body shifted into relaxed mode instantly. #ungrading
11:33 AM · Feb 13, 2021

+

A5 How can I help the poorest S, the S who comes in w/o resources or support, the S who has to work FT? Flexible deadlines & redos & taking late work & free #OER txtbks. Their learning will look different than my typical white privileged Ss & I have to respect that. #ungrading
11:51 AM · Feb 13, 2021

+

If ANYONE would've approached me w/this years ago, I would've laughed at them. I really "liked" sorting & ranking Ss. I was a jerk. I have proof in my daily journals. But if I had that response, I imagine others do too. #ungrading
11:54 AM · Feb 13, 2021

+

My newbie #ungrading experience continues: I have to reframe the "it's time to grade stuff" feeling; I think this will take a while to unlearn. I constantly wonder if I am giving enough fdbck, too; I think that will always bug me. I'll be tweaking this idea, forever & that's ok
9:20 AM · Feb 16, 2021

+

I suspect the reason I keep outing myself as “the tough T who was once a total jerk w/all the harsh rules” is bc I still need to forgive myself AND I want to remember that if I can change, others can too. #ungrading
8:19 AM · Feb 28, 2021

+

Yet another bonus to #ungrading: I'm swamped this week and feeling rundown/under the weather, so since the Ss have assessed themselves, those grades populate the LMS and I'll give feedback when I feel better.
10:54 AM · Mar 3, 2021

+

What used to be in my Outlook calendar as “grading” or “assessment time” is now changing to “feedback time.” I welcome the change, of course, but it’s a little awkward yet. A shift in theory -> a shift in action. (Also: “feedback time” is much more fluid.) #ungrading
6:54 AM · Mar 9, 2021

+

IF I have to use the LMS, then I am going to plaster FEEDBACK spots all over it. Hi, do you want feedback? Upload your work here. What kind of feedback would you like? Would you like it public or private bc I'll email you no prob. FEEDBACK FEEDBACK FEEDBACK #ungrading
12:11 PM · Mar 29, 2021

+

Two Qs on my mind today, with similar answers: How can teachers demonstrate "growth" in their teaching? How can students demonstrate "learning"? #AcademicTwitter #EduTwitter #ungrading #TeacherTwitter #metacognition
10:33 AM · Apr 1, 2021

+

I realize #ungrading won't solve everything, but I do think ungrading can solve everything.
8:02 PM · Apr 4, 2021

+

I've probably tweeted this before, or maybe someone else has, but you can't really have an anti-racist class by ONLY un-whitening the materials & content. Your policies shouldn't be racist. Your "grading" processes shouldn't be racist. #TYCA21 #4C21 #ungrading meets #OER

3:12 PM · Apr 8, 2021

+

When I see my nieces and nephew, I ask: “What are you learning in school?” I’ve never said, “What grades are you getting?” I bet the former is a common Q for most... So obviously, we intuitively know grades dictate nothing. #ungrading
9:04 AM · Apr 10, 2021

+

I'm trying to extend myself grace as I swim thru #ungrading waters for the first time, & I'm finding the oddest Qs popping up. How much do I back off from the "this isn't the 'level' of work I usually 'accept'" from Ss? If I'm assessing just completion, what does that look like?
8:47 AM · Apr 26, 2021

+

In giving up control, how does that mesh with the occasional S who does the absolute bare minimum? (Yet, what is the "bare minimum"?) Even under this theory & practice, I may not "catch" all of them. A few might still not learn or even be motivated. #MondayMood #ungrading
8:49 AM · Apr 26, 2021

+

I know I'm worn out - more than "normal" - bc I'm not "excited" to read my creative writing Ss' work. I think they are an awesome bunch, but my motivation is lacking. Embracing #ungrading, tho, means I should probably extend compassion to myself as I do w/them. *deep breath*
12:46 PM · Apr 27, 2021

+

Weirdly, I had a few epiphanies during the summer of 2019 when I ended up down the lovely Twitter rabbit hole of #ungrading. So, I

got shook up JUST IN TIME for the chaos of covid. I sure hope I would've realized it without the major epiphanies, but yeah. #teachinginapandemic
6:40 PM · May 6, 2021

+

And when it starts to feel OVERWHELMING for me, I'll walk away & take a breather & remind myself that if I didn't take late work, these students wouldn't have the opportunity to learn or revise. In the past, they would've failed my class, & that's not cool w/me anymore.#ungrading
8:51 PM · May 7, 2021

+

Has anyone else connected the dots between #ungrading & retention? If ALL Ts embraced Ungrading, how many more Ss would LEARN & stick around? How many do we lose to our harsh policies? Of course, bringing this up at a faculty mtg = "Sybil says we should ditch rigor & be soft."
8:38 PM · May 8, 2021

+

I think I had ONE S attempt to use a classmate's paper this sem,& I reached out to chat w/them, but they didn't respond. That STILL seems like a win bc I teach about 100 Ss/semester&anecdotally, it seems like I saw more plagiarism w/ a more traditional grading system.#ungrading
8:44 PM · May 8, 2021

+

I'm taking a moment to sit w/ these S responses to #ungrading in my #creativewriting course b4 I review more student work... the prompt was "What was your initial reaction to the lack of focus on grades? How do you feel about it now?"
7:10 AM · May 13, 2021

+

"I love it. It increases confidence in ourselves, because all of our writings are different. Because we have the freedom to get good grades on what we all individually work hard on, it has become much easier to write in my style." #ungrading
7:11 AM · May 13, 2021

+

"I really like that, college should be more about learning, not about punishments, it takes the fun away." Bingo. #ungrading #learning #fun #ftw
7:16 AM · May 13, 2021

West Fargo Journals.

02.22.1999

This morning's weird dream ended with the alarm going off. I really didn't feel well, mentally or physically. I called Mrs. Frandson to tell her I would come in later. I got here in time for 4th hour. We will be watching the movie *Anne Frank* this week as well as testing on Anne Frank. As for next week, we may be starting on Nouns or my unit. Both next week and the week after will be interrupted by testing (CTBS, etc?). So, we are basically in limbo right now – at least I am with my unit – try to get everything figured out and understood as to the days I will have. I am also in limbo with my gigantic job search. I should be going nuts or becoming frustrated, but I am okay and taking it day by day. I am glad to not have a job, so I am roam and do others things. Like the racism meeting tomorrow. I am also tutoring at nine dollars an hour. I just wish I had a job settled and knew where I will be in a year, etc. I found great "question of the day" ideas for starting points in each classroom. I have a goal of being better at my voice and control of the classroom for the next time the NDSU overseeing professor comes.

03.01.1999

Today was screwy. Mrs. Frandson told me to prepare for today "just in case" and told me to teach the whole day. Well, I was flabbergasted and not prepared, so I winged it. She evaluated me also. That's kind of a wild way to do it, I suppose. I admire her and all, but I don't like to play games.

Besides that, school was okay. It was a boring catch-up day. Tomorrow and Wednesday are testing days, as are next Tuesday and Wednesday. Pretty nuts if you ask me. My unit starts March 15th, so I am excited really for that week to begin. Also, our apartment lease is up at the end of April. I may have a job in my hometown for the fall taking Mr. B's spot. That means I would work next to Mr. Wall and teach my brother. I almost wouldn't mind it. I would be closer to my current boyfriend (compared to Crosby or Minnetonka) and could get a good start in a familiar school district. It only pays $17k/year, but that is double what I make at Target right now!

03.09.1999

Well, the first day of this week was all good. Tomorrow, we start CTBS testing which will just be loads of fun. The sub I am working with is one I worked with before. I hope she doesn't mind me teaching the whole time or at least most of it. I think it will be interesting – that is for sure.

[...]

We got tons of snow overnight and I got stuck at school. We got five inches just today and that doesn't count last night or what we will probably get tonight. I am enjoying my free night. The rest of the days will be spent grading quizzes. Maggie and I were total slackers yesterday. She slept most of the day, and I painted and watching some big-league basketball games. I slept too, but slowly, it got more and more snowy out, so I got into a blizzard state of mind. I just printed out some resumes and letters to go to Breckenridge and West Fargo High School. Both are looking for English teachers. I hope I can get my ass in somewhere. Minnesota schools are my best bet for getting paid well – Wahpeton and West Fargo would be worth it, too.

03.16.1999

Well, my unit is going well. I was pooped after today's lesson. It was fun to listen to them talking and creating – I felt like the oddball out – I should have created another one or kept myself busy somehow because otherwise I feel like I am a babysitter. Other than that, I felt very comfy and happy having them roam about and CREATING! And some of the things they came up with. I should have asked them to do the 3rd person idea with the notion in mind to have that person describing them try to get into their personality more. Some did that and some didn't. It was my fault, but they still turned out fantastic as far as I am concerned. I am glad to have them doing something that doesn't make them complain, and it also gets them using their CREATIVITY.

05.27.1999.

I GOT A JOB!

Yep. Battle Lake Public Schools! With $27k/year starting! And it sounds like a great little school to teach at. I may just stay there the rest of my life.

Now, I have much to do to, of course. Suddenly, this job with Dakota Boys Ranch really does not suit me at all. I haven't worked much, but I honestly don't care, and I know they have plenty of people to do whatever they need. Besides, this is my last summer to myself and already I need to start thinking about curriculum. I have a busy couple of years ahead of me. It should be interesting and challenging and possibly even rewarding.

I have to find a place to live, and I want to maybe purchase a car.

I went to see my kids and Mrs. Frandson the other day which was awesome. I saw Dr. Cummings, too, and she gave me a big hug.

The college boyfriend and I are back together; he said that he looked at me a little differently after I got the job, and he has said a few times that he would easily move out there.

All is well. I just have lots to figure out now. MN residency, license, housing, car, etc.

+

"You can do almost anything you want," says Carol[106], beaming, when I ask if I can decorate my classroom.

+

---

[106] One of the amazing administrative assistants I got the pleasure of working with. The staff at many places I've taught have ALWAYS made me feel at home. They are underappreciated.

When I graduated from college in 1999[107], I applied everywhere for a middle school or high school English teaching job. I bet I sent out ten letters and resumes to surrounding schools. I received a rejection letter from my hometown – due to not having any teaching experience.

For weeks, I waited and waited. Finally, a call came from a small school in Minnesota.

I interviewed. I toured the facility. At the end of that interview, where I compared the act of teaching to a religion, I was offered the position. I believe the actual play-by-play was the superintendent asking me how long it would take me to accept the position, and I said: "30 seconds."

By the time I needed to move into the lake town, I was single and somewhat devastated over the breakup. I had stopped eating (anorexia had reared its ugly head in the past when I dealt with the end of other relationships), but luckily, an apartment opened up ($300/mo?) on the main drag, AND beyond a new living space, I had a classroom to decorate. I poured my heart and soul into those two projects the entire month of August. I befriended the school's secretaries, and hours into the endeavors, my appetite returned. I celebrated with a burger combo at the town's Dairy Queen. It might've been my first "meal" in days.

Decorating my huge classroom, learning the program that would put together the school's yearbook, reading up on all the materials I would teach, as well as meeting new faces every day that I would eventually remember. I was naïve, that much is obvious, but I had high hopes for myself. I listened to everyone's advice; I kept my mouth shut when gossip would arise. For that first year, I just tried to be the teacher I thought I was in my head.

---

[107] Please note, this part is a reflection on the chapter.

The Basement.

There is an old home video taken by our mom. She's walking down the basement stairs. My siblings are in old desks. They might have old textbooks open, they might not. I think my brother – the youngest – is coloring something he shouldn't be coloring. The recording comes to me at the chalkboard, and I frantically erase what looks to be a Mad Lib. I was possibly trying to teach my siblings nouns and verbs and adjectives using a silly Mad Lib. And this is perhaps where my teaching career began. Haphazardly, in a basement, with pupils who did not care about what I was saying.

Not much has changed.

Battle Lake Journals #7.

02.25.2000

I originally went into architecture my first year of college, and I was pretty serious about it, but when I look back at my childhood – I was always playing school with my younger siblings, and I could always relate to people younger than me. Once I realized in college how much I loved to write and read, I thought – where could I do this for a living and the answer was the English professor and why not teaching? I adored my English teachers, and I could easily be in front of a bunch of kids, plus I had the "role model" aspect down: I didn't smoke, drink too much, have sex, do drugs, etc. Students could look up to me, and I believe that that is what has happened. I don't have all my basics down, but I do have the relationships figured out between the students and I as well as the colleagues and me. I took on a lot my first year, but I have always been an over-achiever, and somewhat of a perfectionist so it all combines and works well. If only I could be more of a disciplinarian, but would that be outside my personality? I would like a bit more control, but I am young and at least they didn't walk all over me this first year. I was ready for anything, though, that first day. Right now, I love this "job," and I am proud of my decision. Sometimes, I don't feel accepted because of my age, but that, too, will pass and, hey, I'll miss those comments down the road.

03.04.2000

As I read about the different categories of teaching English, I find that I am somewhat in the "teaching for inspiration" category, which, unfortunately, doesn't please me. This category of teaching has teachers who "wing it" a lot and don't plan much. They simply hope that the students will focus in on the issue, assignment, or project and go from there. I want to jump more into the "teaching as discovery" mode. These teachers:

- Don't avoid questions that have no answer or mind saying they don't know.
- Let students talk.
- Allow pauses in the talk – just like in a real conversation. This means there are periods of silence in the classroom.
- Ask, ask, ask, and fall out of love with telling.
- Start teaching where the students are, not where the book is.

They also give ideas on how to teach *Their Eyes Were Watching God*, so I better show Mr. Peterson.

05.08.2000

It's getting towards the end of the year, and I thought this week would be an okay one, but it has already started out on a bad note with Carr circling some of my usage on a faculty survey, and then a parent called and needed to vent about getting the students together to tape their movie when – according to the parent – they could perform it in class. Ah! I understand, BUT they don't have to do it that way.

I have got to not take things personally and realize that not all parents will like me, or administrators.

If I would've done this same project in March, I would've run into basketball, January – bad weather. Any month is not always the best, and May is a finals month. This is a final project. Sheesh. Get off my back, people!

05.14.2000

That whole last week sucked big major ass, but there is only seven fucking days left, so everyone can take their complaints with me and stick them in their backpacks and take it home with them. I almost lost it in front of the kids, and that is a first. All my days are blurred together, so I can't even recall what day that was.

Parents need to be BEHIND the teachers and know that the teachers are taking full responsibility to get the kids the best damn education they can give them. Jeezus. I may be young, but I do know what the fuck I am doing, and if I need help, I go to Mr. Peterson, the whole faculty, or books.

Summer is coming at the perfect time.

This must be a tad bit what burnout feels like.

05.18.2000

I am already turning into a "I will kiss your ass if you leave me alone" type of person. If I am going to have people constantly looking over my shoulder the rest of my teaching career, that is just going to suck. Yeah, I said it: Suck suck suck. Jeezus. You'd think I had said "fuck" or something! I almost wanted to quit today; I really lost it in the bathroom 3rd hour.

Goddamnit I am so sick of parents NOT coming to me and instead complaining to others. WHY the hell don't they come to me? It's pisses me off big time. I cannot explain how much it ticks me off. I'm looking forward to my summer. Thank god. Hopefully, by June, I won't flip out on anyone.

+

I was having an okay day. I then talked to Carr this morning about Michelle being late, and he let me know again that parents were upset with my goddamn projects, so I called one who is on the school board and straightened out shit. Then later on there are these feelings of people against me, through talking with the school board member and Carr.

[...]

It feels as if he talks down to me; it pisses me off. Plus, when I walked into his study hall, he smiles at me as if everything is happy. Fuck that shit.

I talked to Maggie and bawled a bit (I cry the most when I am angry). She agrees totally. It doesn't shock me. I need to get a hold of my former teachers – some people who can make this all into a perspective little package for me.

+

Memo:

This first year for me was flying by fabulously until two weeks ago. Now, I realize and apologize for my stupidity that appeared in my previous memos. I am not only beginning to learn how to teach, how to take criticism, and honestly, the second is not an easy one for me, but throughout all of this conflict, I have done more thinking in these last weeks than I ever did in college about the educational system we have, about professionalism, and about who I am as a teacher and what my goal is through teaching.

I thank all of you for your patience with me this year and also your support. Your anonymous criticisms have made me think, made me turn myself inside out trying to figure out what I have done incorrectly, or correctly. I thank you for questioning me, challenging my motivations, my projects.

I ask, though, that in the future you would put your name to your comments to me. I would appreciate it. Thank you. I wish all of you a relaxing summer and hope to see you all around. Until next year...

Quotes, Take 2.

Thursday May 10, 2007

One student's feedback:
"She wears too much black clothing."
Huh?
Posted 5/10/2007 at 9:31 AM

Wednesday October 6, 2010

"All students are super smart until proven otherwise."
Seriously, I know my students are smart; that's why I don't let them get away with much.
evil laugh
Posted 10/6/2010 at 10:8 AM

Thursday February 17, 2011

"I didn't want to destroy my paper by adding too many words." - student in my online course.
What the What?
Posted 2/17/2011 at 12:2 PM

Friday March 18, 2011

"It's really hard to teach those who know it all." - Him, sarcastically after trying to give me ice-fishing advice. Me: "I know! Ask my students."
Posted 3/18/2011 at 5:44 PM

Monday September 26, 2011

New motto for students:
Life is Homework!
Posted 9/26/2011 at 1:15 PM

November 10, 2019.

Someone probably needs to hear this, as it is a metaphor for life, but you need to plug in the crockpot in order for it to work.

Outside and Inside Forces.

Sunday September 14, 2008

Cookies, camels, and lists:

I'm one tough cookie. This I am very aware of. I've been through some major, major dips in my life. Sometimes I've had people at the edge, throwing a rope at me. Friends telling me I have to eat or I have to cry to get it out of my system. And, sometimes, I have not had people with ropes and pizza by my side, either by choice or by chance.

Now, in recent years (all post-undergraduate years), when I am at my most frustrated, I don't get depressed. It's like that option has been completely deleted (or drained of it's energy). Instead, I get really, really angry. From that point, I jump into a hate-filled hibernation, really. Things like, "FINE, if X doesn't X then X won't X; I'll show X to mess with me!" [How I've gone from using formulas in the classroom to formulas for emotions is beyond me right now.]

I pretty sure that psychologists would frown at this defense mechanism (or whatever the term is), but it's better, in my mind & opinion, than just being depressed and having constant pity parties.

Essentially, to continue my very abstract post here, many people have been added to what I call my Sh*t List. Yeppers. With some, they have officially used up their "last straw" or killed the camel's back or whatever the stupid metaphors are. The List was fairly empty for a time. Typically, in the summers, I don't see enough people to be involved in adding to that List. But now, heading into week four of the semester, I have probably 5 or so people on there! Some students (I told one straight up that he was on it the other day when for the third time I had to help him log into [the LMS]!), some family members, a sprinkling of friends... it's a nice mixture, and they are all at different levels of "dislike" right now. I'm sure I'm even on some people's (student's & neighbor's) Lists too, and I'm okay with that. I'm aware of how I can occasionally piss people off. Tough cookies really don't care.

Do YOU have a List like this one?
Posted 9/14/2008 at 5:34 PM

Wednesday November 3, 2010

Lately, it's been my theory that for the rest of my life, the world appears to be out to get me. Just when I start to feel up, "they" bring me "down a notch."
It feels that way, even, with family and friends and apparent "loved ones" which is the most insane part.
But maybe that doesn't have to be my perception.
When we start to feel beaten down by everything and everyone around us, it's easy to point finger or just fall into a heap at the end of the day, depressed and full of "eh." But here's my latest thought on that... if, when we feel that way, we can recognize that everyone feels beaten down, repressed, by someone or something, then it's easier (and maybe mental-healthy-er) to think, "Okay, they have their own crap going on; it bugs me that they try to beat me down, but how can I blame them? Only I can pick me up; I'm the only one in control of me."

For instance... my students. Some of them are awesome (85%); some of them need to wake up and smell the salsa (15%), but when I walk into the classroom, I can only control me. I attempt to control them, and they usually listen, but, really, they have their own crap going on. Maybe they just broke up with someone or maybe, like me at their age, they constantly fight with their parents because they want more freedom. That's stressful.

And, basically, those "Negative Nancy" teachers and administrators out there are just people who didn't pick themselves up enough times. They got run over by the freight train of life or something (maybe they view it as a train they can't run away from or a train they didn't jump out of the way of?); it's too bad. It's not our job to point that out or try to change their attitude. I think we can only lead by example.
Posted 11/3/2010 at 1:20 PM

January 19, 2016.

I had a thought recently that I forgot to document. It wasn't a pretty thought, but I'm sure for most people – especially those in the upper Midwest in the winter – it's a relatively common thought. The thought was how easy it is to slip into depression. I've been sad, then realized I was just uber pissed, and then I've been through sadness again with the death of family members, and then I've worked through that by living the way they'd want me to, etc. Sadness is different than depression. I've had suicidal thoughts, but they aren't as prevalent as they were when I was a freshman in high school... and then a freshman in college. It's odd that at turning points in my life, I have found myself either thriving on the chaos of it all or completing falling victim to that black hole.

So, last week was tough, is what I'm getting at. I started to battle myself:

Voice A: "Well, I guess I'll just focus on my classroom. It's the only control I have."
Voice Z: "No, you have to push for change on our campus. Don't give up."

Voice A: "But I'm exhausted. No one listens to me, no one cares."
Voice Z: "You have to use your voice. If no one speaks up, who will? Don't let the status quo win!"

May 5, 2017.

[...]

Anyhow, I'm finding it easier and easier to let go of my anger with the few students that conjured it out of me recently. While the acupuncture pins were in me yesterday, I let myself tear up over the frustration of it all. And I remember saying to myself, "You can go ahead and overthink this. Go ahead and think too much about it because eventually, it will go away." I push myself – and probably others – to get over things with students quickly because students will always do that to us, but it's okay to dwell before releasing the anger.

[...]

Now, onto bigger, cooler things. I'm going to flip my projects in English 110 next fall. Start with the Wildcat (media + multi-genre + a wee bit of argument) then the Panther (visual essay) then the Elephant (Fake Company) then the Camel (interviewed research) and end with the Alligator (letters). I'm deleted the Tiger from the line-up because I'm sick of seeing the same answers along with shitty in-text citations. The new Wildcat Project will absorb the lessons I thought the Tiger would teach.

Josie and I have had at least one conversation about "being on" and how that's the extrovert in us – how we need the hermit side, the introvert, to counteract the need to always feel "on" in the classroom or just while on campus in general. I think that's why I get a little anxiety about Math Olympics[108]. I have to "be on" in a different way with a different audience who

[108] Years ago, Lola convinced me to dress up for Math Olympics - a math competition for grades 4-6 in the region - as the Number Fairy.

is unpredictable to me. And, due to what happened last year with me helping out Charlie in the grading room, I might have additional responsibilities to just the dressing up and handing out stickers.

[...]

Well, time to wrap it up in this office... for this week at least. I'll shut down the iMac, head home for a bit of rest and lunch, and then pop back onto campus as the number fairy around 3:30 or so. I think it will go well; I can always "disappear" for a while and even if that pisses off someone, that just means they'll ask someone else to be the fairy next year OR they'll realize that I shouldn't have to be anything more than the fucking fairy.

Because being a fucking fairy is fucking exhausting as it is.

Peace out.

August 3, 2018.

I can't pinpoint exactly where this little funk has come from... the slight feeling of a summer cold coming on yesterday morning? Or the constant "summer went so fast" message from everyone? No matter the cause, I felt it very necessary to meditate last night and the night before. I also had to just stop giving myself a guilt trip for not doing more Wednesday and yesterday. After a fun lunch with the girls – which included a gummy bear martini that added to the funky feeling – I was simply tired, and since lunch went almost until 2pm, I said FUCK IT to the pool and napped. I asked myself what would make me happy in that moment, and it was rest. Done. Over.

[...]

With all this said NOW, I unfortunately started to fill my head last night with Brene Brown ideas that appear to conflict with *The Untethered Soul* ideas and then I realized that some thoughts connect between the two... the one thing I wondered was how I can be vulnerable when I'm supposed to just observe my thoughts and transcend. Can one transcend the noise of their own minds and still be vulnerable? Then again, if 90% of my thoughts are totally unnecessary, I should be able to focus in on the ones that cause me to be vulnerable – the ones regarding creativity, etc.

And still, I have to remind myself that I won't always remember to put into practice the lessons I've learned this summer from Brene and Jes Baker and Michael Singer (author of *The Untethered Soul*). Somedays, I'm just going to be in a funk and then I'll need to turn on my meditation music and read quotes from those authors to remind me of what I know already about myself and life. Somedays, I just won't feel like ME and that's okay because it's just momentary and I'm human and it's okay and FUCK IT.

I'm wondering right now if this journal subconsciously – or even consciously – places pressure on me... something to the effect of I MUST DO ALL THE THINGS SO I CAN WRITE ABOUT THEM and also LOOK AT HOW PRODUCTIVE I AM. Sometimes, dear Sybil, "time wasted" isn't "time wasted" at all. You know that you know that, honey pie, so what the hell? Let it all go. Take a nap, don't take a nap. Organize that fucking closet, don't organize it. Go for a swim or don't. No one really cares. Do I care if anyone went kayaking on 15+ lakes this summer? Nope. Do I care if anyone went on a summer vacation or napped every damn afternoon? Nope. Don't give one shit. [...] Don't glorify busy, kids. And I should follow that lead. Boom.

Okay... I'm going to go do whatever this fucking Friday decides it needs me to do in the moment. I would like to drop off some Amazon returns because they are taking over the damn home office, and I would like to get some water and sun because those two things seem to reset me a little bit... but other than those tiny goals, the day will be another summer day that I refuse to feel the need to FILL to the MAX. Yep.

Well, the semi-helpful meteorologists in our area said that the southern part of the valley could potentially see the most rain chances today, and they were actually correct. After a tiny morning snooze (yes, I wrote the above post around 5am), I packed up three boxes of returns to bring to the grocery store, and then brought Sadie outside... JUST as we walked out the door, I could see a flash of light behind me and then BAM a massive crack of thunder boomed right above us, and poor Sadie didn't know what the fuck was going on. She eventually peed, and I went to the store.

As I got home and parked the bug, it occurred to me that it was going to rain, and I remembered the promise I made to myself to get out on the fat bike at least once this summer IN THE RAIN. So, I unpacked the one bag of groceries, found a hat, and tried to explain to Sadie what I was about to do. The rain started to come down harder, but before I could back out, I pumped up the tires and WENT. Puddles were everywhere, my legs pushed this heavy bike (that gave me more trouble in the winter) happily, my body got extremely soaked, and I eventually found an eye-witness on campus who just looked at me like I was a kid in a candy store. I was. It was the best feeling. I didn't want to stop, yet eventually, the rain lessened and then splatters of mud were probably going to end up on me, so... yeah. Once I got dry clothes on, I just felt this content feeling. As if I had been baptized in the rain[109]. A reset for the tiny funk I've been in. Who knows if the pool opened this afternoon because I don't feel it necessary to go down there... my joyful movement – with water – has already been taken care of. Done. And now, post-lunch, I think it's time to do what rainy days are for: naps. Okay, they are also for reading books and drinking hot cocoa, but I'm mentally and physically just flushed with contentment. Who knew I needed a ride like that? And maybe another storm will pop through later, and I can do it all over again.

September 26, 2018.

---

[109] It's such a spiritual event, for me, to bike in the rain.

I was feeling weirdly emotional just a bit ago, and it's coming back as I type. I don't know where it's coming from. I'm trying to observe the sadness (or frustration and anger, since I tend to process them with tears); where is it coming from? [...] Am I in need of some quality sleep – is that where this is coming from? Is it how I noticed the headaches I was having weren't connected to anything recently (like they typically are)?

[...]

I think – no, I KNOW – it's okay to not be okay, yet I'd like to find the source. It's probably a combination of body image crud in my head with not sleeping as well (even though I do crash quickly) and then the political white noise and general headaches and guilt trips. Sybil, just like after the triathlon, here's another damn pep talk: You do you. [...] You are a strong woman; crying every so often to get it all out does not make you less strong. The shit that you are placing on your back is not for you to carry, necessarily. Drop it by the wayside for a bit. Put it telepathically on someone else or in some other time period. If you need a Xanax, take one. You might need to just start planning the self-care you said you would this year. The acupuncture with Tasha might not help your hormones, so maybe you need to jump those green pills. Maybe you should consider going to the Southpointe chiropractor again even though he was spendy.

Okay, those pep talks always help... deep breath. I can and will care for myself the best way I can. I'm very glad I'm writing about this. I was about to go into a vent session about the two students who are showing just enough disrespect in class and in my office but eff it. Instead, I'm thinking about tonight and tomorrow and how to include some self-care. Meditation, yoga, a bike ride? One moment at a time. [...]

September 30, 2018.

I cried the hardest I've cried thus far over Sadie's health today. I finally sought out Cochise in the garage to talk about her, how she's not putting weight on the one leg anymore, how she seems sadder, how her breathing seems different, how I don't want to wait until she fractures the damn leg to put her down (how painful and abrupt!), how I want this to be a join decision between us (he said he'd make the decision for me – I was somewhat relieved at that; I thought I'd have to be in this alone), how I don't want to keep her around just for me... he said we just let her be today. It might be a bad day. We'll observe her this week (he has it off – is already working on the bathroom), and I noted that I have drugs for her for 1.5 more weeks. Not that that matters maybe, but it could be a weird sign... if she's starting to not want to walk on her own. [...]

May 20, 2019.

[...]

Wednesday was a bit of a depressed day. It was tough to get out of bed that morning. I tried not to guilt myself into doing much. Rest is okay. [...]

The View had Craig Ferguson on their Wednesday episode, and he was there to promote his memoir called *Riding The Elephant*. I've never been a massive fan of his, but I do find him funny and charming (could be the accent). He explained that the memoir's title meant this: when you are on an elephant, you think you are leading the elephant, but it is leading you. This is life, he said. And that was helpful for me to hear on that somewhat-sad Wednesday. So, thanks, Craig?

[...]

"You're not required to save the world with your creativity. Your art not only doesn't have to be original, in other words, it also doesn't have to be important." - Elizabeth Gilbert

September 3, 2019.

[...]

Unfortunately, in other news of crud, I wrote this on Saturday (August 31):

Their issues - with writing and English classes - are their issues. Somehow, they've decided my class sucks, without taking it. This is not on me. They need to ask themselves why they detest writing and English classes because it's not on me to change their mindset = none of the outcomes state that a goal is to make them like it. If they want to detest the class all semester, well that's on them.

And I'm giving them choice and voice, so why complain? You want to write about your hunting adventures? Then find the outcomes that suit that goal. You want to create presentations about the pros and cons of dating older women, put it down. You want to design a "How to Plan the Perfect Party" brochure, figure out how that fits.
I don't think they realize how long writing courses have been around... How these classes are important to employers and a necessity for accreditation. And let's say they were passionate about changing the accreditation? IMAGINE THE WRITING/COMMUNICATING YOU WOULD HAVE TO DO TO CHANGE IT!

Mindset > Situation: English classes suck, so this class will suck.

Situation > Mindset: This might not be like other English classes?

Yep. See? Always thinking academically. And I think it's a good line of thinking. I mean, it truly isn't my goal to make everyone love my class or like me or remotely love writing. They need to see it – I suppose – as a tool to help them accomplish things now and in the future. I can push them to SEE that, but again, it's not a fucking course outcome... and it's not achievable (isn't that part of that SMART goal crap?).

[...]

October 3, 2019.

[...]

I've been exhausted lately, once I've arrived home. Last night was no different. I was in PJs by 5pm with a burger in my mouth, and I could've easily fallen sleep. For a nap, or for the night. Who knows. I'm unsure when it all began – when we had

Sadie or before my last diet or after I stopped going out after work – but it's annoying. Am I just tired? Is it adrenal fatigue? Is it the underlying hum of stress from the national administration? Is it my hormones and another symptom of perimenopause? Perhaps it's a combination of never really having had a good sleep schedule. From looking back in my journal entries, I see that before Sadie and while in the middle of my last diet, I also wasn't sleeping all the way through the night for a variety of reasons – too much on my mind, unable to crash after getting up to pee in the middle of the night, possible hungry stomach, Cochise's snoring...

So, the solution lately has been to go to bed early and I've started taking supplements that might help – melatonin and magnesium worked for a while, but then they started to give me headaches.

[...]

Anyhow, it's my latest quandary – why am I so damn tired? Some might say that I should throw exercise in the mix, and I might once I figure out if these supplements will help with the WAKE UP part of my day as well as the SHUT OFF part. My guess is that perimenopause is the main culprit and once one starts to lose sleep on a constant basis, it's a slippery slope into trying to gain back that rest, and I'm unsure if I'll ever hit that sweet spot.

I might also need to meditate and take more breaks from screens – the tiredness is compounded when my eyes are as dry as deserts.

[...]

I'm evolving, people. A student – who slept in – just popped into my office to find out what we did. I didn't chew him out, nor did I only harshly refer to our schedule like I would've in the past; instead, I explained what's up in a nice way and even gave him a Frayer for the hybrid homework. Yeah. It takes nothing to be kind. I hope I never return to that jerk-off I was before; why did I need to make them feel badly?[110]

Huh.

Okay... well, I'm going to head home.

January 22, 2020.

[...]

The 3pm went well. Better than expected, really, even though I couldn't figure out the copy/paste thing on that computer because it's a PC keyboard and a Mac system. Ugh. Anyhow, I divulged to that 3pm class how I used to be an "asshole" teacher. Yep. Dove right in. Told them I didn't want to be a dick for another 25 years. I think they got it, and maybe it helped lighten up all the angst some of them have.

Oh, I also talked about how if they are sick, they should stay home so their germs don't come to class and have sex in the air and create a super bug[111] and then kill us off. I should tell the 9am this, too, as well as the asshole teacher part. Yeah.

But, for now, I'm content with how this is going.

April 1, 2020.

[...]

My recent (and very private) Facebook post:

Hi. I'd like to take a moment to have a teeny breakdown. I just listened in on our college president's first virtual open forum since the pandemic crud started. And I could not keep myself from crying. I miss campus. I miss my crazy-ass students. I miss my colleagues. I miss my office and my little fridge that has half-drank Diet Dews in it. I know I am so very freaking privileged to be working at home, and I'm not sick, and I haven't lost anyone to this illness, but... shit.

October 19, 2020.

---

[110] It's a really good question, actually.

[111] Foreshadowing?

[...]

Got my third COVID test today before picking up an "eh" lunch. As I wait around for my 3pm class, I had a realization from all the work I did this morning (email and feedback in Peer Review for the English 110 courses' Large Project 2s):

I didn't realize that I get much more "mean" at mid-term. A whole lotta sarcasm and sass coming out of this face... "I KNOW you all read the schedule RIGHT?" "Um, no, you don't get to decide what projects are group projects."

The two students who may or may not have worked together on LP1 (the Fake Company) handed in a "group draft" for LP2 in the peer review. Here's where the narrator comes in and says, "It was not a group project." I'm not sure where the guys got this idea. I never said it was group-based, it's not in the instructional guide, and all of their classmates uploaded their own individual survey reports. Huh. So, I emailed them that they could both use the survey findings, but they had to write up separate reports. Hopefully, they don't try this with LP3, but if they do, I guess I'll have to state it AGAIN. I can see these two – one of them was the nimrod who told me he didn't have to wear a mask over his nose because he'd already gotten it – also stating that they don't have to put charts into their reports because their link (to SurveyMonkey?) contains them. Um, that's great guys; take some fucking screenshots then. Why do you think you get to NOT do the things your fellow classmates ARE doing? C'mon now. Shit.

I don't know if it's because it's mid-term or what, but I'm losing some of the calm-happy-whatever from early on in the semester. Like, this weekend, I was thoroughly annoyed that students emailed me. One was from a student who left her self-assessment on the teacher station in the classroom, thinking that was my goddamn office (there's always a few). Another one wanted feedback on Saturday for a project due Sunday... when I had had optional writing conferences ALL WEEK. I realized that trusting them meant I had to trust them to troubleshoot without me because I need rest. I need to decompress. I need to reinstate my out-of-office replies. I thought they were unnecessary last spring, but they are now. It's as if we/I've moved from "teaching with strategy and to inspire" to teaching to get by, to survive. That's what the tweet is today.

October 26, 2020.

Two students physically in class at 9am, with two virtual. No one f2f or virtual at 11am. It could be the temperature outside, it could be covid concerns, and it could just be that time in the semester where everyone is tired. And now it's like covid-anxiety-election tired, which is a whole new fucking tired. Yeah.

I hemmed and hawed this morning, wanting to take a mental health day, but then I guilted myself. I hadn't been around anyone since Wednesday – what was my problem? I was fine. Plus, trying to take a fucking sick day is almost more exhausting than dragging my ass out of bed, fluffing my hair, and putting on a decent outfit. The guilt trips are highly unnecessary, I realize, but I am glad I got to talk to Zooey for a moment this morning… which brings me to my next paragraph:

My email to my department on this chilly Monday morning:

So, I was telling Zooey this morning that it's been harder and harder for me to get out of bed, and I've always been a morning person – even with daylight savings. It's probably existential dread mixed with anxiety, but it's sucks. And I know what depression is like, and I don't want to go there...

BUT THEN just a few minutes ago, my TYCAMW friends alerted me to another TYCAMW person and how he posted something stupid about PDF rules on FB.

And now that I've expressed myself (see below), I feel so much better. Being angry is so much easier, and more fun, than being sad.

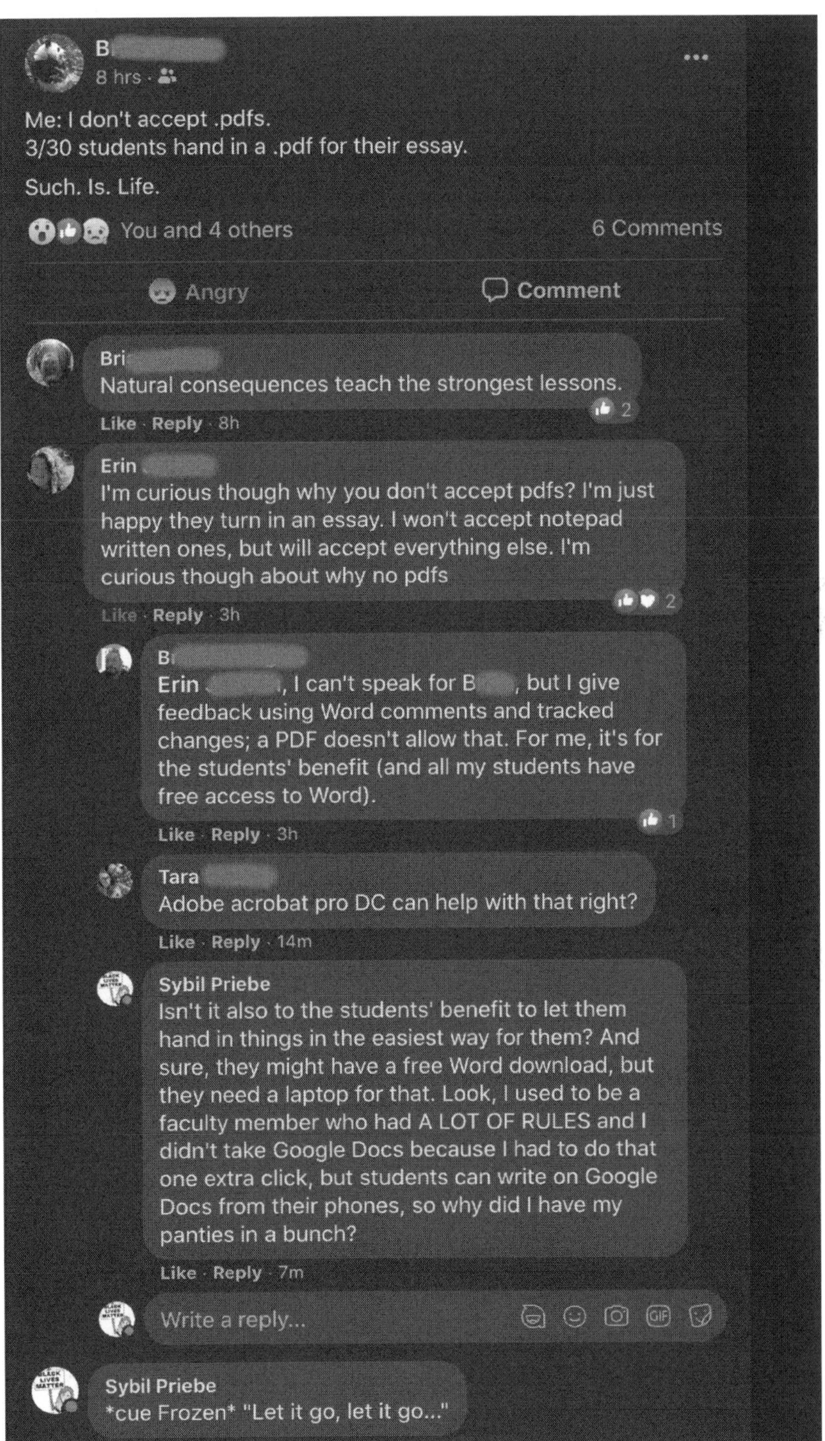
B
8 hrs ·
Me: I don't accept .pdfs.
3/30 students hand in a .pdf for their essay.
Such. Is. Life.
You and 4 others
6 Comments
Angry
Comment
Bri
Natural consequences teach the strongest lessons.
2
Like · Reply · 8h
Erin
I'm curious though why you don't accept pdfs? I'm just happy they turn in an essay. I won't accept notepad written ones, but will accept everything else. I'm curious though about why no pdfs
2
Like · Reply · 3h
Br
Erin , I can't speak for B , but I give feedback using Word comments and tracked changes; a PDF doesn't allow that. For me, it's for the students' benefit (and all my students have free access to Word).
1
Like · Reply · 3h
Tara
Adobe acrobat pro DC can help with that right?
Like · Reply · 14m
Sybil Priebe
Isn't it also to the students' benefit to let them hand in things in the easiest way for them? And sure, they might have a free Word download, but they need a laptop for that. Look, I used to be a faculty member who had A LOT OF RULES and I didn't take Google Docs because I had to do that one extra click, but students can write on Google Docs from their phones, so why did I have my panties in a bunch?
Like · Reply · 7m
Write a reply...
Sybil Priebe
cue Frozen "Let it go, let it go..."

January 7, 2021.

Each day seems like a week. It sometimes feels like the mornings are one 24-hr period, then I nap and wake up to another full day.

And we only made it five days into 2021 without "incident."

Meanwhile, covid deaths are hitting records every fucking day. Yet those scary numbers are ignored due to everything else.

[...]

I think I sent out the liquid syllabus links/emails to students before having some lunch and napping. If I don't specifically record this crud in my iPhone notepad or in here, I lose it... and not because my memory necessarily sucks, but because with everything else going on, it's hard to concentrate. And time has no meaning.

Change (verb)[112]

- to make different in some particular
- to make radically different
- to give a different position, course, or direction to
- to replace with another
- to make a shift from one to another
- to undergo a modification of

Change (noun).

- alteration, transformation, substitution

[112] "Change." Definition. *Merriam Webster*. https://www.merriam-webster.com/dictionary/change

{This page intentionally left blank.}

October 30, 2018.

October 23, 2018.

[...]

Sadie's leg definitely looked bad last night; either she bruised it, or the skin is darkening as it's getting stretched out by the "tumor." I gave her some meds when I got home, and then her nighttime meds were pushed back a few hours. We both slept pretty darn well, so that's a relief. We both needed it. I can foresee her leaving me at a very unfortunate time, like right around the election or right when the holidays pump up. But I continue to remind myself that her not being in pain overrides my need to keep her here. Yes, I still want her to see snow one last time, but... if I were a dog, I wouldn't want to put that kind of obligation on my human. I would trust her to do what's best for me, given the clues to my quality of life. Thus far, the only thing we can see is the oddness in how her back legs operate and the size of the one back leg. She's still eating, she's still peeing/pooping just fine, and she still wants to greet us. I realize that she might have to be let go even while her faculties seem "normal" or typical, based on what that leg does. When I think of them sedating her, and her seeing my face as she goes under, I tear up, but I know she would see me and think everything was alright. And it would be.

Pain-free. Always. For her.

Ugh. Lots of emotions and feelings on a random Tuesday, as usual. I should finish up as much grading as I can and go home to her. I could grade there, too, actually, and my eyelash lady just moved my appointment back to 5:15pm. This way, when I leave here, I can go get Sadie more treats and then be with her until my eyelash/book club stuff. Good call. [...]

October 26, 2018.

Sadie's leg is going to be what "takes her down." On Wednesday morning, I had a headache and some digestive issues.... I called in, informed students, and then I noticed blood on Sadie's leg. That big bad bruise had broken open, as did another smaller spot below the bruised bulge. She was bleeding very little, very superficially, but still I knew this wasn't good. I cleaned it up with witch hazel and used a gauze bandage I found in my medical supplies box. As the day went on, I realized it was never going to stop bleeding. I decided Thursday morning to call the vet and confirm what I was thinking – that eventually it would get infected; it would never heal over because that "tumor" will continue to grow.

I finally got a hold of the vet I had spoken to the most – she had done the x-rays in the summer and had assisted me with the added medication a few weeks ago – and she confirmed what I suspected. I told her that my plan was to spoil Sadie this weekend and then let her go next week. She said that that was a common decision among dog owners, especially those who weren't shocked with an emergency situation.

When Cochise got home, after being gone all week, Sadie was happy to see him and when he saw her leg, I think it dawned on him what crummy situation we were in. Her personality hasn't changed much, and she still eats and walks, but she is limping more and more, and what I've noticed is that she is simply unable to get comfortable on the floor of the living room. He wants us to see how the weekend goes, but in my mind, she's heading downhill, and I don't want her to deal with much pain at all. Last night, she woke me up at 2am and then at 4am to go outside and then she paced for an hour. I finally gave her some meds, and she zonked out until 8am. This morning, when I left for campus around 10am, she didn't want to go outside. I gave her the other half of a vetprophen and came here to get distracted for a bit. I've caught up on my grading, and I have one class: after that, I'm back to her.

I've started cutting up old white sox of mine to use to bandage her leg. This morning, there was blood on the carpet where she had been sleeping, and I said (thank goodness for comedy): "It's okay; I hate this carpet anyway." She sometimes flinches when I touch that big dumb leg, and so I'm sure she is dealing with some pain. She's such a trooper though because she was excited to see Cochise last night, like I said, and she begged for food from him like she always does.

At this point, I want her to have relief. I can control that with drugs this weekend, and then, yeah, we'll see what's up for next week. I cried to Maggie yesterday about her situation, and Maggie wants to be there with me when she goes, and if Cochise can't be with me/us, then I do want her there. I could do it alone, too, because I trust those vets out there.

When I talked to the vet about the appointment next Tuesday (1:30pm), she asked who I would want there –which vet. And I said any of the females. For some reason, losing my shit with them feels like a better plan than crying in front of the older dude. He's nice and professional and all, but I just feel like the ladies get me, and this is a moment when I will need that comfort.

October 30, 2018.

We got Sarah – a good friend of a friend – as the vet. She was sweet, gave us time, and was just the perfect person to put Sadie out of her misery. She gave me tissues and a hug and was so gentle about it all.

She went peacefully, after snoring a bit. I gave her a kiss on her head, told her I loved her a few times, and both Jan and I told her she had been such a good dog.

I go from moments of missing her to moments of relief. Maybe it all hasn't hit me yet, but I remind myself that she definitely needs to be out of her misery. Her last moments were good ones with us, and I know we gave her a great life.

My IG/FB post:

We said goodbye to Sadie today.

Last week, the skin on her enlarging left back leg (probably osteosarcoma) got so stretched out, it started to crack and bleed superficially in two spots. I made the appt then for today to relieve her of her pain; I figured we'd spoil her over the weekend. Then yesterday, that same leg fractured.

For those who don't know, she was surrendered to 4LuvOfDogs with her Newfie brothers in the summer of 2014. Just as we finished our privacy fence, my sweet friend Megan notified me of Sadie's profile. She was a senior dog (9) who was good with cats and kids, and I knew we'd be a great retirement home for her. In August 2014, I picked her up at Nikki's (fantastic foster!), and we listened to Elton John all the way home.

She was the best dog. She loved rolling around in the snow, eating pork rinds with Cochise, sniffing everything in our big yard, and occasionally getting in Sushi's space. She comforted me when campus stuff got chaotic and was the perfect napping companion.

She spent her last days eating fun human food (pumpkin pancakes!), completing one last adventure around the yard (including getting muddy), and receiving lots of hugs and attention. She was still in good spirits this morning when we shared a Pop Tart.

I feel relief that I no longer have to worry about her falling downstairs or getting sad over my absence. I will feel a little lost without her, and extremely sad, but I'm so very, very grateful she was in my life.

#StSadie #RIP #AllSaintsGoToHeaven

I'm sure memories of her will cause me to tear up, I'm sure I might have a full body cry left in me over all this, but we made the right decision for her.

As comments come in on Facebook, I'm weirdly not choked up as much as I thought I would be. Am I exhausted? Shocked? Did I already grieve her loss earlier (remember my post from September 30 when I full body cried about her) and last week? Maybe. Maybe it'll come rushing at me later, but right now, I am okay. I'm okay with the decision, how the weekend went, how peacefully she went… yeah. She was meant to be in our lives, and it was just a win-win all around.

Cochise and I want to put her ashes in the soil of another tree in our yard (maybe an evergreen in the southeast corner); I plan to get a little heart necklace that holds ashes.

Well, maybe I'll be more of a wreck later, but for now, I might zone out with some TV or a tiny nap before we go out to eat (already texted Dad to join us if he wants).

Oh, p.s. I just wrote this to Maggie:

As she passed away, she snored a little bit. It was so cute. And then her face just got peaceful. We left as her bladder released... so there was poo, pee, and blood all over; if you're going to leave a party, leave it like that!

October 31, 2018.

For some reason, I'm second-guessing how her final moments went. Like, I'm wondering if we should've been more concerned with how anxious she was, but she was just skittish and that's how she's been at the vet before. AND since she couldn't move on her own, that compounded her ability to move about as she saw fit as well as observe – little supervisor! – what was happening outside the door. But as the sedative kicked in, she had both Cochise and I right by her. We had our hands petting her and I hope that the smell of us and our voices and the touch helped calm her soul. Once the sedative fully calmed her, she was pissed about Sarah touching her front paw, but… then she just slowly left us. Her face looked so peaceful. I keep that memory stuck in my head, along with the fact that she snored a bit – I hadn't heard her do that since she slept upstairs – and left pee, poo, and blood all over – if you are going to go out, go out big!

I slept like a small tornado last night. I dreamt of her and students, and it was all a mess. It was nice to sleep in a bed finally, and I realized that the couch had been softer. Cochise cautioned me as I threw away her toys yesterday, and I'm sure he's just concerned about me and my mental state with all this, but I'm okay with changing things up... slowly moving into a new normal with new habits and new layouts. I really want to clean up the house now, even though her fuzzies will be a permanent fixture in that home now, and switch up the living room furniture, etc.

I hope all these thoughts I'm having are a reflection of someone who is adjusting well. I'm sure I've been grieving her since the summer when I lost my shit on the phone to Alisa regarding both pets. I've wondered what the house would be like without her large presence countless times, and we all know I've bawled over that dog and her sweet temperament and personality. She loved us, and we loved her.

Lots of dog talk at lunch, and no one ever asked specifically about Sadie. This is fine, and Zooey asked after how it felt to hear everyone's stories. I said that it was okay. And it was. I don't want to put the ka-bosh on anyone's dog life; dogs are great.

In between my 8am and 11am classes, Josie wanted to hug me, and I did lose it a little bit. But it was good to tell someone about her last minutes. I'm sure Maggie will want to hear, too.

[...]

November 4, 2018.

I had some lunch with Charlie on Thursday, and then the "monkeys" met up for drinks around 4:30. Earlier that day, before getting to campus, I stopped by the public library to pick up our book club book and reserve a back-up book to use as a mystery reader Friday. Then I went to get Sadie's ashes. I was fine walking in – seeing her poo in the parking lot was comical to me – but once the vet tech said, "I'm so sorry," I almost cried again.

To add to the bit of humor, they wrote "Sadie" on the bag of ashes that was in the box: correct usage of quotation marks. Perfect. She was a heavy dog, so the ashes weigh a few pounds.

Some will get used in the jewelry I ordered; the rest stored in the garage until spring when we plant a tree in her name.

I told the poo story at drinks and tried not to lose my shit too much. Right before meeting up with the girls (and eventually Johansson), I had sobbed horribly, a full body shaking, with my hands on the box of ashes as they sat on the kitchen island. I think I did this again Friday morning. Full-on sobbing, saying "I miss her so much," with large crocodile tears. My eyes and heart and soul and mind and body have really gone through some shit lately.

My friends have been so very supportive, by the way.

[...]

A week ago, she was still with us. I remember telling myself a week ago that we'd be watching the Bison and Vikings without her a week from then, as if I could completely prepare myself (Sigh). I constantly miss her while also being thankful she went peacefully and didn't end up in a ton of pain... nor did we have to put her down in an emergency situation. It's a weird new normal that I'm trying to create mentally and physically for myself, and I know it will take time.

This process sucks, but yet, I know I'll be stronger in the end. I know she's already made me a better person. So, there's that, too.

Progressive (adjective)[113]

- of, relating to, or characterized by progress
- making use of or interested in new ideas, findings, or opportunities
- of, relating to, or constituting an educational theory marked by emphasis on the individual child, informality of classroom procedure, and encouragement of self-expression
- of, relating to, or characterized by progression
- moving forward or onward: ADVANCING

---

[113] "Progressive." Definition. *Merriam Webster*. https://www.merriam-webster.com/dictionary/progressive

{This page intentionally left blank.}

Bigger and Better.

"You should write a story about this." One of my professors says to me at the English Department workshop[114]. She had asked the deadly question, "Where have you been since you graduated?" and I had responded with a shorter version than what is found here:

The classroom phone rings in the middle of my only freshman class, 5th period. A few students dare me to answer in a particular way, and since I figure it's the main office with a question, I smile. Carol, the secretary, I think will get a kick out of it.

"Jack's Pizza Palace, will this be delivery or carry-out?" My freshmen giggle.

"Sybil, this is Mr. Belchner," my heart rate increases substantially. It's the superintendent.

"Yes?"

"I need to see you in my office this afternoon. To discuss next year's schedule," And with those words, my female intuition kicks in. I am about to get "let go."

The people who couldn't look me in the eyes were the ones who would end up determining my future. At the end of my first year, reflection for next year began and at about the same time that I thought of all my changes I was called into the superintendent's office for a "meeting." He (who had never stepped into my room for longer than a sneeze) proceeded to tell me all the things I had done incorrectly while the principal sat there and said nothing. The principal, a stout fellow who had tried to retire a few times, had given me high marks in

[114] Cindy Nichols embraced me the minute I ended up back at my alma mater's (NDSU) campus for grad school in the fall of 2001. I felt so welcomed.

every evaluation.

He even had a list. Why didn't I learn of these things sooner?

The list included, but was not limited to, my relationship with the students (I was "too friendly"), my attire (my "panty line" was of major concern?), and teaching style (allowing the students to think and feel instead of memorizing facts and how they should think and feel about the literature we were reading). I feel NO need to defend myself because I know that nothing I did was wrong – it was, simply put, different and that scared him. At most, I was a naïve teacher, but, really, when was I going to learn exactly what was expected of me? They had no teacher orientation.

I probably scared a lot of people in that community. I am a young, female teacher that defends her beliefs and ways of doing things. Plus, I didn't want to date (long reasons why) in the community and so that was excessively taboo to them.

Luckily, I was allowed to come back and try to improve myself (which meant to be a little less me and more of someone else I wasn't). I was grateful to come back because of the students. That is the reason many teach. It's obviously not the pay, and it isn't the parents, and it isn't the administration. It IS the kids.

I spent most of the summer as far AWAY from the community as possible. This was the lake town I had fallen in love with at first glance, and I was spending the warm summer back in Fargo with my sister. I began to doubt myself and my teaching and I also thought many people were talking about me. My parents worried about me, and my friends told me to leave the teaching position.

The next school year began easier than the first and like many schools in the area, we had another new batch of teachers coming in. Of all of them, I meshed with three of the ladies, and we all started hanging out. Stress was alleviated with getting together to vent, and, yes, have a cocktail. I make no excuses for these activities because without them, I would have probably killed myself or ended up in a mental facility. And these activities were not because of how the kids affected me, but because of the everyday chaos: parents who think their ideas are better and administration that appeared so shallow even the youngest students could see through their fake exteriors.

It was rough, but with every evaluation from this new principal, I got better and received high marks again. Out of all the bad things mentioned the May before, the outstanding thing I had managed to do was produce an excellent yearbook. So once again, we did.

Flashback to the dialogue at the beginning of this chapter – in March of my second year there, I was informed of a meeting. That Wednesday afternoon, I headed to the same office from the May before. While walking through the Media Center, I took a huge deep breath and told myself that it was happening for a reason. An unknown reason to me at that time, but a reason, nonetheless.

He was blunt. My contract was not going to be renewed; the reason was that I didn't add up to "district standards," and that I should finish up the year "strong."

I sat there as they blabbed on about how "firing people" was not a fun part of their job, and I thought of beating them up. One has to understand that I am not a violent person and here I was with so much adrenaline inside of me that I could have exploded with fire. They made me doubt myself – that was what hurt the most.

In a daze, I returned to my room and e-mailed my family and close friends. I was still in shock as I told my girlfriends throughout the evening, and they took me out to eat because all of them knew that deep down, I needed companions that night. I am still grateful for that and always, always will be.

Before we left the school, we ran into Mr. Kohlmeier, who upon seeing my red, tear-stained face understood what had occurred. He hugged me and simply said, "You are onto bigger and better things, kiddo."

The students wouldn't find out for a week because it had to be approved by the school board the following Tuesday, and I even sat in on the meeting to try to look into the eyes of the parents who had told me I was doing a great job throughout both years. They never looked up and it was all taken care of in seconds. Again, I was utterly crushed.

Trying to teach class the next day and months to follow were difficult. I wrote out what I needed to say to them so I wouldn't choke up. Besides not being violent, I am also not one that ever wants/wanted to show my feelings to the students. They were either completely shocked, saddened, or mad. Many voices were raised in anger towards anything that had to do with it all. Some tried to convince me to stay as if it was my choice. I received hugs the entire day and frequently until the end of the year too. Heart-wrenching is not the word for it.

I am still recovering.

I used many things to numb the pain from that day on. Denial, partying on the weekends, and various trips to see friends to simply get away and drown myself in my music while driving in my car. My decision as to what to do next, however, was made only hours after being "let go." I was going to Graduate School. I didn't want to deal with any school politics anymore. No one deserves to have to question themselves constantly, to doubt themselves, or to get such little respect.

On graduation night that May, the girl who spoke first on behalf of her class, Natalie, brought me to tears as soon as ones started to stream down her rosy cheeks. I finally cried, and it hurt. Yet, as she spoke of going onward on their paths through college and life, I realized that that pertained to me too.

The First Days.

- I remember wearing my hair up in a bun and fake glasses during my first days as a Battle Lake high school teacher. I wanted to appear older than the high school seniors I would have first period. A senior girl called the only Asian in school an offensive name, and I sent her to the principal's office only to hear later that "it's just how she was raised."
- Minard Hall at NDSU was terribly hot that morning. A girl fainted on my first day, and luckily, I knew what to do because I had experienced fainting once. A few students lifted her legs, and one ran into the hallway to call 911 from the wall phone (yep, that was pre-cell phone 2001).
- I cannot pinpoint my first day at NDSCS, but I do recall that I taught five English 105s in a row on MWFs. The early morning commute caused me to witness the wheat fields swaying and the sun rising. The afternoons saw a tired me return to Fargo. I only lasted one year as a commuter; the winter made that decision for me.

Holiday Letter, January 2005.

Dearly Beloved,

I have officially decided that if I see one more tapered leg jean on someone in this town, I am going to freak out. Sure, maybe it's got something to do with the fact that I am obsessed with *Sex and the City*, mainly Sarah Jessica Parker (I clap like a 5-year-old who just got a pony every time I see her on TV), but some people have no clue. I, apparently, have no clue as to when to properly send out holiday cards, but I really don't give a shit.

Essentially, I will finally be getting my ass out of graduate school come May 13th (Friday the 13th, mind you). Jodi and I both graduate, so it's going to be a big deal and a big party with a big keg. Before all that, I am teaching three classes of first-year English Composition at NDSU, and this semester I landed a small gig with Aaker's Business College on Wednesday nights teaching their Foundations of English class: a class NDSU should have.

After I graduate, I would love to get a teaching job in Duluth, have a fabulous apartment near the lake, and maybe write on the side for a magazine or newspaper. I want to stay around here due to the seasons (I like not shaving for 6 months and wearing tall boots) and the cost of living.

As far as the boyfriend goes, Cochise gave me my first diamonds for Christmas. In the photos, I am wearing the earrings and necklace he gave me: silver, heart-shaped, and sparkly. If he ends up still in my life when I move (or not), then that's cool. I refuse to worry about that. Sure, I'd like to have a family (I think) but having a stable job might be a good idea to begin with. Boy, do I sound logical!

We had a fabulous year of parties at our house: Leap Beer 2004 Party, Pimps and Hoes Party II [left me with a bruised cheek (because I missed the last step of our basement staircase and used my face to stop myself because I had beer in my hands) and a dirty cowboy hat (fell on my dad's dirt pile outside when I tried to pee behind the shed)], and the second annual Halloween Party.

Not much has changed about me. I am still a weirdo, I still have the Bug (turned 5 in December), I still like to rip it up, and I still like Lionel Richie. And I still have a crabby cat named Sushi.

On my plate for 2005: I turn 28 and graduate (damn rhyming!), two of my longtime friends are getting married (Nichole in March and Fran in July), and I hope to find a kick-ass job teaching or writing. If you want to read up on me, check out the *Spectrum*'s Site, or the *BisonBlog*. Take care all. Hope you like the photos! ☺

Maggie's motto: "Staying alive, drink a lot – don't deprive, it's mutha f*ckn' 2005."

Unknown Date.

Periodically, I take a look back at my journal entries to "see" where I have been, and maybe where I plan to end up. At times, it's been depressing; I've fallen into the words and let them consume me too much. But, luckily, at other times, I am able to say, "Sybil, that teacher – that girl/woman/person – brought you to this place. Without her and her mistakes, you wouldn't be HERE, and you really like being HERE, so it's all okay."

In recent memory, losing our St. Bernard Sadie (October 2018) was the catalyst for so much change in my life – mostly professional. I felt the need to cheer myself up after her passing October 30, 2018, and so I placed myself on the Ph.D. path – a path I've thought about many times before. The application went in on Christmas, and before then, it had already led to a conversation with a colleague (Zooey) about how she saw me as a "growth-seeking individual."[115]

The spring of 2019 was filled with much anxiety. I interviewed with the School of Education at NDSU at the beginning of March, and then didn't hear anything until the end of May – my sister's birthday actually. It was as if in that time period, I had convinced myself I wasn't ready or wasn't a fit or didn't want to spend the $20k (my campus would've covered some tuition), and I even found myself on Easter diving into Twitter like I never had before. I found webinar after webinar about OER and Instructional Design, and the universe decided for me: use Twitter to educate yourself.

That summer, I signed up for the Creative Commons Certification course ($500 – money well spent) and a free Wikiversity course on OEP. I continued to follow fabulous people on Twitter and signed up for anything that sounded remotely interesting. I also checked hashtags from time to

[115] One of the best compliments I've ever received. Truly.

time, especially #OER, and found so many helpful textbooks, materials, and articles. I started a Google doc titled "My Twitter Education Blog" and posted URLs to everything I wanted to read or had read, etc.

The one hashtag that "haunted" me (unsure if that's the verb to use here) was #ungrading. People were discussing the removal of letter grades, the necessity of feedback over points, and other ideas that had alarms in me going off left and right.

STUDENTS ASSESSING THEMSELVES? WHAT?

I ignored the hashtag and told myself it wasn't for me. I loved my rubrics; I liked that they "seemed" objective to me... that they covered "the requirements." The course revolved around my needs, but surely, it was engaging and interesting and fun and all the other damn words teachers use to convince themselves their courses are student-centered when NONE of the materials are centered on anyone but the teacher.

Oooof. I said a lot there, yes?

Yes.

Eventually, ya'll know what happens. The hashtag got IN. Last fall, I sat at my office desk often wondering what it would look like to completely release control of grades. To give students choice and agency. Weirdly, the pandemic was the first "test" of these new ideas. A more inclusive pedagogy and ungrading followed me as we went remote in March, and students were granted extra time on projects. I wasn't full of angst when they emailed me with issues. I didn't stress out when I assessed their work.

As the world was freaking out, everything in me chilled the fuck out in regard to late work and grades and, yes, even the language used in student writing. At the 4Cs in Pittsburgh back in the spring of 2019, Asao Inoue delivered a "controversial" keynote that I missed out on, but I heard so much about. Essentially, he was harsh with us: we need to stop propping up "proper English" as the "best English" and instead include all sorts of English, including Ebonics/Black English/African-American English. After taking parts of his speech in and reading comments from experts on Twitter, I agreed. I looked back on how I had taught enough students of color, and I wished I could go back and instruct them differently.

I also wish I could go back and ask myself, "Why are you being such a dick?" When I tell my department members this, they say I wasn't a dick. But I was. And I'm unsure why. Sure, in college, we were taught to have policies, and I was given the advice that I should be a bitch to students for the first few weeks of teaching, but where did I get the ideas that my English class had to be so STRICT? And all along, with these stupidly strict policies, I bragged about how fun and student-centered my class was. What a joke.

At least I can admit it. The old ways were shit. Yes, students still enjoyed my classes, and I enjoyed them most of the time, but things could've been more inclusive. I could've done better, and now that I know better, I will do better (I am paraphrasing Maya Angelou). In wanting to do better, my anxiety levels have lowered… I have less students failing the classes, and assessment doesn't give me high blood pressure.

I'm so grateful for being denied entry to a doctoral program, I love what Twitter did for my professional/pedagogical development, and I cannot say enough good stuff about the Creative Commons and OER and the people connected to those entities.

At the conclusion of this last year (19-20), I had officially been teaching at NDSCS for fifteen years. I foresee the next twenty years to be filled with less hateful email messages and more passion projects.

Quotes.

March 26, 2020.

One quote from today's Zoom meeting and something I said while chatting on someone's patio.

- "I've snorted a lot of things up my nose in my day, but I've never done that" (a colleague, in regard to what people were doing – blowing a hair dryer up their noses to prevent COVID-19).
- "This pandemic shit is like porn for worrywarts" (Me, venting about my mom looking for TP upon their return to Wahpeton in a week).

Reflection.

Saturday March 24, 2007

Questions:
Which way is the path to getting students to learn? [There are many.]
In having to defend myself constantly, am I only realizing how more on track I am? [Perhaps.]
If one feels in defense, should they ask the same of others - to defend their practices? [Maybe.]
When does one know they are trying to do too much in a class for one semester? [I don't know.]
When should one just let situations & problems "roll off" his/her back?
Posted 3/24/2007 at 12:2 AM

Thursday December 20, 2007

Maybe I am wrong. (*It's happened before.*) But when I am not at on campus in my office or in front of students, I am still thinking about how to improve it all. I'm thinking about education and how it can and should impact everyone's lives. I'm thinking about how to better my teaching methods, how to make practically everything in my classes relevant, how to connect this with that, how to make it all worthwhile to even those who come in with the "it's just bonehead English" attitude. What I may be wrong about is that I assume (eeek) that others of other professions do not do this when they aren't at work, if ever. Do bankers think about how to make things easier on their customers, or real estate agents think of trying to only sell "green" houses, or lawyers about how to make the justice system work faster and better for all involved?
These constant thoughts are what possibly keep me from enjoying my breaks, yet I need them to continue to be

passionate and current with what I am doing, with what is going on.
Now... I've heard my own dad say, "Yea, he takes his job too seriously." Am I doing that too? And if I am or if people do, is that such a bad thing?
[I wonder if I can use any of these thoughtful blog entries in my tenure-track portfolio? Now, that's a better, more-light-hearted thought for the season. :-D Thank you to my sister, Maggie, for making me laugh very hard yesterday and today.]
Posted 12/20/2007 at 5:16 PM

Wednesday December 3, 2008

It smacked me upside the head today (again), sitting in my English 110 class. It's going to sound really dumb, really dumb, but my students, when they write about themselves, they are so honest. BRUTAL. And this particular paper ("Who Are You?" multi-genre) always brings out the best writing. Due to that, I sit there amazed. I sit there thinking, "Wow. These people have lives outside this classroom." That's obvious; it sometimes takes a good ol' roundtable peer review session for that thought to reappear in my melon. Like a long lost commercial: "Hey, these 'kids' have been through some crap. What can I possibly say as feedback?"

So many of my colleagues are quick to judge and say that students a) don't know how to write, b) can't write about themselves well, and c) are too involved in themselves to understand the world around them... All these things, for the most part, are just way off. Way off.
[...]
Posted 12/3/2008 at 9:24 PM

Sunday May 2, 2010

In the middle of a dream, I came up with a motto or something... and I remember most of it. A paraphrase: "There are students who want to learn and those who don't.
It's my job to encourage the first bunch and change the minds of the other."

Something like that. It was a re-do of Friday's Party, almost. It was a large room with more empty space than people, and my dad was there. I gave a speech about loving my job and how:
"Many people in this spot have said that they didn't think they'd teach forever or that they'd be here long. I'm different; I knew I would retire from here." Again, I'm paraphrasing my own dream. So weird that I recall some of it.

I did have a year or two *way back when* when I thought teaching there was not going to *pan out*. But things were *taken care of*, and even though the situation wasn't completely resolved, I found supporters when I hadn't at my first school. That was the defining moment. Maybe I knew after all that, that this was the place for me. My two bosses weren't going to let others get in my way of good blasphemy.
Posted 5/2/2010 at 10:16 AM

Wednesday May 5, 2010

My sister said something last night, as we hit up the McD's drive-through, that she's said before. She said, "Well, Sybil, you've had a lot of luck getting to where you are." I agreed. *At that time.*
But now, I'm thinking... about how I've told that to others, mainly my boyfriend, and he said that it was hard work that got me to where I'm at. And I agreed with him. *At that*

time.

So, now, I'm wondering which it is. A little of both? *Let's recap*:

It definitely wasn't luck that lead me to getting "let go" from my first teaching job. It was an adminstration's judgment of me + my stubborn-ness. I'd say it was more them screwing up than me screwing up, but I'm biased. Anyhow, it wasn't luck or hard work that got me into grad school. I simply sent in my application, and since they knew me (and I had all the stuff in the application/had most of the grades - found out later that one professor who looked at my application commented in print that since I had a "C" in a few literature classes, I shouldn't be admitted; it was in print, after that, that someone else stated, "Dude, she wants a Master's in Composition; who cares about her literature grade?"), I was admitted.

Hard work earned me an "A" in most classes after that. It was my non-literature background and brain that lead to my only "B" in Hippie Literature (also called Literature of the 60s and 70s), but other than that, I did what I was supposed to do. I accomplished too much in some courses, and maybe only the minimal A (which is what an "A" student says?) work in others.

Then, I took my sweet-ass time with my thesis. I was about ready to graduate in 2004, but my advisor suggested sticking around for another year to conduct another month-long research study[116]. I was okay with that; I was not in a rush to get into the real world of hunting down a community college spot.

I didn't grab another job for that last year, just lived off my loans and stipend. I worked on the thesis, defended it at the end of April, walked through Graduation in May of

[116] My research was on blogs, and I have so many old blog entries about the process of writing the Master's Paper. I might have to turn that into a book, too?

2005. Then, I applied at many places; more spots were open in 2005 than in 2004 - coincidence or luck?
Well, I didn't apply at an overwhelming amount of schools, by any means, but most the area - even to places without ads online and in papers. I had a boyfriend, and I wanted to be close to family.
I got a skinny letter from Duluth first. I was heart-broken. Then I had an interview way up north on the MN side; I thought it went well; I found out later that they hired 3 of the 4 people they interviewed. That felt awesome! No, not really. Then came the interview in the F/M area. I walked into the interviewing room, because I was early, and accidentally interrupted the interview before me. I found out later that they were looking for traditional, literature-based instructors. A colleague of mine from NDSU didn't get hired either, and she's a fabulous teacher! Neither one of us had luck there.
Then came Fran's wedding in late July. One of my best friends, and I was a bridesmaid. NDSCS called to schedule an interview for the day after I returned at 8am. At that point, I was semi-defeated. I had told myself at age 18 that I didn't want to move "home" and live in my "stupid hometown."
But I went out to Portland and celebrated with Fran and Josh. I got home, barely slept, and then drove to my interview. I barely remember that morning; I recall telling the committee that it would be really neat to work on the campus where I learned to ride my bike. Later, Walter stated that it was cool that I was a "hometown girl" but that that didn't seal the deal. My attitude and knowledge did, and that's not luck. :o)
Has it been happy days ever since I got the call from an administrator and screamed into the phone? No. But it's about the majority of time. The majority of my days are filled with creativity and fun and ... overall enjoyment. I

look forward to coming to campus; I come early and stay late most days when I don't have to.
If that's luck, fine. If it's hard work, cool. At this point, I'm just happy and want others to find this as well.
"Most people would rather be certain they're miserable, than risk being happy." ~Robert Anthony~
Posted 5/5/2010 at 9:42 AM

Wednesday March 30, 2011

In my giddiest daydream about how my teaching can affect students, I dream that they see writing as fun and not something they are incapable of. In addition to that, I dream that they find a book, an author, that they look forward to reading every day or every week. In that goosebump-induced dream, I don't even care if they only like to write erotic poetry or read about serial killers or research anarchy. The dream doesn't even include them putting down the Crackberry or logging off Facebook; it's just an addition to their lives. They read The Onion, perhaps, via Facebook and laugh. They read from a slang dictionary to their friends over lunch. It doesn't have to be boring, and it doesn't have to be appropriate. Language and books and writing spans too many genres and generations to limit what I want them to do, love, and learn.

Just writing that made my day start off ... on a lighter note.
Posted 3/30/2011 at 9:17 AM

Wednesday June 6, 2012

...19 in each section, as of today.
And, as of today, I have not received an email that made me think, "WTH," so that's good.
I have a feeling that these online sections will be good batches of students.

Maybe I just feel better prepared - every semester, I feel more prepared than the previous, though.
:o)
Will I ever feel like I have "mastered" all of this? Probably not. I'm okay with that.

I have buddhas surrounding me in my new little home office. They will keep me creative & calm.
Posted 6/6/2012 at 2:48 PM

January 6, 2016.

Ever since talking to the neurologist right before the end of the year – and even before then a bit – I started to feel a shift in how I viewed my body and mind and life. I may not have a lot of time left. Hell, we all might not if Trump becomes president... I "joke," but seriously, I figured for a long time that I would end up being someone who would die of old age. I'd be farting around at age 99, cursing out relatives that still came to see me, etc. But maybe I won't be around that long, and I don't know if I am that distraught about that possibility. Sometimes, I'm just really tired of people and of trying to convince people to THINK. People, all around me, seem pretty sure that they are on the RIGHT path – that they are doing everything we're supposed to do as good humans, but they fail to recognize even the SLIGHTEST possibility that I – yes, nerdy, sweary, Sybil – might have her poop in a group MORE than they do. What if I HAVE IT FIGURED OUT and they don't? Has that occurred to any [...] out there? Has it? Probably not, those judgey-ass Judgey McJudgersons.

The fact of the matter is that I might be a "visionary[117]" who is completely misunderstood... so much so that no one will ever know it in my time on earth. No one will give a shit now, and

[117] The definition of a visionary - courtesy of *Merriam Webster* - is "one having unusual foresight and imagination" or "one whose ideas or projects are impractical" or "one who sees visions."

no one will probably give a shit later, but I will have said it. I have written it down that perhaps the world's problems lie in what we think we are supposed to do. We are supposed to NOT challenge the authority around us, we are supposed to NOT burn bridges and tell people off, we are supposed to be GOOD little consumers and continue to pop people out of our lady bits so they can be good consumers of materials and churches and all that... we're not supposed to question why we aren't all driving electric cars or why marijuana is still illegal when it's obvious that those things are happening because of money and greed. Money and greed have fucking ruined humans. And I'm – daily, fucking hourly – trying super hard to look past that to the good stuff out there. I'm trying to find pepper in poo, though; it's difficult. It's almost impossible.

So, no fucking wonder I look forward to new semesters... new classes of students where that little classroom is just for us to be around other humans and talk about writing... no greed involved, no money, no Trump. Just us and our voices. I hibernate there. I hibernate even in the students who drive me nuts. Why? Because their complaints aren't even greed-driven or money-driven; they are just baby egos that need reassurance, and don't we all want that?

I'm getting way too philosophical for a HUMP day, so I had better go home... pet my dog, take a nap, and then sweat my balls off at hot yoga.

January 25, 2016.

As the oldest, I've had to do everything first. Well, almost everything. And that can take a toll, no? When you are the only person you can truly rely on, day in and day out? Yes, it has caused some major independence on my part as well as – on the opposite end – major commitment issues (I don't think I could depend solely on another person forever?).

Another epiphany I had this morning was that I'm glad I have started to write these books. Sure, they are mostly about teaching, and I've fictionalized them to protect idiots, but I am recording my thoughts. If no one ever reads these fucking journals, they will at least be a record of my thoughts. Whether those thoughts are nasty or not, is not for me to decide, sometimes. And this is nothing new to me: the writing of my thoughts. I kept journals for years and maybe they should be put into digital form. I like being able to look back and see what was going on on Day X.

[...]

November 30, 2016.

So, on Monday, the day of rest I gave myself before the chest pains started, I watched *Wild* – the movie based on the book we read for book club recently. Some of the ladies in our book club complained about the book – finding feminist issues with it – and some complained that the movie wasn't that great either. I disagreed on both accounts, slightly. I think I watched the movie at the right time, perhaps, which is why I don't find as much fault with it. For instance, right now, I'm trying to find peace. I know I have to let go of the regressed anger from my childhood; the movie touches on this... the main character had to let it go, had to let it be what it was. Now, do I have to "let things go" in the present when my mom (or dad) says something that's not quite right? No. This is the present.

The person I was last year, in the last decade, in my past life (for those who believe in reincarnation) is a person who brought me HERE. She has evolved. She has gained experience and had insights and been through turmoil. She's been defeated and depressed and had dangerous thoughts, and it's ALL okay. IT IS ALL OKAY. All of it. All of the good and bad brought me right fucking here, and I can't judge them anymore. It's exhausting.

As for the present, I am stressed. The muscular chest issues yesterday and Monday night clue me into that. As does the pimple (small as it is) on my face; I never get zits. Never. I'm not bragging; it's just a tell-tale sign that something is fucked in my system. So, I need to de-stress even as the semester is wrapping up.

June 3, 2018.

[...]

On Friday morning, I cancelled my eye appointment; everything was feeling much better. Maggie texted that she'd be down by 2:30pm, and her and mom took off for downtown (Blue Goose Days) while I waited around for the plumber, who was slated to come down around 3-4pm. Once he gave me a $1200-1500 estimate, I biked to meet up with those two at the Brew. I thought it was going to be a short trip of a few drinks and then dinner, but we were there – or at the street dance a block away – until about 10pm. Yes, we all walked home, too. Nut jobs. We ran into all sorts of fun people, we took a good selfie with James Wateland in between sharing funny stories, and I ended up talking to a former sand volleyball friend who talked so much about himself that I was only able to get in like two sentences about myself. Some people apparently don't know what a dialogue is; most just like their monologues, but hey, if he needed to tell me all about himself to make himself feel better, whatever. Some people simply need reassurance or some sort of boost to their self-esteem or some sort of weird acknowledgment that they are doing cool things. I don't know for sure, but even in my drunken haze, I noticed how little I spoke. I notice stuff like this all the time now... my parents didn't ask for more info the night I went to their place and vented about campus. I mentioned the mayor idea at Lizzie's wedding Saturday, and no one really said much except Lola pretended to hit me in the forehead (which I assume means I'd be stupid to consider the idea).

All this intrigues me. The people who need to speak so much versus those who are interrupted or ignored. The people who don't ask how others are doing. The people around me who claim to be friends of mine, but who don't want to hear about my reflections or ideas. Is that why I write? Do I feel that much kinship with the page that I find solace here instead of with people[118]?

I just called Maggie to vent about these things... is this why I feel more loneliness AROUND people than when I am by myself? Probably. I get around other humans and realize that I'm not playing by the right rules or something. Maybe I should be interrupting people more? Maybe my listening skills don't matter? Then again, those things aren't me; it's not authentic.

I guess that all this is a possible mind fuck for most people? Maybe I'm not saying anything new. Maybe this isn't an original thing to be speaking to; maybe everyone feels like we're all not being listened to. I can only speak for myself, of course, and I realize my perspective might be off. It's just one perspective; maybe I talk too much, too. Maybe I'm hogging up air space without knowing it. And maybe because I reflect too much, I notice it. Everyone else – the friends I saw last night, the former sand volleyball comrade – perhaps is walking away from the interaction thinking it went well. That it was fine and dandy. I have no idea, truly. And here I am shitting on it with my reflection. Oh well.

June 22, 2018.

[...]

Each day is about just taking care of me. My mental health, my physical health, and everything else in between. I've found myself worried about not using my summertime "correctly," and I think I do that every damn summer, so I simply have to stop that. Or the mantra that needs to pop up when I "worry" about my time management should be: One Day At A Time. Same during the school year!

There is no "correct way" to use the summer. Look at poor Mr. TM who finally didn't go into campus yesterday; it was his first day "off" since the school year wrapped up. It's not like he's doing summer "wrong," but at least that's not what has

---

[118] Yes.

happened for me. I've been able to just concentrate on shaking off all the shit of the school year while bulking up the tools that will help me in the future. If I can do anything for myself – for Future Sybil – it's to prepare myself now for the crud that will be tossed my way. Like Tasha[119] said, I can control me; I can't control the path in front of me.

[...]

July 13, 2018.

It's going to sound cheesy to anyone I tell it to – if I do – but this summer has definitely been about soul-searching. It's not like I don't think I CONSTANTLY search for truths and spiritual guidance anyway, but this summer has definitely been about that very cheesy endeavor. And I'm transferring fucking knowledge all over the damn place, too, as I read. With Brene Brown's theories on vulnerability and shame come some of the same echoing thoughts of how people have to be open to change and not base their happiness on external shit. Then from those ideas come the theories that Mark Manson has regarding not putting your fucks into everything others give fucks about. Overall, observation of thought is SO DAMN IMPORTANT because if you are guilt-tripping yourself or saying you SHOULD want to do something or waiting for some "shoe" to drop before you attempt something risky or cool... those are fucks you don't need to be giving.

Clear your mind and jump in the damn pool already!

[...]

Boom. So, of course, now I want to read that book. But first, I want to finish up Brene Brown, and I do have another one of her books on loan from the library (due in a few days). *Braving The Wilderness* starts with her disagreement with a quote from Maya Angelou about belonging. She tells the story about not fitting in with her family, and how that's the basis of belonging, period. It got me thinking about my first experiences with

[119] My first acupuncturist; she was amazing and is now helping out vets!

family troubles and belonging with them and with school mates… I had to come to this journal and write about what I remember.

I definitely remember connecting with our dad the most. Mom was so hard to read at times – I still can see her face as she'd come home from work on a Friday, and how we would wait to see if she was in a good mood or not before asking to do things (stay over at friends' houses, order pizza, etc.). Dad worked hard, and long hours, and yet never took the workplace angst out on us. Yes, he was stoic at times and drank beer to probably numb certain things, but he was the more consistent parent. Even when our parents fought, I don't think I ever thought they were fighting because they disliked us. […]

As far as belonging in our family, I remember being told I was stupid a few times which didn't immediately send me to tears (again, from what I remember); instead, I was very stoic. This non-emotional part of me was brought up at least once when I was watching *Beaches* (or some movie like that) with my mom and sisters. They were crying, and I wasn't. My mom said I was cold-hearted; I'm possibly paraphrasing, but yeah. And I know it bothered her that I didn't love the sport of volleyball as much as she did. I played the damn sport – liking it most of the time – from about 4th grade until I gave it up in 11th to just be a manager of the team. The coach didn't like me, and I cared WAY too much about tennis. I tell this story a lot, but my parents made it to very few of my sporting events compared to my youngest siblings. Dad's work schedule rarely allowed him to attend anything, but when it did make it to a tennis match, he tried to understand what the hell was going on. Mom, on the other hand, didn't try. And when it came to volleyball, she'd comment on how often I didn't play. Sure, I wasn't as good as the others – I will admit that – but perhaps she didn't see that they were all going to camps in the off-season; these camps were out of reach financially for my family even if I did want to attend.

Anyhow, when it comes to school, I wasn't popular, and I didn't really try to fit in by being like everyone else. My earliest memories of elementary school show a girl who got teased for not brushing her hair by the more popular girls. I had one best friend, and once we hit middle school, she bumped up the ranks, and I just coasted between random friend groups and loner-hood. I'm sure this bothered me somewhat, but I don't remember how much I cared. I knew the popular crew was drinking and hanging out on weekends; I strongly recall loving Friday nights to myself in my room to read. I also recall loving Friday nights when our family was together and doing the pizza/movie thing. As chaotic as our home life could be, it was a norm I could manage. Or maybe I numbed it all out with Danielle Steele books. Who knows.

I was pretty smart (top 25% of our graduating class of 99) and fairly good at athletics (nominated to Miss Tennis of ND), but I doubt anyone I graduated with would say I was extremely memorable or out-spoken. Once at college, I blossomed a bit finding more friend groups, discovering alcohol, and thinking about what I really believed in (compared to my parents' political and religious leanings). Maybe what all of this is telling me is that I do agree with Maya Angelou's quote about not belonging and how that is a great freedom. I don't have a problem not fitting in, and I belong with the right groups for me at the right time. Like, when I went to TYCAMW for the first time; those people felt like MY people immediately. Perhaps my upbringing has led me to that agreement with Maya that Brene didn't have, and that's okay.

I don't know how much more reminiscing to do today.

August 15, 2019.

[...]

Okay, so I started thinking about this "20 years" post I want to publish on FB. Yep, it's been twenty years of teaching for me. We partied like it was literally 1999...

I suppose it'll go something like this:

Date: August 1999

Scene: A brand-new high school English teacher decorates her classroom. She places knick-knacks near her desk to remind her of family and friends, she looks through the books that have landed in her cupboards (Yay: Fahrenheit 451; Boo: Shakespeare), and she reads through the Minnesota Standards, planning the lessons and projects of the year for her seniors, juniors, and freshmen. She educates herself on the program that will help her students create the yearbook; she educates herself on how and where to make copies and the names of the secretaries and other teachers.

She doesn't know everything she needs to know, but she's ambitious. She's creative. She's new to it all and wants to figure out how this teaching thing will look on her.

+

A lot has happened since then, of course.

I bought my bug, I've rescued a cat off the "mean streets" of Fargo, I've found a partner-in-crime, I've purchased a house, I've become an aunt, we've adopted an old sweet dog, and on many occasions, I've attempted to "kill myself" completing triathlons.

I've educated myself in numerous ways and met so many wonderful people. I've read SO MANY PAPERS.

It's been twenty years. And I wouldn't change a thing.

Not the break-up with that one guy in 1999, not the return to grad school after not seeing my contract renewed for year three at BLHS, not the chaotic department I walked into here at NDSCS, not the doctoral program rejection I received a few months ago... and definitely not all the student words I've gotten to read.

I still don't know everything I need to know, and somehow, that excites me.

September 29, 2019.

I made the executive decision at some point this week that since I was finished updating the hell out of my/our OER textbooks, I would focus in on me... I would start to edit my teaching books/journals. It's been a LONG while since I published Book 1; thus, I cracked open the journal entries attached to Book 2 (Year 2015-2016). This was the school year when we "lost" Lola. This was the school year Brit left and Josie joined us.

Because of this new immersion in Book 2, I wanted to spend the weekend reading and editing, and I have. What I've learned is that my teaching style and history definitely parallel the diet stuff I've gone through. What I mean is that I didn't know what I didn't know, and I was just doing my best – doing what I thought was best. But now as I read these entries, I sigh with how angry I was at students (at times), how weirdly attached I was to my "policies," but... when you haven't fallen into a Twitter rabbit hole and done some heavy self-reflection... when you haven't taken a summer to focus on yourself... when you have been overwhelmed with negativity from others (and sometimes yourself), things happen that you aren't able to SEE right away.

I regret feeling that way and writing in that way to a certain degree, but if it's a true memoir, it is what I was feeling at the time. I can't change it, and I think I was meant to feel all that then and I think I was meant to find the Twitter rabbit hole this last spring when I was wondering what the fuck happened to my doctoral program application.

When students can't get their poop in a group, it's easy to be upset with them. I don't think anyone can or would blame teachers for that, but as a teacher who is slowly moving away from that harsh reaction, I see how unhealthy it was for my mental health and classroom environment. I doubt that I have gone from average teacher to amazing overnight, but shit, my anger has died down... it's saved for worldly politics, perhaps.

Life is definitely made up of these moments of reaction, and I'm learning that they are better ways for me to react that still keep my boundaries intact but don't intimidate students to the levels I once did. If that makes sense.

[...]

Yesterday, I re-read Book 1. I wanted to make sure the vibe was similar in Book 2 and reading Book 1 brought back SO MUCH. I drank so much more and was probably focused on food and exercise too much (lots of double workouts). I did find a few errors – the code names I gave to people were so good; I can't recall who the hell they are – but otherwise, it was okay. I can see a non-teacher getting confused by the jargon, but oh well.

What I've noticed thus far in Books 2+ is that I'm pissier with the out-of-class issues on campus, and I don't mention what I'm doing in the classroom much. So, perhaps I'll try to be more intentional about that in this set of journals, and then when I edit Books 3-5, I'll attempt to go back through and add in the assignments, at least in the Appendix[120]. I mean, when did I stop using the Grading Contracts? I think I phased them out without trying? Or maybe that was on purpose? I've read, too, that when it comes to the T&R committee[121], I let that whole Helpful/Instructional Booklet and New Process (portfolios go straight to committee) to die out at the end of the spring (2016) when the admin didn't put me on their agenda for the department chair meeting. I suppose by the time Fall 2016 came around, we were too deep in budget shit for me to notice that those two items got thrown away. I'm sure admin appreciated that.

[...]

---

[120] Maybe I'll do this, but maybe it's also another book project: the book of wacky assignments?

[121] I have a lot more to say about this committee and "leadership" and "professionalism" in another book I'm working on. Yes, after compiling ALL of my old and new journal and blog entries (etc.), I had 2-3 books' worth of stuff. So… stay tuned?

October 17, 2019.

[...]

And I just read some more passages from Becky[122], which made me reflect. She wrote about how certain events have brought her to this spot in her life. It was all meant to be the way it was. I've noticed this semester that I've been getting down on myself for the attitude I've had in the past with students. There's a part of me that says, "Hold up, now, missy, some of your students do deserve some tough love and sassy response and the occasional silent treatment; you are simply choosing now NOT TO rely on those techniques. It's not bad, it's just a DIFFERENT approach." It's too easy to say, "Oh, I should've done this sooner," because I didn't know then what I know now.

Last summer didn't have the same conditions as the summer before. In the summer of 2018, I was sleeping in the living room with Sadie. I'm sure I still nerd-ed up on things, but it wasn't as passionate as this last summer, and that's okay. I didn't want to take a class about Creative Commons Certification, nor did I know about the Wikiversity stuff because I hadn't been sucked into Twitter as much.

And then – beep – like that, after Sadie passed, I wanted to turn inward to me and care for my sad insides. So, I applied to the doctoral program, and in realizing that that wasn't going to happen, I moved to a different sort of education for myself. Each step led to where it was supposed to lead. The same could be said for my job here; if I would've graduated in three years with my Master's, this job would not have been open. Sometimes the universe screws us over – this can't be denied – but sometimes the universe is looking out for us. George Carlin whispers to my subconscious in my sleep, perhaps, that the doctoral program is not the way to go: "Save yourself $20k little lady and fucking do your own thing." Amen. Truly. Amen.

So, yeah. How's that for some reflection before noon.

---

[122] Former student turned k-12 teacher who wrote her own book!

[…]

December 23, 2019.

[…]

Anyhow… before I log off and plug in this beautiful MacBook (so glad I purchased her, by the way; I have a plan to recycle the iMac upstairs soon and use the credit for a new iPhone – hopefully, this can all wait until next Christmas. I'd also like a new modem & router next year, but yeah), I'd like to reflect and compare this year to last. Last year, I had a student call me a bitch, and I was pissy with Walter about the English 120 online blowing up for spring. This year, no one called me a bitch and Walter figured out a new plan for Online English 120 – I teach one section and Cecila the other and now I will officially ONLY TEACH FIVE SECTIONS[123] for the first time in a LONG time. Like probably a decade.

When it comes to academics, I submitted my doctorate application on Christmas Day last year. I was so hopeful and optimistic that that was the next path for me, and the universe had other ideas. Since I didn't hear boo by Easter, I went on Twitter seeking out training and BOOM, now I am Twitter nut and I've attended a BUNCH of webinars and I have kept a very helpful (and private) Twitter Education Blog that is many pages long. […]

I miss Sadie, but I feel I'm on some track to eventually adopt again. Maybe a few German Shepherds. Maybe after Sushi is in heaven. I will definitely wait until after the trip to Milwaukee next year after spring break for TYCA National and the 4Cs.

I bought a new car this year, I paid off my student loans, and I got my own office. The latter has been a big adjustment, but I think I will be kinder to Josie without having to take on her drama daily like I was. Yes, the drawbacks are more

[123] Yes, I taught overload – 6/6 plus summer school – for many years.

isolation, but with that isolation comes creativity, too. And like I said, less drama.

I love the Jeep, and I haven't had one ounce of buyer's remorse or regret over saying goodbye to the Bug.

This next year will be interesting, for sure. Rumor has it that Theo Brokaw is retiring, so I'll have a new faculty member next door... presenting on OER with Tom at TYCA National could be fun and insightful... continuing to work on our own TYCAMW conference has been fun, too (hopefully, we nail down Louise Erdrich!), and gosh... I think I'm just hopeful. Oh, right, there's an election next November; I hope that goes as BLUE as it can.

April 4, 2020.

I'm up early, again. No matter what time I go to sleep (9pm or 10:30pm or later), my body wants to be up around 4am or 5:30am. I think yesterday was the first time in a while that I woke up past 6am. I do like to be up early, but isn't 4am a little excessive? It reminds me of when I commuted my first-year teaching at NDSCS. I'd leave Fargo between 5-7am, and it would sometimes be dark, and I would sometimes catch the sunrise over the fields – the wind pushing the product in those fields in one particular direction. The color of the sky and the earth. Those mornings were so calm; they were the calm before the storm of the chaos of the day's events. And now there's calm all the time with most people working from home and/or children schooling from home, and I suppose the chaos – if I need to be metaphorical or philosophical at this hour – is within us instead of outside. Okay, I guess if you lived in a larger city there may still be chaos outside – at stores and at hospitals, but here in the upper Midwest, it's an inner chaos of what's going to happen, and will my family be okay and how will this affect x, y, and z in the long run?

April 23, 2020.

It's a different lens with which I see life these days. And I doubt I'm alone. COVID-19 has pushed us to look at ourselves, at each other, at the nation.

Usually days are specifically organized into "the day this person pissed me off in this meeting" or the day I assessed a truck load (which was typically Tuesdays – now those are ultra-zoom zoom days) and then went home to nap. Now, there are long spans of time when nothing seems to occur, or a teeny speck of a moment will matter. Time shortens and elongates. Days feel quiet and loud, chaotic, and streamlined, red alert and blue skies. (Oh, yes, sometimes I'm poetic.)

One minute, I miss Zooey terribly, and I'm so grateful for my department; the next, I'm annoyed by others. One minute, I'm in the house alone without the TV on, and I'm straightening up things, wrapping up tiny projects, being productive domestically, and then next I'm zoned out to some show – tired and wanting to nap. Then post-nap, I'll wonder if I should go outside and play in the dirt. Sit on the deck and sniff in all the good oxygen. Bike ride up to campus to cry and holler at the world.

One could argue that it's not the way to live, but how was I living before? What can I learn from this kind of life?

September 24, 2020.

[...]

It does bug me, instead, that they[124] haven't found a nice nugget of compassion to extend to their students. They're keeping track of those who are technically quarantined and those who are not, and I wanted to say – as we discussed this with Johansson in the hallway yesterday morning – who the fuck cares? It's on them to watch the videos or log into whatever. Why not focus your energy on anything else? But, you know, I was there. In any other year before I realized I was being a dick to students, I would've been keeping a list, too,

[124] Other teachers on campus, regarding students who were absent for covid reasons.

and checking it twice. Hell, it was only a semester or two ago that I was logging every student's late pass to make sure they only used three. It's quite interesting to step back and see the policies in action that I once embraced like a beloved long-lost relative. And since I was a dick to students and had an epiphany about it, I also realize that other faculty will have to find their way in that respect, too. I can't force this process on anyone any more than anyone can change someone's drinking or smoking habit. It had to occur to me. I had to go through an uncomfortable stage of ignoring the #ungrading hashtag on Twitter, thinking "that's not for me."

[...]

December 15, 2020 – Tuesday of Finals Week.

Happy birthday to he-who-shall-not-be-named on the Facepage. I bought him a different whiskey from the Proof company (based in Fargo) along with some cinnamon liquor from a different North Dakotan company.

I popped onto a Zoom last night with some "TYCA National" people. And I had originally told myself that I wasn't going to say much, and then I wouldn't shut up. Or so it seemed. I really need to calm down the anxiety I get with that, or with rounding up the troops for when we all used to go out, or when I'm trying to fall asleep during a pandemic and I don't feel awesome so therefore I think it's the virus. I got tested yesterday, so that should put my mind at ease?

Anyhow, I wrapped up the second-to-last batch of grading this morning, and it's not even 8:30am yet. I have a 1pm "ECOR[125]" meeting this afternoon, and that's it. I did just send a print job (more pictures for frames in the kitchen – I'm slowly starting to tweak that room and wrap up the living room;

---

[125] Electronic Curriculum Online Resources. This is a statewide taskforce that has the goal of creating fully online courses that use free materials; these courses will be available to all students at all ND campuses. I hope it comes to fruition.

yesterday, I put up the Desiderata[126] frames and redid the lights on the tallest Christmas trees) to the Copy Center, so at some point, I'll go grab and pay for those, as well as pop by the parental unit's house to check on their mail; they went to the cities and will return Thursday.

[...]

The piece[127] that sticks out: "You are a child of the universe no less than the trees and the stars; you have a right to be here." I agree, wholeheartedly. Even the students who have pushed buttons on me this semester – Cole & Caleb. They are here to teach me. They give me the lessons. The show me the way to let go. And if my legacy is just writing, so be it. And if my legacy is improving learning for students, so be it. And if my legacy is increasing affordability for my students, so be it. I am here for a reason, and those might be it. I am proud that I have come to this spot. I am letting go of the harsh rules, and it feels lighter. Life feels lighter, especially since the election. Life doesn't have to be about complaining that students didn't introduce a source in their paper. Life doesn't have to be about responding to every outlandish opinion and bitching about late work and getting anxiety over new ideas or the fact that I think I talk too much.

I am striving to be happy. Sometimes, that means rest and tinkering in our house, and sometimes, that means redoing the course shells in Blackboard. And sometimes, it's a mish-mash of activities in one day combined with reality TV watching. Either way, I'm inching myself in an evolutionary manner away from certain parts of me that are no longer necessary. What is the use in holding onto strict rules? What is the use in many of the things I used to hold dear? They did not serve me. They didn't serve others, either, but they most definitely didn't serve me, and that should've been a wake up on call on its own.

---

[126] The first one can be found here: https://www.desiderata.com/desiderata.html
[127] From the Desiderata.

I would like to be a better person coming out of this pandemic. If not for others, then for myself. There is no need to put that kind of pressure on myself, but if change happens in tiny spurts – me noticing my old self in complaints from others, etc. – then change is happening.

Yeah.

Okay. Time for some breakfast.

Student Note.

December 11, 2003.

Sybil, I am really sorry about leaving all this crap until the last minute. I feel like a big jack ass. I really need to stop my procrastination; I think that's going to be my New Years resolution. But anyways I am glad you gave me the opportunity to make up some points for doing this, and thank you again very much for putting up with all my crap. You are an awesome teacher. I really like the way you teach, not out of the book so much, but talking about things, and having group discussions. I wish I could say that I would see you next semester but I can't because I couldn't take your class because the times conflicted with my other classes. By the way thanks for the email informing me that you wouldn't be in your office tomorrow, because it's freaking cold outside. But thanks again for an easy semester of English.

-JB

{This page intentionally left blank.}

{This page intentionally left blank.}

Timeline.

- May 1999: Graduated with B.A. in English Ed
- August 1999 – May 2001: Taught at Battle Lake High School and bought the 2000 VW Beetle
- August 2001 – May 2005: Graduate School
- July 2005: Accepted position at NDSCS
- School Year 2014-2015: First book published, *The Big-Boobed Bridesmaid*
- School Year 2015-2016: Second book (*teaching: with a side of chicken wings & a shot of vodka*) dedicated to John Wall; Brit and Lola leave the college; we create our first OER the summer of 2016
- School Year 2016-2017: Massive budget cuts; Josie's first year
- School Year 2017-2018: Professorship attempt and Faculty Council President chaos
- School Year 2018-2019: Sadie passes away, Ph.D. Application, Easter Twitter rabbit hole, Creative Commons certification, OEP class via Wikiversity, lots of webinars and epiphanies
- School Year 2019-2020: New offices, new Jeep, and Covid
- School Year 2020-2021: Covid and retirements

Acknowledgements.

Thank you to me for keeping all my old journals. They were tough to read through at times; the writing was fine, but the content hurt to digest.

Thank you to me for researching my own emails and tweets and more recent journal entries to find the entries that said the good, the bad, and the ugly things.

Thank you to my sister Maggie for listening to me hash out this book and what it could look like; thank you to my sister Jodi for letting me read your copy of *Untamed*, which was possibly my first lesbian/bisexual author (?).

I think it's wise to thank my partner-in-world-domination, my cat, my friends, and my family.

It's probably not a horrible idea to thank my students who gave me the material for this book. You nutty humans are the reason I do what I do. True story. So, when I'm frustrated in your general direction, just know that any mental f-bombs that I might be tossing your way are with love.

Always with love.

I'd like to thank my colleagues and my campus, too. Sometimes, ya'll are a fabulous support system, and, sometimes, I just want to bash my head against a brick wall in your honor. Either way, the students need lots of good teachers in their lives, and when I'm not it, you all are. Or maybe we all work together in that respect? Yeah, that part.

+

**The image on the cover of this book is from the lovely web site Unsplash; it's by Glen Carrie = https://unsplash.com/photos/JiSkHnWL020 I added the title/my name over the top by using Pixlr.com.*

About the Author.

Sybil Priebe lives in the upper Midwest and teaches at a rural community and technical college. She likes books, bicycles, and blasphemy. She can be reached at: sybilannpriebe@gmail.com

+

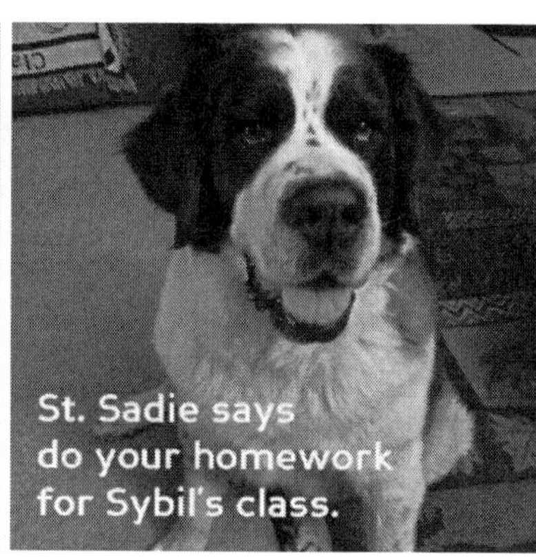

Made in the USA
Middletown, DE
17 December 2021

56086257R10170